The Exile

A Devoted Son's Spiritual Journey

Book One of the Exile Trilogy

L. Arik Greenberg, Ph.D.

The Exile: A Devoted Son's Spiritual Journey
Book One of The Exile Trilogy

Copyright © 2023 L. Arik Greenberg, Ph.D.

First Edition

Published by Enlightened Religion Press, LLC
Los Angeles, CA 90045
www.EnlightenedReligionPress.com

No part of this publication may be reproduced in whole or in part, or stored in a retrieval system, or transmitted in any form or by any means, electronic, mechanical, photocopying, or otherwise, without the written permission of the publisher. Requests for permission to make copies of any part of this book should be submitted directly to the publisher. You may contact the publisher through the following website address: www.EnlightenedReligionPress.com

Hardcover Edition:
ISBN-13: 978-0-9600889-4-2

Paperback Edition:
ISBN-13: 978-0-9600889-1-1

E-book Format
ISBN-13: 978-0-9600889-3-5

All rights reserved.

Library of Congress Control Number: 2023934854

Cover design by Barbara Groves, Broken Candle Book Designs
www.brokencandlebookdesigns.com

DEDICATION

For my parents, Richard and Barbara;

For all those who have suffered child abuse;

For the compulsive hoarder who still suffers.

And for those who helped us through the period of the Exile, and beyond;

Those whom I have called herein by their real names;

And those whose names I have altered for the sake of their anonymity.

For Melissa, my *beshert*, who became "One of Us", whether she liked it or not.

Thank you all.

CONTENTS

Preface	i
Prologue	v
Chapter One: Introduction	Pg 1
Chapter Two: The Making of a Hoarder	Pg 9
Chapter Three: Abuse Memories	Pg 43
Chapter Four: The Pre-Exilic Period	Pg 73
Chapter Five: The Exile	Pg 111
Chapter Six: Aftermath of the Exile	Pg 183
Afterword	Pg 217
Bibliography	Pg 219
About the Author	Pg 220

DISCLAIMER

The Exile contains graphic descriptions of child abuse, compulsive hoarding, as well as other disturbing imagery. Those of sensitive disposition, or those who are easily triggered, should take care before reading specific sections of the book.

PREFACE:
INDISPENSABLE NOTES FOR THE READER

The Exile is the record of a spiritual journey. Originally written as a single monograph from 2009 to 2011, the events of the subsequent decade demanded to be included in the narration, causing the manuscript to swell far beyond its original size and scope, and requiring that it be presented in the form of a trilogy. This is the first book in the series and should be read as such, continuing onwards to each successive volume.

This memoir—that is the trilogy, in its entirety—is not for everyone. Just as the artistic expressions of the painter or sculptor may not be understandable to the hard scientist, or the language of mathematics may not be comprehensible to the musician or poet, some may not appreciate or even be ready for this work. Some may even be offended or disturbed by the raw and candid discussion of theological and spiritual despair, or the wrestling with God, which is a uniquely Jewish endeavor, a tradition seen throughout the Hebrew Bible and continued by those like Elie Wiesel. It is my belief that this memoir is for a very advanced questioner of theology and spirituality, and there may be things about it that are offensive and antithetical to those of a more fundamentalist and traditional outlook on theology. I am aware of this, and I ask their forgiveness.

Is this a true story? One may ask what constitutes a true story. After all, one always leaves out the menial and mundane portions of one's experiences that do not contribute to the overarching story, that would bore or distract the reader. All truth, as told by an author, is subjective; even historical truth is never objective, but an admixture of subjective testimonies gathered from various voices. Therefore, as much as anyone can claim that a non-fiction account is true, the majority of this text is as much as possible a true account of the things that I remember, having edited and curated them together to make sense.

Therefore, this memoir is intensely personal, and largely autobiographical, as if I have given the willing reader a glimpse of my diary, having bared the innermost rooms of my soul. It is therefore intensely honest, as a record of what I have felt and thought and prayed in certain very specific situations, yet may no longer think or feel. In many cases these may be quite embarrassing, even shameful; things I would never want anyone to know about me. But I have chosen to record them here nonetheless, in hopes that they may help others who have experienced pain and loss and despair of a similar sort or magnitude. They record my struggles, my wrestling with God, as I understand that being. It is a record, a testimony of my evolution, my theological development, as a spiritual person, a person of immensely deep faith.

Thus, there may be moments in which the willing reader will not like me or my thoughts and deeds and choices of that moment. There will be places where one reader may dislike me for my persistent captivation by old and outdated theologies, the reader perhaps considering them too conservative. There will be moments where yet another reader will dislike me for entirely the opposite reasons, for my being overly disrespectful towards God or dismissive of more traditional theologies. Too liberal; not liberal enough. Too conservative; not conservative enough. Too theistic and captivated by a personal God; too rebellious and rejecting of a traditional Christian God—or harboring a loss of God, for that matter. Too willing to entertain non-Western theologies and conceptions of the Divine; yet too critical of any deity altogether. Or that I am too wordy. That I embody a certain privilege and that my suffering pales in comparison to that of others. Or where in my pain and grief, I may record a moment of snap judgment or callousness towards another person, judging them by their appearance or their ethnicity or their gender. These are not depicted here as a final and definitive declaration of my belief—in fact many of these moments I am profoundly ashamed of and they do not accurately characterize the final state of my beliefs—and for these I ask the reader's forgiveness. I ask the reader not to judge me too harshly, but to just observe, to wait and see where I wind up, in as much as one would not judge an infant too harshly, but should wait until they are grown before judging their merits as a human being. And that is what I am, as are most of us: infants in a complicated and confusing cosmos.

As such, providing a record of these moments is a sort of act of confession, that my soul be shriven of a secret sin that otherwise might have remained concealed. Furthermore, they form a momentary account, a record of my feelings of that moment, a confession of what I have done and gone through that have led me to my current state of spirituality. And I ask the reader's forgiveness not as the perfect and impartial judge of my conduct and crimes, but as witness to their own foibles, which if they choose to recognize them, are much like my own, and make them all too human as well.

I say, "willing reader", because I am aware that the full text of this memoir is long—very long. And the willing reader may suffer. I am also aware that there are episodes which record and retell incidents in my life, and the lives of those I love, which may be triggering to those who have undergone similar types of abuse, or have experienced similar types of trauma and loss. With this, I give **fair warning** to those who may be triggered by the graphic descriptions of child abuse, of sexual abuse, of compulsive hoarding, of severe mental illness, of bedsores and surgical wounds and lesions, or of descriptions of death of loved ones. These are not included to sensationalize, to fetishize, to scandalize, to titillate, or to provide voyeuristic and pornographic entertainment. Far from it! They are intended as a testament to the things that happened, a record of the suffering that the most important people in my life had experienced. It is an accusation leveled against those who caused the suffering, ensuring that these events are never forgotten, giving some level of tangible form to memories that otherwise would be lost once the last generation that witnessed or experienced them, or had been informed of them, had died out. These stories, told to me by those who have gone, are now mine to tell. The most central of those whose testimony I provide herein, had systematically informed me of them, and gave me permission to write them in this book. Now that they are gone, I am the only one who can tell them, to bear witness to what they endured and suffered. These stories are now my responsibility.

The reader will surely notice that I approach religion from a pluralistic standpoint. I do not claim that all religions are the same—for they are not, as sameness is fundamentally an illusion amidst the beautiful diversity of the world's religions—but that they each have value to the people and the cultures to which they were revealed by a Divine source. Several of them speak directly to me on account of my interfaith upbringing. I approach religion, and my perceived truth of the cosmos, my internalized cosmology, as both a Jew and a Christian of sorts. I am not an observant Jew of a modern Rabbinic variety, nor am I a Christian of modern Trinitarian variety. My approach to these is deeply rooted in the standpoint of my academic studies, incorporating mystical understandings of Greco-Roman philosophy and proto-Gnostic ideas. I am also someone deeply steeped in Buddhism and to some degree Hinduism, through and by way of my New Age upbringing, as well as my academic studies and interfaith work. All of these inform my understanding of the Divine in a pluralistic sense. This may be anathema to some readers, and welcome to others.

What makes this book different from others? Many others can write well. Perhaps much better than I. What is the difference between them and me? Is it because I have experienced a loss of loved ones in a way that others have not? Because I experienced a closeness, a bond, a cathexis, with certain loved ones who were then ripped from me by fate? Have not others experienced this? But perhaps I am able to characterize it in a poignant way that will give others a sense of comfort, that they are not alone in their grief. Most people never have the opportunity to proclaim their grief publicly. They live lives of obscurity and their grief (which all of us experience) is left to the silent corners of their lives. But which of us has not wanted to scream out publicly the ardor of our agony? The utter depth of our loss? Few of us have ever gained that opportunity. But fortunately—if you are reading this—I have that forum.

THE EXILE

I have described this text to friends, colleagues, and confidants, during the writing process as a necromantic incantation, meaning that it is in some ways a prayer, or a ritual in attempt to revive the voices of those who have died and left this plane of existence, and exited my life. It is thereby an attempt to speak to them beyond the grave, perhaps even to *revive* them—in the truest sense of the word—for but a moment and consult them—as Saul sought through the Witch of Endor to prophetically and mantically consult the dead prophet Samuel—thereby ensuring their immortality through words and memory. As such, it is a rumination on the essence of death and memory. And in putting my soul into a book, I am ensuring my own immortality, for as long as this book, these words, exist in some form. And that is one of the major themes of this book—memory as a form of immortality, as both the Greeks and the Egyptians conceived of it. As it was said, "when we speak of the dead, they live again".

As mentioned above, *The Exile* was originally written as a single manuscript, later to be divided into multiple parts, as needed. Each of the books in this corpus functions as part of a larger journey, and should be read sequentially by the serious reader, but the casual reader can still possibly gain something valuable, edifying, from each volume. The foregoing preface pertains to the corpus as a whole—three distinct, but sequentially iterative books in a unified story. As such, I say the following about this first work. It is a work of spiritual simplicity and is thus accessible to the spiritually ingenuous. It is optimistic, trusting, pious, faithful. It presupposes an omniscient, omnipotent, loving, and omnibenevolent God. It is a book that will satisfy the spiritual and intellectual cravings of most people of faith, as it ends on a reasonably happy note. But the last lines allude to the impending challenge to my faith, sequels to the book which chart my more advanced journey on the choppy waters of wrestling with God, incorporating esoteric material that will be anathema, confusing, and even offensive to those who are spiritually conservative. For the religiously and spiritually ingenuous—those on the beginning of their journey, unquestioning and exceedingly literalistic in their faith—I say beware of proceeding beyond the first book prior to being ready to explore a deeper faith that questions, like Job, and that challenges, wrestles with God. Tread no further, but be happy with this tale. But for the more spiritually curious, the open-minded, the intrepid traveler on the road to the Divine—for those who can recognize my apparent blasphemy as a deeply reverent work of faith—I invite you to proceed.

PROLOGUE

First Entry

August 20, 2009

When I arrived at my parents' house, I was greeted with some of the most horrible filth that I had ever seen. Even the driveway was strewn with plastic flower pots, many broken, a shopping cart, baby carriages, an old rocking horse, bottles, cans, leaves, all manner of debris and refuse, all placed very carefully according to the careless plans of an ill mind, seeking to make sense of the pain in her world and in the world we shared.

When I approached the front door, I saw the usual debris and junk that was perennially on the front stoop, obscuring the otherwise magnificent, deep brown stained hardwood double doors that were once a signal of our welcoming intent. And when I saw the large, 11 ½ by 14-inch rectangular yellow poster board sign that had been thumb-tacked to the right-hand door of the once beautiful entryway, it gave a sense of numbing realism to an otherwise surrealistic situation. I was disappointed, as if there was still a chance that this may have been a dream, or a simple misunderstanding. I quickly read the code.

DO NOT REMOVE

DEFACE OR MARK THIS PLACARD

UNDER PENALTY OF LAW

This Building is hereby declared unsafe and unfit for human habitation pursuant to the Code of the Town of Huntington.

The occupancy of this dwelling or any part thereof is unlawful.

It was now a reality. I could not deny it.

****

The front entry being inaccessible, circumstances required that I enter by a rear sliding glass door, around the back of the house, beyond the nearly impenetrable jungle of brush that stood between the front of the house and the rear. I was overwhelmed by a flood of emotions at this point: fear, anger, sadness, even shock and the denial that this could happen to our kind and compassionate family. We were special, weren't we? Or so I thought.

I pulled the heavy, metal-framed sliding glass door to the right, with great difficulty as its tracks were loaded with dirt and plant matter from years of neglect. I was exposed to the interior of the house for the first time in two years. The feeling that I had in the pit of my stomach—knowing that this was undeniable evidence of my parents' sickness and also the moment in which I was required to become an adult—I cannot describe in words. My viscera, the entire front of my body, all ached with a cold groan, a diabolical, icy tingle in my chest and solar plexus. I stepped up upon the elevated ledge and climbed in…. When I peered into the living room of my parents' house, all I saw was horrible things. Evidence of a beautiful life turned very wrong.

I was struck by the utter volume of material in that room. Not only were the two original 1972 chocolate-brown and cream striped tweed couches still in place where they had been for nearly forty years, but also several other large sections of a newer couch that had been bought second hand about two years prior were stood upended in the room, covered with various things, never put into place in a usable position. Surrounding them were piles and piles of newspaper, old phonograph records, furniture, potted plants, and every manner of detritus, so that I had to literally climb on top of everything, perched flat on my belly approximately four to five feet off the ground, squirming forward like an eel in order to be able to move to the dining room and then toward the front door. This newer sofa, in several sections, was brought in to replace the older ones a year or so prior, when my mother noticed that rats had entered into the house through one of the minute holes in the floorboards where heating pipes were directed in from the basement, and then had subsequently begun to make a nest in one or both of the older sofas. Unfortunately, even though our friend Phil had helped bring the sectional sofa in, the older matching sofa and loveseat had never been brought out. Evidently, the sentimental connection to them was too strong for my mother to overcome the need to expel rat droppings from the house.

I moved toward the dining room, once the heart of my family's home, and location of many happy dinners, holidays, adolescent sleep-overs with friends. It was now a place that would have horrified even Dickens' Ms. Havisham, the vendetta-driven, elderly, jilted bride from *Great Expectations*, a hoarder in her own right. It was she whose table was adorned by the petrified and spider web encrusted, erstwhile wedding cake from decades prior, now attacked by rats.

Perhaps those rats were the archetypal forebears of the ones we would eventually find.

I had to move very carefully, so as not to fall over. There were many pitfalls and places where there were simply not more than a few inches of floor space to safely stand upon and balance before moving to the next location. I moved through the dining room as quickly as I could, rounding the head of the great hardwood table, which was completely covered with junk, sheets to cover the junk, and then even more junk, resting about chest height, preventing it from being usable. All of the chairs were covered with bags of unidentifiable items, almost completely obscured as to their identity as chairs. The kitchen—also completely full of material both kitchen-like and not—which adjoined the dining room, was now to my left. With great difficulty, I moved past that and into the short entryway leading to the front hall.

The front hallway was now also full of junk. As I moved toward the front door in order to unbolt the deadbolt and begin to air out the house from the intolerable stench of decay and mold, I had to step over more and more things to navigate. There was not a single space in the house that was able to be called clean or clear or livable. I can say, categorically, that the house was worse than ever before. I had seen it briefly two years prior and it was terrible, but you could still get inside. To this day, I cannot believe that my parents lived like this—in the worst of conditions—for over a year. Prior to that, it was barely livable. Now, I would not have considered it livable at all. One could barely move around without jumping or clambering over piles and stacks. The term "goat paths" has been bandied about in these situations of extreme hoarding; none such existed in the house anymore. The house was filled inside with many years' worth of newspapers, books, old clothing, chairs, assorted furniture and knick-knacks, in addition to what can only be called refuse and garbage. In previous years, I had seen the mess growing, and when I came in 2007 and 2008 (during the latter year I only caught a glimpse through the front door), it was already shocking. But at least there were still pathways during that previous year. Pathways of about a foot wide, between tall piles of junk, as tall as the height of a human in places. In other places, they were just piles chest high that were precariously balanced so as not to fall into the pathways unless jostled.

But now, you had to jump or climb over short piles of newspaper and magazines and refuse in order to get to the next square foot oasis of floor space. There were no longer any clear pathways. They were strewn with shorter piles every foot or so, in order that one would have to step over each pile into a small clearing, steady oneself, and then jump to the next clearing between piles. And with my father's walking problem, I don't know how he did it. That explains his inability to make it to the bathroom at times, which my mother described to me as a function of his laziness or his emotional deterioration. Regardless of the attendant emotional issues, there were serious physical hindrances between him and the bathroom. And this time, the stench was terrible. Previously, the home had begun to present a smell of mustiness and even mold. But this time, there was the smell that I dreaded ever smelling in my parents' house. It was the smell of fecal matter. It was the smell of two people finally being "over the edge." Continuing to explore, I saw large, fat flies buzzing around, spawned and gorged on the animal feces that was distributed surreptitiously around the house by both rodents and by the dog that had come to stay, ill-begotten decision by my mother to help a dying friend. The flies were not only located where the feces was, but also around various piles of squalor and pestilence. The air was oppressive, unrelentingly stuffy, without circulation, dead.

I considered the couches in the living room as a symbol of our deterioration as a family. I recalled a photo that my father had taken of the three of us in late 1972 or early 1973, having just moved into the house. He had set up the timer on the Canon camera he had bought just after I was born, and snapped a portrait of a happy couple and their two-year-old child nestled comfortably between them on a Winter morning, holding several stuffed animals as family members in their own right. All three were the image of happiness, sanguinary sanity and suburban success: a public-school teacher and a stay-at-home mom raising a bright, healthy little boy, curiosity shining within his hazel-brown eyes. This picture was now sullied by the reality of deterioration, of decrepitude and mental illness, compounded over the next four decades. That image was now supplanted by the reality of the increasing filth and squalor they had been living in for years.

This was the hell that my parents had created for themselves and for everyone who loved them. And at this moment, we could no longer deny our sickness—be it as enablers or the primary party who suffered—we were hoarders. As the only child, I felt it was my responsibility to save them. I had vowed to take care of my parents in their dotage, to be there for them as they aged, as a good son should—but I had failed.

****

CHAPTER ONE: INTRODUCTION

"Strange now to think of you, gone without corsets & eyes, while I walk on the sunny pavement of Greenwich Village."

—Allen Ginsberg, *Kaddish*[1]

It's strange to look back on everything that has happened since 2009, since the time I came to call "the Exile", and to write this introduction. Many times, I thought my narrative was done and the book complete. Or at least I tried to convince myself that it was done. But then the universe would add to the tale, revealing more episodes to me that needed to be included—new events and plot twists that demonstrated that the tale was not yet done. Despite my resistance, eventually I realized the story was not over, and I had to resume writing, adding each new chapter, one after another, that completely changed the tone and direction of the book. In doing so, I realized that any premature attempt at calling it complete would have been hollow, artificial, meaningless. After thirteen years of writing, often simultaneous with the narrated events themselves, I consider myself done, and am able to write this introduction one final time.

Many times I have re-written these opening lines, this introduction to the tale. Many times, I have scrapped my earlier work, thinking it puerile, infantile, trite, hackneyed, cliched, and I searched for a better way to begin to tell this story. It is the story of a family that suffered. Granted, all families suffer. Perhaps we embodied a special type of suffering, and perhaps my skillset affords me a certain capacity to convey this. As such, I felt it would be helpful to others for me to share this with the world, as a testament to my journey of faith, my love for my parents, and my rumination on the subjects of death and memory and immortality. This memoir is not for the fainthearted, or those of simple faith that is unexamined or carelessly constructed and poorly sourced. It is mainly for the brave, the stalwart, who are eager to engage in the deeper

---

[1] Allen Ginsberg, *Kaddish* in *Selected Poems, 1947-1995* (New York: HarperPerennial, 1997), p. 93.

questions of life and the nature of God.

It is also a love story on many levels. A love story between myself and my parents. For my childhood home. For the land of my birth, Long Island. For my family, rapidly disappearing. And for God, as I conceive of that being. It is an exploration of memory and identity and the problem of human suffering. Like many before me, I explore the problem of why a loving and benevolent god allows bad things to happen to good people, especially children, the most helpless and innocent among us.

****

I grew up in a quaint little house on Long Island, having moved there as a toddler in 1972. It stood at the end of a long driveway, nestled deeply in the forest, amidst the oaks and spruce and Eastern White Pines of the Northeast. It was a modest little house, situated in the older and more humble section of a fairly affluent village called Dix Hills—a section of the older and larger Town of Huntington—which village sported all the latest styles of home and had many new families come and move into them. The home was in the midst of a row of houses which abutted the edge of a large forest, and at the northern limit of the forest, there was a great and noble parkway, upon which cars zipped past on their ways to and from work. The home had been built by my Grandfather, Arty Merget, the last home he would ever build.

Contrary to the seemingly idyllic setting and description of my home, this is not a happy book. It chronicles the suffering and torment of a number of people over the course of many years. But it is my hope that by telling their story (and mine is among them) some of my readers may be helped. This book is the story of my parents and their problem with what is currently called Compulsive Hoarding Disorder. My mother, as the active hoarder, had suffered with it on some level for most of my life. Even in my late pre-pubescent years, it became evident to me that she was collecting newspapers. Initially, it was explained to the outside world, to those that inquired about her idiosyncrasy, that she was doing research. One childhood friend of mine, well-meaning enough but somewhat presumptuous in his youthful suggestions, helpfully informed her that she should get rid of the newspapers and do her research at the library instead. He was correct on a mundane level, but he could not possibly understand the full gravity of the situation. As time wore on, my mother graduated to collecting newspapers on a larger scale and by the early 2000s was a full scale, active hoarder, who had a ready (and oft times seemingly convincing) explanation or excuse for every aspect of her hoarding. Her most ready response was that she didn't want all the refuse to wind up in the garbage dump in Hauppauge, Long Island or in a land fill. And newspapers eventually occupied only a small portion of the material she collected in the home, which included anything that had perceived value to it, or items which she fully intended to discard in an environmentally responsible manner. Of course, most of the dross she collected never left the house, despite her best intentions. And in spite of Mom's intellectual brilliance and her tremendous charm and her frequent role as everyone's savior, she lacked a certain capacity for executive function when it came to her own household.

My mother, as it turns out, was a very severely abused child who had subsequently repressed her numerous early childhood abuse memories until a later stint in therapy in her mid-fifties. It is her assessment and that of her therapist—and I agree with them—that her hoarding was a direct result, or symptom, of this repressed abuse and that such abuse may in fact be a fairly common root cause of the subsequent reaction in compulsive hoarders. Throughout this book, I will deal extensively with her story under this operative model of the root causes.

My father, however, might be called most accurately the enabler, but his role was so much more complex than can be conveyed by that simple title. His contribution was of course one of traditional enabler, afraid to make waves or rock the boat, simply hoping that the fighting and the misery would end soon by just going along with the hoarding. However, my mother indicated to me that he was also responsible for much passive-aggressive sabotage, including breaking or losing items of personal and legal or financial importance. He gradually refused to fix aspects of our home, traditional responsibilities of the male in our culture. He stopped taking an interest in the operation of the household, after so many years of asserting his traditional male role in family decisions—emulating his father—but not always having the best suggestions or guidance. In many ways, my father did not have a good role model and his ability to engender closeness with his son or with his wife suffered. In many ways, my mother was forced into the role of dominant parent, while my father sulked or read the newspaper, somewhat disconnected from the rest of the family. He was never cruel to me or cruel to my mother in an overt or physical way. A meek and gentle, mild-mannered but occasionally distant and somewhat ineffectual head of household, he was simply unable to feel a part of things and to take the risk and put himself in a position in which he could participate. But can one blame him for this behavior, given the growing hoarding conditions? Which came first, the chicken or the egg?

My father was an extremely successful grade school teacher, having served for thirty years in the public schools, the majority of that time as a reading specialist on the primary level. He helped many children with learning disabilities learn how to read, and he helped many gifted children go on to higher levels of excellence. Over the years, he, as well as my mother, had been to see several therapists to address their personal issues. From what I understand, some of them had said they were no longer able to help my dad. Not that he was particularly disturbed, but rather he was unable to make sufficient progress with them. At least two of them stated that they thought his problems stemmed from childhood abuse that he was unable or unwilling to recall. He patently denied this.

Over the course of time, he began to have memory problems. Not serious ones at first, but short-term memory issues that seemed to be an intensification of his general sensibilities that I had noticed while growing up. He was always the kind of man that would make simple conversation by asking the same questions over and over again. "How's your friend Eric?" "I told you that your mom and I spoke to Jack, didn't I?" after the fifth time mentioning it. And so forth. Small talk that often verged on the restatement of common knowledge. Questions that had already been answered. But later on, in his mid-seventies, as we approached the time in our family life that I have dubbed "the Exile", his general short-term memory got worse. He began to forget the route home and would need prompting by my mother. He began to forget what chores had to be done. He often would explain, when pushed, that these constant questions were not so much that he had actually forgotten the answer, but that his compulsiveness caused him to need to keep checking. We began to surmise, in his work with the most recent therapist, Kim, that my father's tendency to fall asleep during conversations (and especially in therapy sessions) was most certainly related to his short-term memory loss. Essentially, he was expending a lot of energy trying to cover something up, to avoid remembering something, and it was his concentration on the present moment that would suffer the most. This is what prompted Kim to suggest that my dad was covering up some kind of early childhood abuse, echoing the suggestion of previous therapist, David.

It is my assertion that my parents' highly complex mental situation was a function of their early childhood abuse. As it has often been said that two alcoholics in a crowded room will inevitably gravitate toward one another (sometimes replacing one alcoholic for an enabler), it goes to say that two abused children will gravitate toward one another. As it turns out, there is evidence that perhaps both of my parents were severely abused children, but both in different ways, and neither of them had the ability to remember the abuse until much later in life, belying their brilliant and expansive memory capacity. Their brilliance, similarly, allowed them to make easy excuses for themselves and to go only so far in therapy, having partial successes without complete and lasting progress in the problems that plagued their marriage.

In August of 2009, the hoarding situation came to a head. My parents' home was subjected to a surprise inspection by the local town public safety department, brought about in part by a few complaints from nosy neighbors and partially in response to the accidental death of a dog my parents were caring for who repeatedly escaped the house and ran into traffic. The final time this happened, the police who were called to help with the deceased animal saw inside the house and then alerted the appropriate authorities: Town of Huntington Public Safety and Suffolk County Adult Protective Services. Subsequently, the home was "placarded", and my parents were prevented from living in the house until certain safety violations were remedied. These included making all entrances and exits to the house fully accessible, making the exterior more satisfactory in appearance and accessibility, and in clearing all pathways inside the house so that emergency services could effectively carry out their duties if called to respond to an emergency there. During this time, I had to fly out from California—where I had been living since 1993 to attend graduate school and then begin work as a professor—to help spearhead the operation to cleanse the home. All told, my parents were out of their house for just over four months during the mandatory cleanup. We had to rely upon numerous friends and family to help rectify the situation and even to allow my parents to have a place to stay while they were unable to live at home. It was this time period that I concisely termed "The Exile", named after the time period when the ancient Israelites were in captivity to the Empire of Babylon, from 587 BCE to 540 BCE. The Babylonian Exile, or Babylonian Captivity—as it is variously called—saw the ruling classes of the Israelites deported, or exiled, to the city of Babylon as captives. It was only after their liberation by the Persian Empire that the Israelites were permitted to return to their homeland and rebuild. This period of Jewish history symbolizes to me—being by trade a scholar of Biblical Studies—the experience of my family being "exiled" from our home, from August 19th to December 23rd, 2009.

I do not fault any of the official agencies that levied these requirements. In fact, they were literally the answer to my prayers. For several years prior, I had considered how to solve the problem of my parents' physical safety in their home and had even considered calling the health department myself to request a mandate that my parents clean their environment. As it turns out, the choice was taken out of my hands by the angels and forces that protect us (in my opinion) and the hand of God guided those in official positions to make demands that ensured my parents' safety. As it was, I was too much of a coward, placing more importance on my parents' approval than on their well-being. It is this cowardice that I struggle with daily and which I hope I can dissuade the reader from adhering to in their own lives and relationships with hoarders. Speaking metaphorically (or perhaps not), a burning building must be extinguished at all costs, regardless of who is to blame and whose feelings may be hurt when the emergency call is placed.

As I began to write this book, after the Exile was over, the situation would get worse again. We experienced a brief period of rest and repose, but I knew in my heart that something even more traumatic than the Exile was going to occur. In August, 2011, during Hurricane Irene, a tree fell on my parents' house, causing tremendous damage but triggering a series of events that I can only recognize as embodying the hand of God. The remaining volume of hoarded material in the house was to be cleared out by the construction crew in order to rebuild the house, all paid for by the insurance company. It was as if Providence were intent upon giving us the assistance that we needed in order to clean out our lives on every level. But this was not for the faint of heart; only the strong would survive. This strain on my family triggered deadly health problems in both my parents that, for better or worse, would require that all of us pull together in order to survive. While handling their affairs from a distance, only occasionally being able to be there in person, I came to the realization that the story of the Exile had additional meaning for me as a son, an individual, and as an author. Not only had my family experienced a temporary period of exile from their home, but I had developed an awareness, through the soul searching process of composing this narrative, that I too had become an exile—from my family, from my ancestral home, and from my identity. It is this underlying struggle with which the book also primarily deals. As I continued to write the narrative, the theme of being an exile took on increasingly greater significance. All of us had become exiles, from our hopes and dreams, and from each other. And I continue to struggle to return home from my own Exile.

I ask the reader to note that many of the names herein have been changed to protect the innocent. There are people mentioned herein who helped out during our darkest times, as well as those who were not particularly involved, but still were present. These I do not wish to harm by including their full, real names. In changing their last names, or in some cases their full names, I have attempted to keep the flavor of their name so as to convey the highest level of verisimilitude to the reader. But please note, the stories included herein are true. In rare cases, certain events have been streamlined for ease of description. And I have taken great pains to ensure that the truth is told in the most efficient and complete manner possible.

My sincerest hope is that enough volumes of this will sell so that the people who suffer, like my parents have suffered, and like those in my same shoes—people who care for those with a compulsive hoarding disorder—will be heartened and uplifted. Perhaps they may see similarities between my story and theirs. Perhaps they will be brought to do something about the problem before it becomes too late. Perhaps they will realize that the ultimate source of the problem, aside from any other attendant cause, most often is child abuse or some comparable trauma.

I also hope that by giving others the chance to read our story, they will be able to see that this problem is a very widespread one and that it is not merely something that affects anonymous "crazy" people somewhere else, on television talk shows or reality television, but that it is something that is real and experienced by real people. The hoarder indeed has a face. He or she is one of us. We may become one, or may have one in our family. The hoarder is not a mythical creature, nor are they people to be avoided or shunned, or shot with tranquilizer darts and put into captivity so that we can alternately jeer at or study them. They are one of us; they are among us.

If I must synopsize this story in only a few brief phrases, I would once again persist in characterizing it as a love story: the story of the love that a son had for his parents, and how he tried to save their lives, and what he was willing to do to save them. It is also the story of that son's quest to reclaim his identity, his desperate struggle to return home from Exile, like that of the Israelites who also have struggled over the course of thousands of years, through many periods of exile and disenfranchisement and diaspora, to return to their ancestral homeland, and how—like them—it has shaped and molded him during his long period of absence. It is also the story of one person's emotional and spiritual journey, his struggle to reconcile with God.

Barbara Merget, early 1960s, in her early twenties

Richard Greenberg, Port Jefferson, NY, early 1950s, in his late teens

Richard Greenberg in Korea, 1954-55

Richard Greenberg in mid-1940s

CHAPTER TWO:
THE MAKING OF A HOARDER

My father was born in 1935, the eldest son of first-generation Americans, whose Ashkenazi Jewish immigrant parents in turn had come over from the old country in the early 1900s, fleeing poverty and religious persecution, speaking only Yiddish and seeking to resettle themselves amidst other Eastern European Jews wherever they could find communities of them. Dad's maternal grandparents, the Goldsteins, had come over from Bessarabia—a region that has variously been historically claimed by Moldavia, the USSR, Romania, and is now part of Moldova—and settled in the New Haven area prior to moving to Brooklyn. His paternal grandparents, the Greenbergs, had come from Odessa, which was then part of the Empire of Russia, and now Ukraine. Joseph Greenberg, my dad's paternal grandfather, had been conscripted by the Czar to serve an interminable tenure in the army—a virtual death sentence—and was sent to fight in the Russo-Japanese war. Ultimately, he deserted and fled to the United States, ultimately settling in the New York City area. Neither family was ever particularly religiously observant (Grandma Ethel secretly enjoyed the occasional piece of bacon), but they were like any other Jews of the Reform movement at the time. They thrived within their community and their Judaism was part of their identity—a condition of birth that they could not hide from—and my dad's parents were among the founding families of the first synagogue in Port Jefferson, where they settled in 1940. Growing up during World War II—in an area of Long Island where prior to the war, there was a German-American Bund organization among the German immigrant community, which largely supported Hitler and spouted anti-Semitism, prior to Germany declaring war on the U.S.—my dad had experienced a significant amount of anti-Semitism, which profoundly affected him. My dad had always said that as a secular Jew, you could forget that you were a Jew for only so long, until there was an anti-Semite there to remind you. I embrace this sentiment heartily to this day.

Mom's family was largely Roman Catholic, coming from a number of countries in western and southern Europe. Her father's side, the Mergets, immigrated to the United States in the late 1800s, with my Great-great-grandfather, Andreas fleeing the interminable warfare, when he saw cousins on the other side of the battlefield, and carried scars from bayonet wounds gained during the Franco-Prussian War. A stern faced man with mutton-chops and a bald pate, he emigrated with his wife and children in 1885 from Hesse-Darmstadt, part of the German Empire. His fifth child, Andrew, was the first to be born in the United States. He and his son, my grandfather, Arthur Merget, were skilled construction workers, who polished marble in many of the most important skyscrapers in New York City, and later became builders in their own right, with Grandpa Arty building as many as forty homes on Long Island during his career. Mom's maternal side, Sicilians by the name of Dragna, had emigrated from Corleone in the early 1900s, possibly to flee the violence of Mafia feuds in which their cousins had become embroiled.

Throughout my life, my dad appeared studious in appearance with his horn-rimmed spectacles, a bit paunchy and employing a combover to conceal his bald pate and preserve the effects of the once voluminous, wavy black hair of his youth. In photos I had seen of him in his teens and twenties—not yet wearing glasses—he was a very handsome man with certain dark, classically Semitic features and a prominent nose that betrayed his Jewish origins. He was lean and athletic, having been a runner in high school. As he aged into his thirties and beyond, he took on a more nebbish look, and while one would not typically say that he retained his classic Jeff Goldblum-like good looks, he always retained a certain avuncular cuteness well into his dotage.

Mom was always on the slender side, neither thin nor fat, but healthy in her build. She had often been mistaken in her youth for a French woman, as she had the classic dark features and high cheekbones of her Gallic paternal ancestors. She had thick, dark—nearly black—wavy hair that she usually kept fashionably short during my youth, but which she later allowed to grow into long tresses as she went prematurely silver in her late thirties. With dark, exquisitely heavy eyebrows, she was the epitome of the kind of beauty embodied by Elizabeth Taylor and Ava Gardner. However, throughout her life, she was forced to hide her loveliness behind dark-rimmed cats-eye glasses due to her severe myopia. It was this feature which made her look more intellectual and less glamorous, hiding her looks from the world, only to be revealed in professional photo portraiture. As she aged, she still retained her comeliness in ways that shone through beyond her now large, clear, square-framed, plastic glasses.

My parents met early on in college during the late 1950s, and maintained a friendship, but only began dating in 1965, several years after they graduated in 1961. They were married in the Jewish Synagogue, my mother having separated from her Roman Catholic faith incrementally throughout her college years, when she found pre-Vatican II Catholicism too repressive, misogynistic, hypocritical, and abusive. She had cut her ties by the time she had graduated college, and had already begun exploring Judaism, as she always had exhibited an appreciation for Judaism's love of education and open debate, something she found lacking in her native religion. By the time they were married in 1966, Mom was ready to affirm her chosen Jewish faith. However, by the time I became cognizant of religious identity, both parents had come to feel stifled by organized religion all together and, while I was raised believing we were nominally Jewish, I eventually came to realize that our beliefs and practices were very different from most of my cousins and my Jewish classmates. We were eclectic, New Age Jews, the likes of whom had thrived in the Beat and Hippie countercultural movements—people who prioritized social justice and *tikkun olam* over rote memorization of prayers, the proper execution of ritual, or adherence to tradition. We became denizens of health food stores and spiritual book stores, and I was schooled by aging hippies about yoga and kundalini and meditation. While I experienced much confusion over my religious identity, this gave way to a very deep passion for, and fascination with religion, and played into my eventual interfaith identity, one of the hallmarks of my life, and the focus of my life's work.

Mom had always been a bit of a health nut, most of her life, preaching against white bread and sugar in her nuclear family during her teenage years, much to her parents' consternation, as these were considered hallmarks of progress and plenty. But by the time I was around three years of age, Mom had begun to experience health challenges that orthodox medicine could neither diagnose properly, nor treat effectively. She suffered from a dying gall bladder which went undiagnosed due to her not fitting the usual profile of a woman who was "fair, fat and forty", as the physicians' diagnostic adage had read. Rather she was olive-complected (with dark, almost black hair), thin, and thirty. And so several doctors dismissed her agonizing gall bladder pain as being psycho-somatic, and suggested she seek psychiatric help. After one astute doctor finally recognized what was going on and sought to get her immediately into surgery to remove her gall afflicted bladder, she began to advocate for herself in her search for health. As it turned out, the birth control pills she had been prescribed early on in her marriage were notorious for causing certain B Vitamin deficiencies, which contributed to an early death of her gall bladder and a strain on her liver. No one had told her this. She did not discover this until much later.

A few years later, she had been accidentally sprayed by a careless tree-spraying crew that was hired by the next door neighbors. The service person operating the nozzle had not seen her behind a hedge row that bordered our property, and as she used her body as a shield to protect me—her toddler son—from the full force of the spray, he doused her with gallons of poisonous pesticides. After consulting poison control, who determined that she would be fine and that there was nothing further to do, she began to experience symptoms that would later come to be identified as consistent with mercury poisoning. The fly-by-night tree spray company could not be reached for information, but evidently, the pesticide used by them had been an illegal mercury-based spray. Mom began to suffer, once again without any respite or help from orthodox medicine. It was a holistic nutritionist named Sandy Schwartz, who had co-founded a holistic health center in Manhasset, who diagnosed her. His partner, a medical doctor named Jeff Fisher, confirmed this line of inquiry with heavy metal tests that showed her levels of mercury toxicity were far beyond normal levels. Only with highly unconventional therapeutic methods such as intravenous chelation, dietary and supplement-oriented detoxification, as well as Chinese herbs, was Mom able to eventually bring her mercury levels back to normal. But following this, she suffered through many years of side effects such as low energy and depressed immune system, due to the damage done by the mercury. Mom had become fanatical about restoring her health and safeguarding Dad's and mine. She was adamant about eating all organic food, and fortifying our health with vitamin and mineral supplementation. This was the environment in which I grew up during my pre-teen years. Mom's health always occupied her attention at every moment. It was always a concern, and diminished her ability to maintain the cleanliness of her home (as Dad was the primary breadwinner and Mom was the homemaker—a traditional arrangement), and this ultimately became a handy excuse for her hoarding.

****

Nothing that I write herein should be construed as an assault or a condemnation on my parents' respective character. I write this to demonstrate their humanity, with all its flaws. I would describe my parents as beautiful, generous, loving, brilliant, and accomplished people who would be generous with their time and money, almost to a fault. One family therapist even commented, admiringly, on their brilliance. But behind closed doors, their demons, their idiosyncrasies, their foibles, were very evident to me.

My mother would describe herself as a basically neat and orderly person, explaining her hoarding as a reaction to past and present conditions. I believe that she was, largely, correct. I had seen this neat and orderly side of her. In my early youth, she kept a fairly neat house. And things were relatively well organized. But on some level, in my opinion, the preliminary signs of hoarding were always there. And with good reason. As we would discover, much was taken from her in her youth—materially, physically, and emotionally. Severely abused from an early age—sexually, physically, and emotionally—then repeatedly deprived of her prized possessions, it is no wonder that she continued to cling to things for safekeeping, and for stability.

From an early age, in the 1970s I remember two rooms in the house that were the storage areas, the repositories of what could not easily be sorted or disposed of. And of course, most people—most families—have a storage closet or a garage like this. It is stereotypical in American society that a person has a closet full of things, stuffed in, humorously ready to fall out as soon as the door is opened. But Mom had two entire rooms that tended toward this, to a greater or lesser degree. The worst of these was "The Middle Room", as my mother's sewing and crafts room was called. It was originally designated to be a bedroom when my parents worked with the architect to design our house. It was about 10 by 18 feet and had a great window at the exterior side and a door that opened upon the main hallway that connected most of the rooms in that part of the one story, L-shaped ranch home. It contained Mom's beautiful old Singer sewing machine, which she had since before I was born. It also had several chests of drawers, usually covered with fabric of various colors, textures and styles— linens, muslins, cottons, and the like. As time wore on, more things were put into that room. A large dining room table, made of hard wood, elegantly carved, was secreted away in that room, to save it for future use and meanwhile to employ it as a work table. A china cabinet was then socked away in the closet of that room, never to be seen again except in glimpses from behind bolts of fabric. Subsequently, yards and yards of fabric were collected there, obscuring even the largest of furniture from view.

Mom prided herself in being very eccentric, describing herself "crazy", as a virtue. She had a very silly, playful sense of humor, when at her best. She was always a woman of many projects, a brilliant craftswoman who always had some skill she was teaching herself. But as time wore on, the projects took longer and longer, and ultimately a project begun was likely a project never to be finished. Projects and materials for projects, textile or otherwise, continued to be stuffed into the room, regardless of the lack of usable space. By the time the Exile happened, there was nothing more than a tiny walkway down the center-left portion of the room, no more than a few inches wide. Things which were piled high on either side of the walkway would eventually and suddenly avalanche down into the walkway, covering the path and making it hard to traverse without hopping over piles that had fallen.

The other room that I mentioned was known to us as "the Den". It had a sliding pocket door that disappeared inside the wall to the left of the jamb. A corner room in the extreme eastern part of the L-shaped ranch—which was longitudinally oriented southwest to northeast—this room had a large, southeast facing window, and a smaller northeast facing window. Mom used this as an additional project room and it had a larger, round Formica table in the middle, which had once served as the dinner table in their previous apartment. She tended plants in here and there were many, many books filling built-in bookcases that lined the two interior walls of the room. When my grandparents had sold the nursery school and day camp that they had owned and operated from 1959 to 1971, many of the children's books came to rest here in this room. For me, as a child, it was a gold mine full of fun things to look at and read. As a point of interest, my first word was neither "Mama" nor "Dada"—but BOOK, very deliberately enunciated, as if a proclamation. At first, the room was not particularly full, but it was certainly kept as a project room and not an entertaining space, like the living room was. And over the years, dirt from potted plants became ground into the 1970s white shag carpet so that it became gradually more and more matted and felted, and less and less white. A few years before my grandfather passed away, he spearheaded a project to clean out that room, re-carpet it, and furnish it with a sofa and loveseat, which we purchased used at a local tag sale. When he would come to visit, he would enjoy the simple act of sitting and reading in that room. So when he passed, we lovingly christened it the "Arthur A. Merget, Sr. Reading Room".

He died on January 3, 1987. Within a few short years, the room began to fill up again.

Looking back on my mother's transformation into a hoarder, and having discussed this with her at length, both she and I agreed that with the passing of her protector—her father, my Grandpa Arty—she began to feel vulnerable and she began to surround herself with things—items—to make her feel fulfilled and safe. As we mourned Grandpa Arty's loss, more and more things began to be stored in the Den.

For several years prior to my grandfather's death, my mother had begun to enjoy the hobby of going to garage sales to get good deals on furniture and things to decorate the house. Partly, she justified this with the excuse that my dad had never let her buy proper kitchen cabinets or bedroom furniture when they got married, as they were still on a newlyweds' budget and my father was always cautious about unnecessary spending. True, they had installed kitchen cabinets in the bedroom, taking advantage of a deal on the cabinetry when originally furnishing the house—and to me, that seemed normal, reasonably frugal; there was a certain charm to that. But with this new realization, my mom began to go antiquing at tag sales, yard sales, garage sales, estate sales, and the like. She began to buy beautiful furniture with her household savings—lots of Bennington Pine, among other types, but mostly dark woods. By all accounts, she was brilliant with the household finances. As my dad used to say, "she could squeeze the nickel so hard, she'd make the buffalo tinkle," referring colloquially to the old buffalo head nickels. So her extra funds were used to buy furniture to replace the older stuff. But the older stuff was never given away or disposed of. The old furniture was thrown upstairs in the unfinished attic with the excuse that she would one day need it for the charitable foundation she was planning to build.

Many years before my mother ever began to uncover her numerous repressed abuse memories, she had a novel idea for a working farm that we would buy and keep in the family as a place to which we could retreat if there were ever any economic or political problems facing our nation. In my mom's reasoning, if the government came toppling down due to foreign or domestic terrorism or collapse due to simple incompetence, at least she would have some place to retreat and wait out the hard times. This was based on the rational idea, promoted by Grandpa Arty from learned family history, that even during an economic depression, farms can still produce food and help a family weather the storm. To this day, I still believe he was right. Distant cousins of his who lived on a farm in upstate New York weathered the Great Depression with extra produce to spare. And this idea was not too different from the bomb shelters built by people at the height of the Cold War. And in fact, the roots of my mother's plan were very much a New Agey permutation of that basic idea of a Cold War contingency plan. And the birth of her idea came in the early 1970s, when I was still a small boy, and the Soviet Union was then considered to be the arch-enemy of the United States, later called by President Reagan "The Evil Empire". New Age apocalyptic predictions were, back then, characterized within that particular socio-political climate, further fuelled by the predictions of people like Edgar Cayce, Ruth Montgomery, Hal Lindsay, and others. In such a scenario, spiritually oriented, natural living committed individuals like us believed we might have to rebuild society on a cleaner and kinder model, should the U.S. and the Soviet Union destroy each other's governments. And there was nothing illogical about this. Many people around the world have apocalyptic leanings. Millions of Christians have a theological standpoint that is hinged upon the idea of a Judgment Day. And they somehow find a way to correlate it to the current socio-political stage and the potential political, economic and meteorological issues facing us. But beyond simple disaster preparedness, the idea of building bomb shelters and hoarding months of supplies went out of style with the end of the Cold War.

So from the early 1980s, we began to search for property to house such an agrarian retreat. Initially, we searched in Ohio, looking for pure and pristine land in rural areas. We continued, every Summer, to travel further and further west, spending several Summers in Kentucky and later in Indiana. My mother was looking for some kind of angelic sign that we had found the property that we were destined to buy. But no sign was ever given or perceived. So, by the mid- 1980s, we then turned to Upstate New York, to Delaware County in particular. We searched there for several years. Then, when my grandfather died, the search for property was put on hold. But the idea persisted and subsequently evolved and transformed into something much more altruistic and charitable, something of perceived cosmic significance.

Tal Uriel (or Tel Uriel in its earlier forms), a rough approximation in Hebrew for "Mound (or City) of Uriel"—often thought of as the archangel of lost causes—was conceived of by my mother as a charitable foundation that would serve as a haven for abused and abandoned children. Tal Uriel became my mother's brainchild and served as the successor idea to the original farm foundation of years prior. It had begun as a getaway plan for family and had become a *mitzvah*, to be organized for the greater good of society, and still provide us with safe haven, should the need arise. And in the process, she would be doing charitable works for abused and abandoned children. My mother conceived of the original idea well before she had rediscovered her repressed abuse memories; she always had a soft spot in her heart for the most downtrodden of our society, helpless children. And so, a charitable foundation would be set up and settled upon a farm, intending to provide the children who were brought there not only with a place to stay, but food to eat and basic skills to learn, as well as counseling and comprehensive healing therapies. And as a component of this project, people we knew who had different talents would be invited to the foundation in order to teach and help run the place. It was a noble and brilliant idea, which I still think should be pioneered in the future. Other organizations have done similar things. I still harbor hopes that in the future, this idea will come to fruition after all.

But the primary step one would take to found such an organization was not to begin buying supplies and furnishings for said organization and begin to store them in one's attic. The logical first step would have been to incorporate and to begin fundraising and development. Then, only after buying property upon which to settle, the organization would need furnishings and supplies. But my mother did this the other way around. Still fearing some type of impending apocalypse in which she would not be able to get normal everyday supplies, she often used the idea of Tal Uriel as an excuse to satisfy these apocalyptic leanings. Claiming that there might be some kind of shortage when we finally purchased the property, she hoarded items of everyday usage. Fearing that we might never be able to get these items at the same sale prices we had access to now, she collected and stored them.

And upstairs into the unfinished attic went not only the furniture and housewares that were replaced by second hand and antique items from garage sales, but also went new sets of bedsheets, linens, table wares and so forth— anything of potential use that she could get on sale. Without having a plan of how big the foundation would be, or even what would be needed, more things were bought in preparation. And much of it went upstairs.

And it got worse. When neighbors renovated or refinished parts of their homes, I was tasked with helping to take window frames and door jambs and used construction materials out of their dumpsters and bring them to our house, carefully fitting them into the unused left-hand bay of the two-car garage. What had been a normally used storage bay of the garage, still able to be navigated with relative ease, had now become a warehouse of things we would never, ever use. I began to see that there was a certain level of illogic to this kind of thinking. That we would be able to reuse twenty or thirty year old window frames from someone else's dumpster was less than logical to me. I tried to convey this to my mom. Her usual answer was that we would be saving money by reusing these when the time came to build the farm foundation. And so, in went bed frames and mattresses from garage sales. The piles in the garage got higher and higher. What began with a second-hand red velvet couch from my friend Todd's family's basement, that my mom intended to reupholster and later re-use, now grew into a veritable warehouse full of unusable items.

Later, after Grandpa Arty's passing, we adopted furniture from my grandparents' apartment, and other items that had been kept in storage in my aunt and uncle's basement while they had their garage converted into an apartment so Grandma and Grandpa could move in there—the apartment they occupied until their eventual deaths. Rocking chairs, easy chairs, tables, chests, and so forth, all came to live in our garage, now located on the previously usable right-hand bay of the two-car garage, while the left-hand side remained as tightly packed as ever.

Throughout the 1980s, as I grew to become a fairly strong teenager, having embarked on an obsession with bodybuilding, I was commandeered to help with moving antique furniture that we continually bought and located in novel places within the house. To a large degree, I enjoyed this. It showcased my newfound strength—a much needed activity as a formerly scrawny teen with a self-confidence problem and body dysmorphia. And I also had the opportunity to meet many interesting people in many upscale neighborhoods who were happy to swap stories with my parents and me after we had purchased their unwanted or antique furniture.

Furniture and housewares began to be stored in every room. All spare space was taken up. We stored a beautiful cherry wood table, disassembled for space savings, in the Arthur A. Merget Reading Room. Other things were nested inside the table trestles. Books, books, and more books. The room that we had renovated only about five years prior had now begun to fill up again and was no longer extensively usable, either as a guest room or a family room.

But the major problem, however, was still newspapers. The active collecting of them began about 1979 or 1980, after a major blizzard had caused an ice storm a year or two prior—commonly known as the "Ice Storm of '78" or the "Blizzard of '78". That year, my parents decided to buy a wood burning stove to help defray the heating costs and further ensure our safety during future blizzards. Our home lacked a fireplace, which many of our neighboring homes had, a dilemma which used to facetiously concern me as I would playfully speculate how Santa Claus would ever enter the house—if there *were* a Santa Claus, which I was never encouraged to believe in anyway—and I mused that if he entered by the chimney of our home's furnace (which like many Long Island homes was designed to burn home heating oil), he would be instantly incinerated. At any rate, about a year or so after the Ice Storm of '78, my parents went to the local wood stove and fireplace store and carefully selected an Efel Kamina woodburning stove, the newest model. The whole concept of wood burning stoves and the culture that surrounded them fascinated me as a nine- or ten-year-old who had been exposed to pioneer culture and lifestyles from watching *Little House on the Prairie* on television. In my mind, this now made us homesteaders and neighbors to the Ingalls family. I remember timidly exploring the dimly lit store, steeped in the aroma of charcoal and hardwoods, lined in dark wood paneling of frontier homesteads, and discovering all manner of previously unknown wood stove related decorations and paraphernalia—bellows and coal scuttles and the like—while my parents worked out logistics with the staff members of the store, and I was transported back to the frontier with Ma and Pa Ingalls and the children.

Despite the fact that the salespeople and the service reps told us in no uncertain terms that burning newspaper produced excess creosote and that it should not be used any more than necessary as a fire starter, Mom discovered that burning newspaper was much more economical than buying cords and cords of firewood. Newspaper was a plentiful resource. This was in the days before recycling was widespread and supported by the municipal trash carting services. People were always trying to get rid of newspapers. And that worked to our advantage—for a while. Everywhere we went, my mother would ask people to save their newspapers for us and we would take them and burn them in our wood-burning stove. And they would usually oblige. I particularly remember my piano teacher, Mrs. Elder—a cultured woman of European sensibilities and breeding, but raised in Idaho—saving newspapers for us, giving us a small stack every week. It was my chore to carry the stack out to the car, usually right after the lesson was over. It had become a ritual. Even on weeks when lessons had been cancelled due to illness, we still stopped by briefly to pick up the newspapers from her.

And so my mother began to collect newspapers from everywhere. We stacked them in the house, initially on the concrete brick platform upon which the stove was situated. The heat produced by the newspapers was no less effective than wood. We packed it into the stove very compactly, usually placing one major log into the stove along with a huge amount of paper. It burned warmly and steadily. I used to spend hours next to the stove—usually behind it, where the heat radiated with the least hindrance—either drawing or reading or petting the family cat, whom I had named Catnip Racer and who kept me company in that spot of warmth. It was idyllic for a young child. But I did not see the growing addiction that was looming over our heads.

Around the age of eleven or twelve, the newspapers began to stack up more quickly than they could be burned. Mom usually spent hours reading them prior to burning them. She would inform herself through these papers, voracious reader and knowledge chaser that she was. And she would save articles, carefully torn out and put aside for future reference, if they interested her. She had been an unpublished writer who was, despite her brilliant writing, always suffering from repeat rejections of her work. So, the newspapers provided subject matter of all sorts for her to write about, and which inspired her next essay or short story or article. We all noticed that the pileup had begun to be a problem. Some of my friends from school, when they came over, noticed their imposing presence. I recall Gerard particularly, my classmate and friend from down the street, innocently but somewhat presumptuously advising about how my mother could better organize them. She humored him, but had a response for every suggestion, explaining why she had to keep them exactly as they were. He did not see that this was a sickness. Few, if any, of us did.

A Religion of Collecting

While I was growing up, whenever we would take vacations to various areas, to find land for our foundation, Mom would always stop to pick up brochures from the rest areas. But it was never just one or two. It was usually one or two of each brochure. And there was usually a rack of brochures for all the tourist attractions in that area—dozens perhaps. So, she would wind up with one or two small shopping bags of brochures and flyers at the end of each trip. She would claim that she was doing research on the area, to see what kind of area it was so we could get to know our neighbors, should we decide to settle there. Later, as she began to do more artwork and ink drawings, these became the source of her subjects, or so she claimed; she liked the designs that she would find in generic pamphlets. At first, my dad would balk at having to have so many flyers filling the car as we drove. But after several years of arguing and seeing no positive results, both he and I began to lovingly roll our eyes at Mom's predilection and Dad would often joke that "it's her religion; she has to have one of each." And we would all chuckle together, disarming any disturbance of the peace. But the problem was that none of these ever got thrown out. And after thirty to forty years of collecting these pamphlets from everywhere we went, it contributed—as did everything else in the house that was compulsively saved—to the overall volume that was in the domicile. When we executed the cleanout of the Exile in 2009, I most certainly found evidence of pamphlets for kiddie rides and tourist attractions from Elizabethtown, Kentucky in 1981 and '82, and Nashville, Indiana from 1983, and so forth.

At some point in the mid-1980s, the school where my dad presently taught as a reading teacher, a junior high in Northport, was getting rid of old textbooks, to be unceremoniously thrown out. The teachers were notified of this. When my mother found out, she had my dad question the administration as to why they were not donating the books to some needy school district in a less affluent area. The answer, in the height of the wasteful 1980s, was simple: it was too expensive to ship them elsewhere than to just discard them. This answer was unacceptable to my family, and Mom insisted that we go over and save as many of the books as possible, so we could donate them ourselves to a worthy recipient. And I still believe she was right. But one person cannot rectify the iniquities of a wasteful and narcissistic society. When all was said and done, the underlying illness which caused my mother to hoard won out over the simple need to find a new home for these books. I cannot say how many of the books were actually donated to a recipient, but I am sure that the vast majority of them never were. Finding a way to ship them to a school district was far more tasking than my mother had anticipated and her need to start new projects got the best of her. And so the books, perhaps hundreds of identical textbooks—math, science, and so forth—were stashed upstairs in the unfinished attic, or the crawlspace below in the foundation, or in other nooks and crannies in the house; wherever we could find room. And so, open space continued to be scarce in our home.

While I was still in high school, one friend, named Mike, who had been over to the house had commented that he thought it was "cool" that my mother collected things. He stated that everything in the house had a story. And I appreciated his understanding—since others were not as accepting of the sheer eccentricity of it, choosing to be much more judgmental—he had no idea of why this collecting took place. He was right that there was a story to everything, but he did not know the half of it. How could he know? As the house became more full of things, we had people over less and less. My mother was certainly embarrassed about the house and we eventually ceased inviting people over as guests. I still had very select friends over on rare occasions, but my parents encouraged me to go over to my friends' houses instead of having them over to our place.

After I left home to go to college, the problem continued to become worse. More newspapers were collected. We began to run out of usable room. No amount of reasoning with my mother would convince her that we did not need to keep these. She even took to having my father place stacks of them downstairs in the unfinished crawl-space that our house had instead of a basement. My dad later admitted to me, somewhat sheepishly, *sotto voce*, as if telling me a horrible secret, that there were likely thousands of pounds of newspaper that he had put down there. When I asked my mother about why she did this, the answer was that she thought we would need them for burning in the stove if the winter became particularly cold. I feared what would happen if there were an electrical short downstairs, caused by a rodent chewing through electrical wires. This scenario, it turned out, was far less of a stretch of the imagination than one would think. During the Exile, the presence of rats became abundantly evident to us. My trepidation was not unfounded.

While I was growing up, I tended to have a lazy, dreamy, oblivious quality, eschewing chores in favor of daydreaming. Kids tend to do that; and more so boys of intellect, I suppose. When my mother was able to get me to do chores, it was usually vacuuming. As I grew older, the amount of space that was able to be vacuumed gradually, but steadily, decreased. It was impossible to move piles of books out of the way, or vacuum under large, immovable pieces of furniture. So, quite comically, my job got easier as time passed. But nevertheless, I began to realize, by this litmus test, that there was a problem developing. When I began to have a better grasp of the fact that my mother had a problem with collecting, I started to take more of an interest in cleaning. As such, I wanted to help reverse this trend that I had realized was potentially dangerous. When I would come home from college or graduate school, I would ask her to let me help discarding and clearing things out. But she would very forcefully state that what she really needed help with was dusting; that the house was so dusty and she needed me to vacuum or to dust the ranks of old hardbound books that were lined up below the cabinets, servers, and buffets in the dining room and kitchen. She needed me to dust. And I would usually oblige, reluctantly; but as I dusted, I felt indignant, as if she had asked me to polish light bulbs, stressing the crucial nature of that task.

More and more often, I would take initiative and clean things that she would not want cleaned. During breaks from grad school, I would often clean out the refrigerator when she wasn't home, purging it of much of its waste and duplicate matter. Having suffered from moth infestations years ago, infecting boxes of rice and other grains, Mom took to keeping these dry goods in bags inside the refrigerator. Of course, I would have suggested airtight containers instead, unrefrigerated. Nevertheless, they took up huge amounts of room in the fridge, while they did not actually need to be chilled, just defended from bugs. The presence of these many bags and other substantial items, jam-packed into any available space, would impede the flow of cold air within the fridge, preventing proper cooling of perishables, thereby causing their early expiration. And on more than one occasion, the lack of air flow contributed to the early demise of the fan motor, rendering the whole unit inoperative. Several new fridges had to be exchanged, some thankfully under warranty, and others not.

At times, I even took it upon myself to clean off the long prep table that was positioned in the middle of the kitchen and taking up all usable space, having once been our brand new white Formica dining room table. When that table was replaced by a beautiful, hand-carved nearly antique table, replete with "pineapples" on the legs, we moved the old white Formica one into the kitchen. But the space that it provided for prep did not last long. Very quickly, it was covered with several layers of projects, mostly plants and seeds, half-germinated and ready to be potted—or not. The tea bags which Mom insisted were good compost for the garden were saved almost indefinitely, ready to be torn open, the leaves scattered in the garden and the torn bags garbaged; there was always a backlog of these. One of the other major pet peeves I had was that there was a certain rice milk drink that she would perennially buy, having become largely vegetarian at that time; and the packaging of the drink was not properly biodegradable. And so we had large numbers of these cardboard boxes, in which the rice milk drink was packaged, which had to be torn apart so that the petroleum based plastic liner inside could be garbaged, while the outer cardboard layer could be composted in the garden. These, of course, tended to get backlogged very quickly as well. There was always something standing in the way of something else, preventing the task at hand from being streamlined. Nothing could be easy. And this was one of the personality quirks that I noted about my mother. Unnecessary obstacles were created in order to stymie her progress. Evidently, somehow, this helped maintain her personal narrative of failure or martyrdom, or whatever it was that she derived from it. The frightening thing to me is that I have some of that in myself. I have often jokingly commented that nothing in my life is ever simple to explain. That is—despite the humor of it—somewhat scary.

We were always in a catch-22, as we were prevented from cleaning the house in an effective manner, since my mom wanted to keep everything. She gave lip service to wanting to clean. But when push came to shove, and we were ready to clean, she persisted in having me dust off books. This was a frequent argument, almost programmatic. But somewhere along the way, perhaps when I was already in grad school, there was a particular family argument, which occurred when I was home on break, and in which my mom was demanding more help from us in keeping the house clean. Something snapped, and she threw large swaths of yellow fabric from her sewing room over all the random items that were piled on top of the servers, buffets, and cabinets in the kitchen area, in order to cover the clutter. Somehow this was expected to fool imminent visitors into thinking that we were redecorating. And they stayed there for perhaps a decade, those yellow cloths. I remember their still being there when we began the cleanout during the Exile, now covered in even more layers of refuse, like strata from an archaeological site, a ruined city of several epochs.

The composition of the amassed volume in the house was certainly quite varied. Mostly, it appeared to be comprised of newspapers. But there were plenty of other things, including what was mentioned above, along with empty vitamin bottles that needed to be recycled, cardboard boxes, unclassifiable items, many books, magazines, and so forth. But the majority of the mass did still appear to be newspapers, or at least the most obvious item comprising the clutter was such. I will later elucidate some of the theories we came up with as to why the newspapers were such a prominent item.

As a side note of interest, it was later brought to my attention by Jack, my father's oldest friend, that in the 1930s and '40s, there were two brothers living in New York City, by the names of Homer and Langley Collyer. Both brothers being eccentric landowners, they retreated from public life, ceased paying their bills and became recluses, compulsively hoarding newspapers as well as valuables and trash alike. Both were discovered dead in their home in 1947 when neighbors reported to the police a stench coming from inside the home. Over 130 tons of trash were removed by emergency personnel from their Harlem brownstone. One of them died of complications related to malnutrition. The other was crushed to death by his own piles of hoarded matter. One brother had gone blind, and it had been the assertion of the other that the newspapers were important so that his brother could catch up with current events once he regained his lost eyesight. He never regained his sight, and both died within their newspaper-filled hoard, a veritable prison of their own creation. I could not help but note the uncanny similarity to my mother's penchant for collecting newspapers. And as my family's illness became worse, and hit its peak in 2009, I feared that death by hoarding would become my parents' fate as well.

Curbside Express

At some point while I was still in high school, my mother began to notice things that people had thrown out at their curb that were still in good condition and should have been given away. Couches, chairs, tables, all manner of things that in our wasteful, American 1980s mentality were simply just going to fill up landfills. It was indeed a tragic waste. I didn't like it any more than she did. However, as we would drive by, she would cry out—somewhat humorously— "OH, GOOD GARBAGE….GOOD GARBAGE!!!" And we would chuckle supportively. But more seriously, she would often ask my dad to stop the car so she could inspect and see if there was anything salvageable. He would balk at this, complaining "Barb, what are you gonna do with that?! It's garbage!" And he would cringe every time we would roll past a large deposition of salvageables at someone's curb, fearing that she would demand we stop and help feed her addiction. But despite his discomfiture, he would usually stop, she would quickly get out, inspect the items, and then come back victoriously with something small, but useable. Early on, we had gotten our first touch-tone cordless telephone (in an age when rotary wall phones were still being used, but the people who were more affluent and ostentatious were already using touch tone phones and specifically cordless phones) at the curb of some wasteful family, still operational and ready to serve us for years to come. The unit just needed a new battery, if I recall, which my dad changed out, and we had a newly usable phone. My mom began to playfully call this salvage activity "Curbside Express". When my dad would resist stopping the car for "good garbage", she would remind him of all the wonderful things she had already scored via Curbside Express. So, he would reluctantly accede and sit in the driver's seat, car idling, stewing and steaming from embarrassment. Occasionally, he would give her a tough time about it, but he learned that it was easier to give in than to resist. The outcome was less turbulent that way. And the several successful finds that yielded beloved items would stand as a testament, a future reminder of my mother's occasional correctness in this.

For myself, I agreed that our wasteful society had to be retrained. I was an impressionable teen who had many of the same sensibilities as his mother and was gaining more. To me, this was largely a good thing. However, there were limits to my complicity, and when I was enlisted to exit the car with her and help carry some large item back to the car, my own embarrassment began. And as an unpopular teen with a very low self image, one who was very susceptible to the popular opinion of his peers (particularly the prissy, affluent Long Island girls), I feared that the longer I lingered next to garbage, the more closely linked to it I would become. I imagined that my entire high school, nay the entire school district, was receiving play-by-play information about what I was doing, was watching a live-feed, like some anachronistic internet streaming as yet to be invented, and they were ready to mercilessly jeer at me and judge me for my differences. And so this played right into my low self-image. At times, we were driving past lawn chairs and patio furniture in neighbourhoods we hardly knew, and I would be commandeered into helping get the chosen items into the car while my dad waited and stewed. As an older teen or young adult, my strength was formidable and I would quickly exit the vehicle and grab whatever large items my mom wanted and I would stuff them in the car, without even needing my mom's help. My alacrity was not out of a desire for efficiency as much as it was a desire to leave the place as quickly as possible and avoid additional social stigma. Mom was nonetheless pleased that she got her treasures. She knew that it caused me embarrassment; she gained no pleasure from that, but she felt this was a necessary evil and it had to be done. She was saving the environment, in her mind. She was preventing the dump in Hauppauge from filling up unnecessarily with lawn chairs and sectional couch pillows. I took part reluctantly (knowing the social consequences for me), but nevertheless willingly, out of love for her. And so I do not remember her giving me grief for my reluctance, the way she did with my dad. She knew I was doing this out of my respect for her wishes and my love for her.

But as things began to stock up in the house from other activities—from antiquing, decreased expediency in recycling newspapers and containers, and other sources—the things we picked up from Curbside Express were less necessary items and more "luxuries", if you will, that would never see any use. They were a mere salve to my mother's wounded psyche. These things would be stashed in the garage, for future repair or use. Items that were broken were still picked up if there was a chance of repairing them. At a point in my late teens, when I had already begun driving, there was a time in which I had indeed expressed displeasure at being asked to stop the car to let my mom pick up a plastic rocking horse that had been discarded. Feeling my newfound teen chutzpah, I just kept driving, denying her the prize. I had been embarrassed, as it was broad daylight and most of our Curbside Express was done at night, under the cover of darkness. She was hurt and angry this time, at my reluctance. Later, I went back on my own and picked up the rocking horse for her. It was indeed still in quite good condition. The only issue with it was that the wooden handle, mounted atop the molded plastic mane of the horse, had broken loose and wobbled wildly, preventing it from being a safely usable toy. It was not an antique; it was probably from the last ten years. But it was fixable, if you had the skill. Unfortunately, at that time, I did not have the skill to fix it. But my mother was pleased that I went back and saved it. On some level, that horse represented her childhood, her innocence, the vulnerable little child that she was, so easily tossed away by her erstwhile protectors, and she needed fiercely to protect it. Years later, I would understand this. At the time, I just knew it made her happy and it stopped the arguments, the yelling, the guilt I felt at denying her wishes. So I acceded. And so it sat in the garage for years. It was never fixed. At some point, it was shifted outside to make room for other things. Its color gradually faded. Its plastic began to succumb to the elements, it began to crack, and it was eventually thrown out during the Exile. It died a slow, lingering death; a fate worse than if it had been simply and swiftly thrown out prior to our "saving" it.

At some point in my late teens as well, my friend Gerard's family had a garage sale. We picked up a wooden desk from his house. We had no room left for it in the garage—that was already full. So it sat, just outside the garage, upended, tightly wrapped in a blue tarp, weathering winter after winter. But the snow and moisture got to it just the same. And at some point, it began to collapse under its own weight and the weight of whatever other item of furniture was placed atop it. And when it disintegrated, we threw it away. And we replaced it with the next piece of furniture that we "surely could use," saving it from "the landfill" or clogging up "the Dumps at Hauppauge". It might have been better for us to have just purchased it and immediately donated it to the Salvation Army. At least we could have gotten a tax write-off for it and not had it decaying in the front yard. When the Exile happened, we had to discard the item that had taken the place of Gerard's desk, its successor, which in turn had already begun to disintegrate after being out there for about a decade of disuse, fighting off the elements.

College Girlfriend

There were always excuses why people were not invited over. It had gone on for quite some time. We were "redecorating", mostly. That was the official story. Of course, we were all embarrassed, underneath. But it was facilely handled by claiming that we were redecorating. Mom was a master at stories, elaborate ones, which charmed people into believing the lies which covered over the symptoms of age-old torments and demons. As I mentioned, many years earlier, Mike, the friend who had seen the house when it was still livable, had proclaimed kindly that he thought it was cool that everything in the house had a story and was a snapshot of life. But not everyone saw it that way. And the house would get steadily worse, following the passing of my grandfather, who was my mom's protector and champion for so many years.

My college girlfriend, Jenn, who had her own emotional difficulties—as, of course, did I—was staying in Middletown (our Connecticut college town) over the Summer of 1992 and she wanted to visit me on Long Island. Of course I wanted this, too—young love. But there was no place for her to stay. We could have found a place if Mom had thrown some things away, but there was no time to do so. She was always "too busy", she "needed help", and so forth. So Jenn had to come for the day time only and go back to Connecticut by night. It would have been too difficult for my mother to have to explain to Jenn why the house was so messy and that it could not accommodate guests. It was my mom's feelings that were the most important—not mine, not Jenn's. She could not bear the embarrassment of people knowing that she was incapable of rectifying this situation; that she needed professional help. She did not count on the fact that many years later, these demons would be laid bare before everyone to see, despite her best efforts to hide them.

But Jenn had to come for daytimes. And one time, she stayed late. We had to ask my friend's parents, the Feuersteins, if they would put her up for the night. My old friend Dave was more than obliging. I'd known him since I was thirteen and he was always the best friend a guy could have. I drove Jenn over there, about three or so miles away. We set her up in a guest room. Mrs. Feuerstein didn't ask questions. She knew; she was wise. We explained the usual about the redecorating—which had already been going on for about six or seven years—but no judgment or aspersions were cast. I tucked Jenn in and went home. I was grateful to not have to show Jenn the surroundings I was in. So was my mother. There was resentment on all sides, however—more than enough to go around. Jenn resented that she could not stay at the house of her adult boyfriend—and with no real explanation other than the facile attempt to blame it on the redecorating. I believe I had told her privately about the mess (there was no word for "hoarding" yet in common usage at that time). But still, she could never understand. There was resentment on the part of my mother, that she had to be saddled with this embarrassment, this problem that she had to dodge. My father was largely passive in the whole affair—not really happy about the potential of people seeing his home in the condition it was in, but he was just happy not to have the recurrent yelling or rages of my mother, blaming and accusing, characteristically shifting responsibility away from herself. But for the most part, it was I who had the most cause for resentment. It was I who was the least culpable party in this matter. By that time, my room was generally clean. I had given up the typical childhood sloppiness, messiness, having learned to live agreeably with apartment-mates in college. But this was my home, too. I had the right to have guests, especially my first serious adult girlfriend. I resented it very much and I had the right to.

Jenn went back to Middletown the next day. And shortly after this, things continued to get tense between us. We had some major compatibility problems. We were young. I was needy. She was deliberately anti-needy, or distant perhaps. She dealt with mental health issues, and each of us was dealing with our parental issues in our own special way. But within weeks, I had begun to clean my room for the last time, perhaps as a response, a declaration of my autonomy. Any childhood mess that I had previously left was now to be cleared out. I got rid of much paperwork and dross that I had been keeping for many years, I put away old toys—not getting rid of them but putting them neatly in storage. I wanted to distance myself from my mother's hoarding tendencies, knowing that I had some of the same. I brought my room to a nice, neat level, and that was where it would stay for several years after that. But my mother took it upon herself to pull things out of the trash and the recycling, against my will, and save them. It was as if she did not trust that I knew what should and should not be discarded. That I did not have the right to my own self-determination. Yes, there were a few items that perhaps I was a bit hasty in discarding and that in the long run, I am glad she saved. But the overall tenor of the action was intrusive and disrespectful. She saved things that I had determined were mere duplicates of other items or documents, as if I did not have the right to discard these. Many of these went right back into my room when I left to go back to college. Others, she saved in her own areas of the house and placed them in whatever haphazard, disordered manner they fell into, in the lack of time to organize them.

Later that Summer, Jenn and I took a trip from Middletown down to Maryland, to visit her parents, my first time meeting them. It was an exciting trip, my first overnight trip with a girlfriend. It was one in which I learned much about myself and about our relationship, some of which was not so positive. But I also was granted insight into Jenn's own parental issues—a medical doctor and a psychiatrist, now divorced—who were both simultaneously distant and controlling. It explained a lot of Jenn's issues, and particularly those that she projected onto my mother.

We had begun the trip in Connecticut with Jenn's old car, an early '70s Dodge sedan—which promptly died on the way. After selling the car for scrap to a local auto-repair shop, we then took the train the rest of the way down to Maryland, and stayed several days with her mother, who subsequently gave Jenn her old van, also a Dodge, which would now become her vehicle to drive back to Connecticut. When we began our trip back north again and I phoned my parents to tell them that we would be stopping by, my mother begged me not to come to the house. She begged me to call my aunt and uncle and ask if we could stay there overnight, trying to avoid a repeat of the experience with Jenn staying at the Feuersteins' a month or so prior. I grew angry at my mother. Was I not allowed to come to my own home to visit? Was I not allowed to stay in my own house? This of course added stress to my already ailing relationship with Jenn, who had formed her own inaccurate assessments of my very close yet dysfunctional relationship with my mother, placing unrealistic expectations on me about resisting my mom's wishes and asserting my own will. But not wanting to disappoint my girlfriend, or miss an opportunity to individuate from an overbearing maternal figure, I supported Jenn's decision to drive right to my house to drop me off there and then for her to continue directly on to Connecticut. But we arrived a bit late in the evening, and Jenn decided to stay in the van overnight—in our driveway. My mother, faced with the obviousness of her own inhospitability, eventually begged Jenn to come inside and sleep on the couch, something that should have been done the first time she visited, earlier in the Summer.

So we fit Jenn into the Arthur A. Merget Reading Room—the room which my grandfather had helped to renovate prior to his death, several years prior; the self-same room that my mother would gradually fill full of junk over the next decade and then retreat to when the hoarding was at its worst and she was effectively separating herself from my father while living in the same home. The room was nonetheless full of newspapers and things, but we hastily cleared the couch and made it cozy enough for Jenn to sleep on, still surrounded by the other dross and clutter. I could tell that she was pleased. I could see it in her smile. My mother was somewhat pacified, too. She realized she had done the right thing in revealing her idiosyncrasies just long enough to make things right with Jenn and to show her the hospitality that was required in this situation. Jenn went back to Middletown the next day, and things inevitably got worse between us over the next few weeks. We had broken up by the first day of Fall classes, senior year. But this series of incidents stood out to me as a signal of the growing illness in my family home.

Garbage Pickers

When I graduated from college in 1993, my parents were there. They had come up to Connecticut for the ceremony and stayed overnight at the university guest house. The evening after graduation, many of the students—both graduates and underclass folks—were clearing out their apartments to go home for the Summer. My mother and I were both appalled at the huge amount of waste that was generated, left outside of many of the apartments in bags, in bins, or just tossed off to the side of the walls. Such wasteful middle class adult children they were, who didn't know the meaning of want. Much of this refuse was still very usable, items that should have gone to a charity or been recycled, but there was little knowledge of that among college kids at that time, nor resources to receive such. I remember that my mother insisted that evening upon going around my apartment complex—twin buildings called "Lo-Rise" and "Hi-Rise", the former of which had mostly outdoor entrances to separate two story units all adjoined in the same sprawling, serpentine, angular building, and the latter of which being a singular eight story apartment building, both of which were of matching tan concrete—to see what garbage could be saved. And while I agreed with her that much of this *should* be saved, I did not want to be involved in picking through other people's garbage, especially when I had my own apartment to clear out before vacating, my own "junk" to deal with and sort through. But she insisted, and I went with her to help carry things— really to try to dissuade her from taking too much or things that she really would never use. By that point in time, I already knew that she was a bit of a "pack rat", as it was termed at the time, and I saw our Long Island home filling up more and more with other people's garbage that my mother saw further use for and had saved through her Curbside Express. As I mentioned, we did indeed get a few good items from this treasure hunting, but as time wore on, the number of these were outweighed by the sheer volume of unusable items. The value of it also was outweighed by the embarrassment my father and I both felt at being guilted into trolling neighborhoods at night in our station wagon and being forced to stop and help her lift refuse items into the car.

But this particular evening in 1993, around twilight, I remember walking through the outdoor alleyways between the two-story concrete buildings that housed the Lo-Rise student apartments, picking up refuse for her—chairs, brooms, clocks, dustpans, whatever. And as we strolled, I had more and more of a sense of embarrassment, of shame.

The campus was abutted by the local low-income housing projects, populated by people of multiple ethnicities. Much of the town was Italian-American, with a significant number of recent immigrants. Many of the residents of the projects were white, some were African-American. This evening, there were a number of little children who were riding their bicycles through the complex, seeing what their neighbors were up to. I had never had any run-ins with the local children. Generally, these neighborhood kids were reasonably well-behaved—well enough. They usually kept to themselves, sometimes wondering what our lives were all about—these strange college students, neither children nor truly adults—conducted side by side with theirs. Occasionally I had contact with their collective parents. They were generally good-natured people, harmless. They were generally hardworking people of little privilege—regardless of their ethnicity—and suffered from a lack of education and a lack of access to upward mobility or economic advancement. It was quite a stark contrast to our college, full of privileged young adults. But the grown-ups usually kept to themselves as well. There were some community outreach programs that the university ran. And occasionally, we would hear of our students babysitting the neighborhood children or mentoring them in their afterschool programs and whatnot. Occasionally, the children would find their way into one of our buildings, like Hi-Rise, the eight-story concrete apartment building where I lived, or wended their way through the alley ways of the adjoining Lo-Rise complex that I strolled through this night; and they would roam around, looking for entertainment, mainly just trying to make contact with us out of curiosity, like we were aliens or wild animals to be viewed with intense interest.

But this night, several little children—about 8 or 9 years of age, perhaps from the same extended family—rode around brazenly on their bicycles. And when they saw my mother and me, they began chanting, "garbage PICKERS!… garbage PICKERS!" repeatedly, taunting us. My mother did not hear or listen to them at first. She blithely continued to roam around on her hunt, smiling pleasantly at these little children, almost with an attitude of "how cute they are" on her mind, oblivious of the fact that they were attempting to ridicule her and deride her—and me as well. I grew embarrassed. I grew enraged. I knew that I did not like what my mother was doing; that she was on some level inviting this kind of derision. In my mind, I even thought to some degree that she deserved it, that if she only knew the derision she was attracting and the embarrassment she was causing me that she might stop her actions and repent. But I grew more enraged at these children, who couldn't understand our particular predicament. They did not know that this woman, with long silver hair, eccentric beyond words, was a tremendously giving and loving and special human being—the likes of which they might never see again in their lives, even living next to a university such as ours that inspired and propagated compassionate eccentricity. I could not help but think that, even turning to my own defense—that I had more education in my head than they had in their entire family, momentarily and defensively indulging myself in a classism that I am not proud of. That they had no right to deride my mother and me when we were doing this not out of a povertous need for goods, or the psychotic need for artifacts in a vagrant's shopping cart, but that we were trying to save the garbage dumps from being overfull; that we were trying to make some kind of sense of all the waste, even at an environmentally aware (often pretentiously so) university such as ours. I wanted to tell these children so; tell them to shut their mouths, tell them that I was better than they were and that they would never know how much better we were than they. But I did not do so. I knew that it would not make any difference, that it would fall on deaf ears, or even do more harm to at-risk children already growing up in the projects. And I knew that my momentary feelings of adversarial superiority were just a rageful and visceral reaction to their insults. That I was momentarily reminded of being a little child myself and having others make fun of me mercilessly, and having no recourse except to quietly mumble, "shut up" under my breath so that my defiance would not garner a larger beating from my tormentors. I was transported back to a moment of being ridiculed for things beyond my control, for the condition of my family, for an identity that I had not chosen and was not of my making. And on some level, I felt hypersensitive about being associated with garbage and vagrancy. All of my fears that I felt during high school when we would engage in Curbside Express, that I would be spotted and ridiculed for my association with trash and refuse, were now coming true. Even though I did not know these children, they were my accusers; they had power over me. I was angry at anyone who witnessed this moment of vulnerability and I was eager to make myself seem better than they were.

And it was only later that I was able to see the irony of the situation, that these children—born and raised in the poverty of the Middletown housing projects—were possibly dealing with their own issues of inferiority as Black youth in the shadow of an overwhelmingly White, middle class university, and saw an easy target of their anger in this eccentric old "bag lady", who was seemingly worse off than they were. And in this moment, infused with an embarrassing thread of classism and subliminal racism, I had temporarily convinced myself that I was better than someone else, when really we were just a son and his somewhat mentally unbalanced mother, picking garbage—truly no better than anyone else, despite my mental gymnastics to convince myself otherwise. That I was, on some level, merely the enabling son of a mentally deranged "bag lady", filling her shopping cart. This is one of the moments I spoke of earlier, that I include as a sort of confession.

After a while of hunting, the children grew tired of taunting us and moved on to more interesting things. We finished up and I went back inside to continue clearing out my apartment, returning to dealing with my own feelings of loss, having just graduated and knowing that I would never return to this, my home for nearly four years—at least not as a student. That even if I ever did return, perhaps as a professor, it would never be the same. This was a life-changing event that I will never forget. And it would be a harbinger of things to come.

"Save that for me; I can use that"

Nearly a decade after this incident, I was in seminary, out in California. I was working with my friend Grant, who had a small janitorial company, and we were taking on jobs to put ourselves through graduate school. We were cleaning an empty unit inside a commercial shopping mall. The unit had been a supermarket that was currently not leased. We were nearly done with stripping, resealing, and polishing the floors of the large unit, when I had to clean something out behind the store, near the dumpsters just in front of the elevated loading dock. As I was working there, doing I recall not what, a young man rolled by on his bicycle. He was about the same age as I was, about thirty perhaps, White with dark shaggy hair. He was relatively disheveled, largely oblivious of the world around him. He stopped his bike and got off; it had some bags hanging from the handlebars and various other points aboard it. He peered into the dumpster, eyed what appeared to me to be a set of Venetian blinds that had been taken down from one of the vacant units and discarded there. The young man spoke, and he said in a clearly audible voice, enthusiastically, but to no particular audience, "Save that for me. I can use that." He was not looking at me. He had not addressed me directly. He was seemingly talking to some unseen party that accompanied him in his journeys, asking them to do him that favor. And then he left on his bicycle, with no word about when he would be back to claim "that". At first it seemed somewhat humorous to me. I callously thought to myself: "No you can't. You don't have any need for that. You're a crazy homeless person who surely has no use for that set of blinds. Who are you kidding?!"

But I began to see the sad reality behind this. Yes, he was probably psychologically disturbed. But this was someone's son, perhaps someone's brother. He had a story. There was a reason why he was there doing that. Whether or not he could be considered a hoarder, it dawned on me as time wore on, thinking of this vignette in retrospect, that there is a fine line between those who suffer from hoarding, and those who suffer from addictions and mental illnesses. As they say in Twelve Step Circles, "Some are sicker than others." Some people that suffer from hoarding, like my mother, are highly functional in every other aspect of their lives. Others may begin to suffer from increased levels of compulsion and anxiety and an inability to keep their affairs in order. It is these that need the greatest amount of care and supervision from their loved ones. It is these who are potentially a step (or an eviction notice) away from becoming like this young man on the bicycle—a transient person who does not have the presence of mind to know that he has nowhere to store the things he is collecting. I know that in 2009, my family came as close to this as it ever had been.

Mrs. Feuerstein's Tile Place

The aforementioned Dave Feuerstein, who was one of my oldest and closest remaining friends, had what I considered an ideal physical home environment. Even though there were definite problems between him and his parents growing up, his home was always immaculate, perfectly cleaned weekly by a maid (but not pretentiously so), and often remodelled by his very interior design-savvy mother. I loved spending time there. They had a pool, and a pool house to boot. Friends and I spent many Summer hours there, as his house was generally at the epicenter of where our group of social misfits congregated—most of us being of the nerdy or geeky variety. And I spent many hours lusting after his curvy older sister, who was of course, too old for me at the time. On one occasion, I volunteered to help Dave's mom do a cleanout of the pool house. When my mother caught wind of my offer, she was hurt. How could I offer to do chores for Mrs. Feuerstein, when I wouldn't do the same for my own mother? Of course, I saw my mother's point and I was sufficiently chastened. But the point still stood that Mrs. F. would allow me to actually clean and throw things out. At home, by this point, nothing was permitted to be tossed out. Any time I spent cleaning would have been occupied dusting old books that multiplied by the minute, and vacuuming a few square feet of floor space that were rapidly disappearing like the rainforests. To me, it seemed like a losing proposition, a waste of my time that in the long run neither effected any change, nor was truly beneficial to anyone.

When Dave's family took in my college girlfriend, Jenn, when she came to stay, they already knew the condition of our home. They had deduced there was some kind of issue there. They were always respectfully uninquisitive about it. We continued to claim that we were still "redecorating" and that was the end of the matter. But some time in the early 1990s, either while I was still in college or had already gone to California to grad school, Mrs. F. opened an interior decorating place specializing in marble and tile. And she always had beautiful remnants of marble and tile behind her shop that were discarded— free for the taking. My mom took little bits here and there, whenever she had the chance, and they wound up in the garage, lining the pathways, making them narrower. One large square foot of half-inch thick marble wound up propped up against the wall inside the master bathroom of our house. Its weight gradually affected the working of the sliding pocket door—one of several incorporated into the design of our 1972-built home. It caused the paneling of the wall to bow inwards toward the core of the wall and it caused the sliding door to catch and make scraping sounds as one opened or closed it. I tested its function and if the tile plate was removed, the door function went largely back to normal.

One night while I was home on a break from grad school, my mother and father and I had some kind of argument. It was most likely centered around the claim that neither my dad nor I was helping my mom clean the house—a frequent pretense of normalcy, while the tide of incoming collectibles was saturating us quicker than we could handle—and that neither was pulling our weight. The matter was complicated, ironically, by the fact that my dad and I both were now opposed to my mom collecting any more things and we often refused to help her collect things. The matter at hand tonight was that she wanted to go and collect some marble from Mrs. F's tile place. We refused to assist, and she had an episode in reaction to the argument. I believe that this was still prior to her first real dissociative episode in which she remembered repressed abuse memories (which I will later chronicle in depth). But her reaction was nevertheless strange. She left the house at about nine or so at night, in the middle of the argument, and began to walk down the long road toward the end of the street. She refused to say anything to me. At times, my mom could be unreasonably rageful—never in a violent manner, but in a cold, petulant, distant, verbally wounding manner, belittling her opponent in ways that they might not recover from for years to come.

I began to follow her, pleading for her to stop and talk with me. Finally, I got her to stop. I offered to get the car and take her over to the tile place, my peace offering. She reluctantly acceded. I went back to the house and got the car. My father, not wanting to be left out of the reconciliation, decided to come along, despite his former stance against this. We drove the mile or so to the store, which was at this time of night closed, now being about ten o'clock. Behind the store were a dumpster and some pallets. We found some beautiful marble and a variety of tiles both inside and outside the dumpster. They truly were a marvel, since they were remnants that could not be re-sold in such small quantities. We loaded them into the car, unaccosted by anyone, and took them back to the house and unloaded them. My mother was finally happy again. We had shown our love for her by helping her to obtain what she wanted. She had grand designs for these tiles, which she had gotten for free. They would be part of some elaborate redecoration that she had conceived of, but which would never, ever take place. By going with her and helping her, we had validated her right to dream and to desire better things. We loved her and wanted to please her, but this only temporarily filled a gaping maw. We helped her to get her "fix", metaphorically speaking. We showed our love by doing what was at that moment the worst thing for her. It would still be several years before we had a name for this addiction to material things—"hoarding".

Problem Identified; Progress Still Unseen

As of 1993, Mom's memories of having been abused as a child began to emerge ever more fervently, like a toxin that simply must be purged. Every now and again, she would have dissociative episodes, which would usher in a new host of atrocious memories. Of course, these episodes were disturbing to my dad and me, being difficult to watch a loved one out of their right mind—even if it was only temporary. She would process these memories subsequently in therapy with David Grand, the family therapist, a brilliant man who had previously worked with my grandparents as a marriage counselor, and she would seemingly become happier and more confident in herself, as if a heavy weight had been lifted from her shoulders. She even began to realize, consciously, that the collecting of newspapers (we still did not have access to the convenient title "compulsive hoarding" until much later) and other such material was indeed related to her childhood abuse. She realized that the worst of the hoarding began shortly after Grandpa Arty died, in 1987, with her unconsciously interpreting his death as both a disappearance of her protector, but also as a mandate of permission to begin to detoxify her abuse memories. That is to say, the one whom *she* was protecting from the villainous abusers was now no longer living; she no longer had to protect him from the horrid truth that he had somehow evaded knowing during his time. She could expose the monsters to the light without fear of their making good on their threats to harm and kill her beloved father if she "squealed" or snitched. This, of course, was all an unconscious line of reasoning, symbolic and even somewhat stilted. But it was helpful to her to uncover this.

Mom also began to reveal that on some level, her collecting of newspapers was somehow related to the dysfunctions in her relationship with my father. At the time, I did not know the extent of these dysfunctions. To me and to the rest of the world, Richard and Barbara Greenberg appeared, by all accounts, to be the ideal couple, but underneath that carefully curated exterior lurked a secret sickness. Yet despite their eccentricities and their dysfunctionality, I do believe they truly loved and respected each other. I still believe that this is true, at its core, but in later years, closer to the Exile, I was granted a glimpse of the hidden sickness in their relationship, to which I believe both of them equally contributed.

And so there was at least an outward attempt to clean the house. Not much progress would be made, but the intent was declared. As I noted earlier, I had cleaned my bedroom in the Summer of 1992, transforming it from a messy teenager's haven to an adult's orderly space. But while I was away in California for grad school, the dysfunction surrounding the house continued to increase. As previously mentioned, I even generously offered my parents the option of utilizing my bedroom, while I was not there, as a "clean room", a family room, for watching television there, congregating there, and so forth. I told them that while they were in the process of cleaning up the rest of the house—their own bedroom, the living room, the dining room, and all other peripheral rooms that were chock full of junk—that they should feel welcome to use my room as a safe area where there was no clutter. They took me up on the first part of that, but they misinterpreted the second part and began to bring more and more clutter into my room. Every time I returned home from grad school, there would be more and more junk being stored in my room. My mother would blame my father—saying that he had taken things from the couch in the living room and brought them into my room and dumped them there in order to make room. And I do believe this. Could one find fault with him? But he would then tacitly blame her, when she was out of earshot, saying, "You know how she is. I just try to keep the peace." He would not really take any responsibility for his own part in it, preferring to appeal to the truth which he and I both acknowledged—that she was a packrat. And corroborating this, there were things in my room that were characteristically belonging to my mother; things that only she would bring in there and utilize—certain books and magazines, little knick-knacks that were stereotypical of her patterns. More and more frequently, she would store things on my bed, as a staging area—boxes of vitamins, linens, sheets, towels, blankets, books, and so forth. And they would not be cleared away by the time I returned home for a visit. And I had to patiently wait for them to be cleared away while I sat nearby in whatever clean space there was to sit, having just arrived by plane or by car and suffering from driving fatigue or jet lag—just so I could have a place to sleep. I didn't mind the simple wait; I minded that my room was being commandeered and used more and more as a storage area. I trusted them and this was a direct violation of what I had asked of them. This was a gross transgression of my personal space. And it was a combination of their doing; my father having no impetus to clean up after himself or dispose of things in a consistently appropriate manner; my mother simply not willing to give anything up or throw anything away. It was a deadly combination.

 Often, we would argue as soon as I returned. I felt violated and put upon and it was difficult for me not to show it, no matter how hard I tried. Mom always claimed to have worked very hard for several weeks prior to my arrival, stating that she was exhausted from cleaning and that I should show her some understanding and mercy. My dad often appealed to me in advance, stating that the house wasn't as neat as it should be, but that my mom had been working very hard and that I should cut her a little slack; that he wanted to avoid having us argue. I would often promise not to make a big deal. But it was difficult not to, difficult to hold my tongue, because I knew that they were lying through their teeth. Her pace of work was hinged upon how quickly she could read every single newspaper in front of her and throw out a small portion of the volume. She worked at a snail's pace, constantly distracted by other tasks and by the interesting features of every piece of paper to be discarded. It was preposterous for either of them to claim that much work had ever been done.

And then when I had finally arrived and was able to view certain areas, particularly the kitchen or other common areas, Mom would claim that up until earlier that week—just prior to my arrival—that "the whole counter had been cleared away and was totally clean," but that my father had "messed it all up." Gradually, throughout the conversation, the extent of the claimed original cleanliness would diminish to only that side of the counter, to only that portion of that side of the counter. But the sense was always the same. He was always to blame. And frankly, there was a significant amount of blame to be shared with him, but it was never as much as Mom claimed. Her entire upbringing, we used to joke with her, was characterized by the phrase, "Blame must be found." When arguments would ensue, her demeanor was always accusatory: "Why did you do that? Why did you get your feelings hurt? Why did you say that?" Responsibility was rarely, very rarely, accepted or shared by her. And when either my dad or I would bring this to her attention—as compassionately and often as meekly as possible—she would exclaim, "I'm not blaming you! Why does everyone think I'm blaming them?! I'm like a scientist; I'm just trying to get to the bottom of this, to find out why you did this." Her accusatory and adversarial tone was never evident to her, but it was to everyone else. And so, this was the nature of almost every argument that she and I had during my adulthood, and the nature of many of them between her and my father.

A few years before the Exile, while I was home on a Summer break, I decided to go into the garage to seek out something in the unfinished attic. I discovered that there were literally dozens of empty cardboard boxes up there for no conceivable reason. I questioned my dad about it and of course, as usual, his answer was, dejectedly, "I don't know. You know how your mother is. She's a wonderful lady, but she does things her own way. I just learn not to question in order to keep the peace." I became irate. I was astonished. My dad begged me not to bring it up to my mother. "Get angry with *me*!" he said, "Blame *me*. Just don't bring it up with *her*! You know how it'll be." He seemed terrified at the prospect of an argument. But I chose to broach the subject with her after all. Her answer was somewhat logical, but nonetheless the excuse of an addict. "I ask your father to bring things up into the attic but he never does. And when I finally convince him to do so, he just loads everything around the opening to the attic and leaves it there so that no one can get in the next time. It's very inefficient use of the space," she explained. And she was right. That was his way, the path of least resistance, the easiest way out. In his mind, half-assed was more than enough for a job that she asked him to do. She continued, "I put those boxes up there so that when we bring things up, we can just dump the items into the empty boxes and seal them up. It's more efficient that way." Still, she was right, to some degree. But frankly, the level to which she had executed this plan was far too much. Like much else of what she did and how she did it, she was like a machine that couldn't be turned off. There's nothing illogical about having boxes up there in the attic. But why dozens of them? And why does half the stuff she was putting up there even need to be there at all? Still fuming nonetheless, I chose to leave the matter alone.

Early Attempts at Cleaning

My mother's friend Barbara Simmons, whom we knew since some time in the early 1990s, was ever willing to help out. She was an expatriate English woman who had stayed in the United States after her last divorce. She had become a very close friend of my mother's; they both shared a passion for all things esoteric and paranormal. When they worked together doing spiritual work, including spiritual channelings and the like, they referred to themselves as "The Two Barbaras." Barbara had gone into doing self-help seminars with a psychic flair to them. She was good at what she did, even though she seemed to retain certain mental and emotional blocks that prevented her from doing this full time and reaching her full potential as a spiritual guide and mentor. But she was always eager and willing to help her close friends like us, being quite the organizer. Her presence in our lives was always a boon.

Around the Summer of 1997, I was home from grad school on break and I was again working at the town's public swimming pool as a manager, the fourth consecutive Summer I had assumed this same position. After several years of the house getting much, much worse, and my returning to a less and less hospitable environment, even my mom knew that something had to be done. So she allowed herself to accept help from an outside party, something that she never would have previously done. Barbara was a tough cookie, one might say. She was a thin, almost gaunt woman of diminutive stature, but her size belied her tremendous capacity for work and the ability to take charge. She had a way of convincing you that something needed to be done. She didn't take any guff from my mother, either. In situations in which I suggested something to my mother that she did not agree with or refused to do, it was easy for her to reject these ideas. But if Barbara suggested them, there was a level of demand there. I respected that about her. The bottom line was she was there to get something done. She wasn't going to have any of my mom's wishy-washy refusals to get rid of things. The downside was that sometimes Barbara would get into a cleaning frenzy and things that should have been saved or simply donated were thrown out in a fit of hyper-efficiency. My mom lost some important family recipes during this and other cleanouts that Barbara spearheaded. But all in all, "them's the breaks," as they say. If my mom had been more on top of cleaning and purging unnecessary items in a timely manner, the situation would not be as drastic so as to require a sudden purge which was often devoid of consideration for the sentimental things, heirlooms, keepsakes and so forth. In fact, I remember my father and I coming home one afternoon during Barbara's cleaning project and we were both remonstrated for not being home earlier to help out—I believe we had gone fishing, in a rare father-son bonding day. I, particularly, was chided for leaving a glass on the table that morning. I explained that I wanted to reuse it as a water glass; I was told to keep it aside and out of the way if I was going to do that. She was indeed a hard task master, a bit of a drill sergeant. But it was her direct and generous involvement, this matter-of-fact, take-no-prisoners attitude of hers that eventually helped keep me going during the Exile, as I will later expound. When I wanted to give up or when the emotions got too much for me, she propped me up. I am eternally grateful to her for that.

I have included this anecdote as illustrative of Barbara's capacity to clear out large portions of the main area of the house in record time. She would come in, take charge, and throw things out. The dining room and kitchen, mainly, were her targets, and by the time she was done—within a few days of work—the place nearly sparkled. And this is saying a lot, considering the amount of sheer volume that was stuffed into those rooms at that time. But my mother filled it up again in just a few years. And from time to time, Barbara would come back—once every couple of years—and give a good cleanout to those areas. At some point in the early 2000s, my mother and Barbara had a bit of distance between them. Not so much a falling out, but a falling away, one might say. So during that time period, there was less of an opportunity to ask Barbara to come and help with cleaning and purging; someone to keep Mom honest. So, when my mom began to collect and build up the volume of clutter, it remained.

Dad's Role

Lest I seem to be painting a one-sided picture, I should elucidate my dad's level of participation in the issues of the family hoarding. As I mentioned before, my dad was more of an enabler. He did not actively hoard. But his enabling role was not as simple as one who enables an addict by helping to buy them drugs, or earning money to pay for them. Of course, there was an element of letting my mom have her way in order to avoid the painful arguments that would ensue if one got in her way. But in addition, my dad's procrastination and his laissez-faire, "why put off till tomorrow what you can put off till the day after tomorrow" attitude provided a handy excuse for my mom not to get things cleaned. He had the tendency to leave things all over the place, like a stereotypical male that will not pick up after himself. There was never any malice in it, or even any element of typical male sexism (as in, "that's woman's work"), as it was with his own father. On the contrary: for my dad, his word was his deed in as much as if he said he would do something, that should be sufficient; if it actually got done was a different story. When I was a young teenager, I would often have breakfast with him in the morning as he got ready for work; my mom would typically sleep later than we did, since she was more of a night owl. In these situations, if I was running late for school in the morning, he would often tell me to leave my breakfast dishes and he would take care of cleaning them up or putting them in the sink. When I returned from school, they were still there on the table. This was a perennial thing which I remember continued even into my early adulthood when I lived with my parents during Summer breaks from grad school and had Summer jobs that began early in the morning. These were certainly good memories, having breakfast with my dad, but the point here is that his promises often lacked a certain follow-through.

And so, he did not take part in the cleaning of the house. Perhaps it was an unconscious emulation of his own father's reliance upon traditional gender roles. Or perhaps it was just a level of resignation to the fact that no matter what he cleaned, it would not make a difference in the overall cleanliness of the house. My mom knew how to quickly fill the spaces that were cleared away. But as time wore on, it became evident to me that my dad's inability to take part in cleaning or keeping clean was not the major dysfunction in my parents' relationship. There were other, deeper problems. It was these which on some level were the impetus for my mom's increase in hoarding activity. What was lacking in their relationship, emotionally and physically, she tried desperately to fill using newspapers and clutter, as I will later address. As my dad aged, his obliviousness and carelessness began to grate on my mom. He had the tendency to disconnect with the world and everyone around him, to sulk, to disengage and go into a world of his own. In more recent years, this even began to affect his short-term memory and resemble a minor level of dementia—which his doctors maintained he did not have. His breaking things, losing things, all passive-aggressive actions, were perhaps a motivator for my mom's increased hoarding, but they were in some ways a reaction to them. In this situation, it was hard to tell which came first. Was it that his oblivious misplacing of cordless phones, bills, checks, checkbooks, cell phones, and other necessities, was a passive-aggressive response to her compulsive hoarding? Or that her compulsive hoarding was a passive-aggressive response to his perennial "checking out" from life and his carefully cultivated obliviousness to the world around him—which indeed included his own wife? That his closing off to her was what triggered her self-medicating response? It was a two-way street. And in my opinion, both of them shared significantly in the blame.

For many years, Mom recounted that he had executed poor decision-making, beginning very early on in their marriage, being somewhat arrogantly adamant about such decisions, imitating the traditional dominant male, but not really using good sense or being open to good advice by those who were on his team. That he often made poor, unilateral decisions, refused to follow or ask for directions, and other mistakes that the stereotypical male makes. This played directly into my mom's sense of having to do everything herself, her martyrdom complex that undergirded her personal unconscious narrative. Later, I discovered that it also played into my father's own issues with his deceased mother—the one person that he trusted growing up, the one who in many ways was his protector, analogous to my mother's father being her protector against the abuse. He would unconsciously play out disobedient boy/angry Mommy scenarios in his marriage to my mother. My mom was, in a way, the replacement to his own mother. The two of them—my parents—

were far more alike than different. As has often been said, two alcoholics will always be able to find each other in a crowded room. In this case, the two abuse victims were able to find each other in a crowded life and were always ready to play out their unconscious narratives with each other in the role of the adversary.

But when all is said and done, when all is analyzed, I still suffered the fate of any good son of two abuse victims. Even though I had nothing to do with how they got to be the way they were, I still suffered from their idiosyncrasies—more so, their idiocies. Sometimes, I would see other people's houses, the homes of friends or even strangers, and I would envy them their cleanliness, their order, their normalcy. I would wish that I had a normal life, like theirs, a normal house like theirs. I would comfort myself by saying that despite their outer appearance of normalcy, I am sure that they had problems that I would not want to have—drug addictions, financial instability, or lack of acceptance of their children's individuality, or divorce or infidelities. Perhaps this was true. Perhaps they all suffered from something, as we all suffer, being human. But it did not stop me from envying them the one thing that I really wanted, the one thing that I could never seem to obtain or create—a clean, safe, uncluttered home. And I would dream about it often at night, that my home was suddenly and decidedly clean. That I congratulated my mother and father for finally cleaning our home. In one dream that I had shortly after a trip home—during which I was again faced with the stark and unrelenting reality of the hoard—I recall obsessively trying to rub out a stain on the kitchen counter, a dark stain that would not come clean no matter how hard or long I scrubbed at it, but I kept on doing so; as if it were symbolic of my inability to have any effect on my parents' intention to clean their environment, or to really allow me to help. Sometimes it was a daydream, a wish that I would even share with my parents: that I could sit on the couch in our living room, and wiggle my toes in the clean, new, white shag carpet of the house from back in the 1970s, before it was matted and covered by clutter and dirt. I would ever dream that our home was, in fact, livable.

THE MAKING OF A HOARDER

The Greenberg Family in 1972-73

THE EXILE

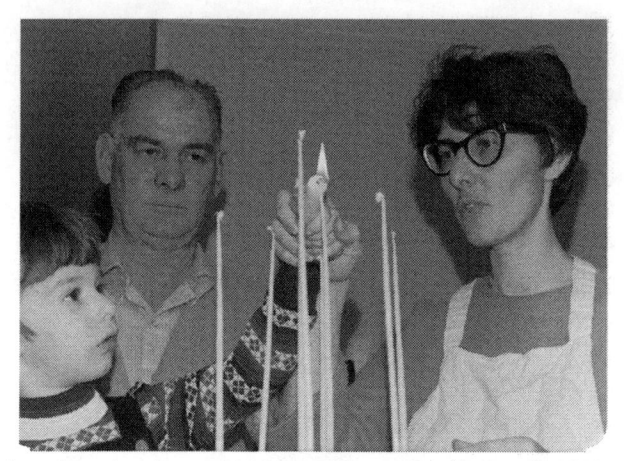

Lee, Grandpa Arty, and Mom at Green Gardens, early 1970s

Dad and Lee, at Green Gardens, early 1970s

Grandma Jeanne, Lee, and Grandpa Arty, early 1970s

CHAPTER THREE: ABUSE MEMORIES

Disclaimer: As mentioned earlier, *The Exile* contains graphic descriptions of child abuse, as well as other disturbing imagery. Those of sensitive disposition, or those who are easily triggered, should take care before reading the following section of the book.

The First Dissociative Episode

I have previously told of the incidents in which my college girlfriend, Jenn, came to visit at a time when my mother was adamant against anyone seeing the messy interior of the house. We had not yet been able to put a label on the hoarding. We just knew that something was wrong and that there must be a reason why my mother was addicted to newspapers.

Later that school year, in Spring of 1993, things changed. My mother's first dissociative episode came in April. I was on Spring Break in my last year of college at Wesleyan University, and was home for a few weeks. Things were going fairly well for me. I was happy in my studies, approaching graduation. And I had also been casually seeing a really beautiful girl named Abby while I was on break, which did wonders for my self-confidence, especially as an odd bird who suffered from living within an odd family. Even with my occasional fights with my mother—some of which would be fairly heated—we were getting along well. I was having a good Spring Break while at home, by all accounts.

On one particular night during my vacation, my cousin Marty was supposed to come over to visit. He was always very close with my parents, and was a tremendously compassionate and understanding individual, as I have noted elsewhere in this book, his having many times come to our rescue. Nevertheless, my mother was still embarrassed about his coming to see the mess, despite the closeness they shared. On this day, she was frantically trying to clear piles of newspapers off the living room couch and throw them somewhere else. They often went into my mother's sewing room, "the Middle

Room", where she tossed anything that was not yet able to be classified or disposed of, and where there were piles of spare cloth and draperies, as well as an antique table and some other bureaus and chests of drawers. There was still a tiny pathway down the longitudinal line of the room, just left of center, barely enough room to sidle in and get to the sewing machine.

Tonight, the sewing room was still a bit too congested, and much of the clutter went straight into my parents' bedroom, later to be a major deposition site for clutter. We began to work feverishly—Mom, Dad, and I—to get the living room presentable before Marty got there. But it was of no use. There was too much to do. Too many piles. My mother began to have a strange reaction. She later described the following to me in great detail, as much of it happened while she was alone, my father and I working in another room.

As we were taking newspapers from under the dining room table and the living room, Mom began to panic. As she moved toward the bedroom, she started feeling fear, but she carried on with her work, moving quicker toward the bed and placing piles of newspaper on the floor or in a handy spot. She was now overcome by terror, while moving newspapers into the bedroom. She went past the bed and into the walk-in closet, looking for a place to hide. She thought to herself, "I don't want them to find me; I must find a place to hide." She opened the large cedar chest, positioned in the closet behind racks of clothes, to hide in there. When she realized she could not hide in it, as she was too large to fit, she then pushed aside clothing near the door of closet, and hid behind the clothes. She was frantically trying to push into the wall, thinking she could hide inside the plaster in the sheetrock drywall panels. She simultaneously realized that this was crazy, and yet still there was a part of her that forged ahead, as if this were her only option. She let out a cry. My dad heard this and came into the bedroom to find Mom in the closet. She gave Dad strange answers about why she was there, so Dad went to get me. I came into the room. We got Mom to the bed, but she remained on the floor next to it, sprawled out with her back up against the mattress, writhing in agony and fear, like a terrified child, unaware of her surroundings. She cried out, in a muffled voice, "She's choking me! She's choking me!" Again and again, she cried out like this. I immediately identified it to my dad as a dissociative episode, having recently learned the term in a college psychology course, and I later found out that my suspicions were correct. We tried to calm her and bring her back to a recognition of the present, but it was quite some time before she calmed down to a point where she was coherent. She later relayed to us that during this episode she could see herself—with the same clarity as if watching herself in a movie—being strangled by Grandma Jeanne, her mother, while still a little child. She was about four years of age at the time and she was trying to pull Grandma's hand away from her throat while Grandma was struggling with little Barbara's—my infantile mother's—other hand. Grandma then put both hands on her daughter's throat, not concerning herself with the little girl's other hand, ineffectual as it was. Little Barbara thought of biting her mother to make her stop this insanity, but she didn't want to hurt her. In fact, little Barbara was petrified of hurting her mother. And yet, simultaneously, she was afraid of being strangled to death. It was noteworthy that in trying to defend herself, the little girl didn't want to hurt her mother, as she was still her mother and she had tremendous loyalty to her.

During this, Barbara (as I shall refer, in retrospect, to my mother during her juvenile years) had trouble catching her breath, but the pressure on her throat was still not enough to make her pass out. Grandma was holding her fingers in the wrong place and her inexperience in strangulation had saved my mother's life. This unprovoked and psychotic attack took several minutes, and then just tapered off. Grandma seemed to stop choking her for no reason. Little Barbara had been trying to fend her mother off while she was in a fit of blind rage, perhaps occupying one of the alternate personalities that we would later discover that Grandma Jeanne suffered under. This episode, we learned, was perhaps the first overt act of violence that my grandmother had perpetrated against her daughter, but it would not be the last. She had already taken part in several episodes which Grandpa Lawlie, Grandma Jeanne's own father, had orchestrated, scenes of such incestuous depravity that only appear in Greek tragedies and horror stories.

While this dissociative episode was going on, my mother being given the painful gift of memory—remembering events from perhaps a half century before during her early childhood—we called her therapist, David Grand, and asked his advice. I had described the incident as such to him, using the term "dissociative episode" and he was duly impressed at the accuracy of my amateur diagnosis. He had just had a cancellation, coincidentally, and he advised that we keep her calm and try to comfort her, but to try to bring her into his office for an immediate session. I tried to reach Marty at home to let him know we would not be there, and for him not to come, but I could not reach him. I left messages for him at his house, but he had already left to come over. This being before the days of mobile phones, I left a note on the door for him so that when he arrived, he would not be alarmed; I stated in the note that we'd call him later to fill him in.

During the therapy session, Mom was hardly able to remove her hat and coat, and largely was still not quite herself. David asked us to bring her back the next day and to continue to keep her calm. In the sessions that she had with him subsequent to this, he confirmed his earlier suspicions that she had indeed been severely abused as a child and had repressed these memories in order to survive psychologically. He worked with her for many years after this, using a variety of effective techniques called EMDR (Eye Movement Desensitization and Reprocessing) and bilateral stimulation, which might appear similar to hypnosis to the untrained eye, although experts would make a very strong distinction between them, and are designed to retrieve and detoxify the memories of abuse so that the patient can live a more normal life.[2] While it certainly helped her to face and detoxify the demons of her repressed childhood abuse, it did not however, help her to cease her compulsive hoarding.

Little Barbara

Little Barbara would suffer numerous times under the multiple personalities of her mother, Jeanne. Many times, the woman would simply slip into another personality, some more deadly than others, and Barbara would have to play her cards right in order to survive or to shorten the episodes. Often, she would be attacked with needles, sometimes with Jeanne's sharpened fingernails, picking, clawing at little Barbara's flesh, opening deep wounds and reopening earlier ones. Jeanne would come out of the bedroom, seemingly changed into a different person, having sharpened her fingernails and polishing their pointy tips, saying "the instruments must be prepared." This phrase struck fear in my mother's heart, knowing that she would soon be tortured. Her scars from former sessions would be opened and she would be made to bleed. This deranged monster, so different from her mother during normal moments, and yet still vaguely carrying the same undercurrent emotional distance that was her constant characteristic—noticed by both her children and her husband—was perhaps emulating some kind of villain she had seen in a Saturday serial at the movies. Who knows? But it was years later that my mother made the connection between these memories and the scars that she still had in various places on her body (mostly her fingers and hands) to prove these events had indeed happened. The injuries had always been explained away as, "Clumsy Barbara....She's always falling, always hurting herself." Once, even, as I will later discuss in detail, Jeanne tried to drown Barbara in the bathtub, while washing her daughter's hair. The little girl barely survived. After that, Grandma never washed her daughter's hair again. It was now up to her to wash her own hair. Grandma came to hate Barbara's hair, a reminder of this incident and surely of her own insanity. This, too, would play a role in their relationship, later in life.

Many times, Barbara would suffer under the torture of her Grandpa Lawlie, Jeanne's own Sicilian immigrant father. Sometimes Jeanne was there, slipping into a dissociative episode of her own, changing personalities that acted as a lackey to the deranged old man. Sometimes, Jeanne wasn't there at all, going out to shop or handle errands, leaving Barbara with her grandfather, and Grandpa Lawlie would have some time to call his group of depraved and perverted friends, who would then descend upon little Barbara like wolves upon their prey. It had been suggested by David Grand during Mom's therapy that this group may have been some sort of cult, performing pedophilic ritual abuse

---

[2] David Grand, *Brainspotting: The Revolutionary New Therapy for Rapid and Effective Change* (Boulder, Colorado: Sounds True, 2013).

on the little girl. Without hard evidence, we can only speculate. But the results were the same. They would have their way with Barbara, their victim, prior to Jeanne's returning. And no one would ever be the wiser.

Over the years after the first dissociative episode of '93, my mom would share many of these repressed abuse memories with me, as a window into her personality and personal history, and I always felt privileged to be her confidant as she retrieved these submerged memories. It became evident that Grandpa Lawlie kept company with some of the sickest and most depraved individuals that one could conceive of, drawn together through common interests, and self-selected in an age well before the advent of the internet, where every perversion and depravity now has its own corner of the Dark Web, protected by not only the Bill of Rights but also by the pretense of privacy and personal freedoms. But in those days, one can only wonder how these people found one another to explore their common "interests". God only knows how they kept it a secret. But child abuse is a common occurrence. Prior to my parents' marriage, sometime in the 1960s, when my father was working for the NY State Department of Insurance Reimbursals, a colleague had told him that incest and child abuse are the nation's best kept secret. It is true that often, people will ignore what they do not want to see, and will allow bad people to get away with bad things rather than taking the risk of confrontation.

There are times when the proverbial elephant in the room was too much for conscientious relatives to bear, and they too become blind to its presence. And this principle of human behavior worked to the advantage of my mother's abusers. As an illustration, Aunt Chickie, Grandma Jeanne's baby sister (who ultimately lived to well over 100 years of age, though she was somewhat delusional in her final years) would often talk about a relative named Benny from Whitestone. He was one of the Italian relatives, an immigrant, who would show up frequently to family gatherings. He had sustained a head injury at some point, making him a bit lacking in the sense department, but not so much that he was unable to function; he was just weird. He worked in construction and was quite burly. He would line up all the boys in the family and ask each of them in turn if they had been drinking their milk. "You drinka you mik?" he would interrogate forcefully, in his Sicilian accent. Then, he would take their heads in his hands, each one in turn, and bash his forehead into theirs. If it hurt, then supposedly they were not drinking their milk. Uncle Arty, my mother's older brother, reported later that it always hurt, and he was no weakling; he most certainly had drunk his "mik". With the girls of the family, it was an entirely different account. He would go around groping their developing bodies, particularly their breasts, and would make inappropriate comments about their growth, "Hmmm,…you get-a big!" as if he were complimenting their progress. Generally, they were stunned by this outrageous behavior, and unable to complain. But the real outrage was that none of the family's adults did anything to stop this behavior. At first, they found his antics amusing, but the more egregious actions were ignored out of embarrassing discomfiture; as if to tell this deranged cousin to knock it off would upset the apple cart too much and cause even greater problems. Once or twice, Aunt Chickie would complain to her mother, Grandma Lawlie, standing there also bemused but helpless; Grandma Lawlie would stammer in broken English, both that she didn't know what to do, but that it was alright, he didn't mean any harm by it. The bottom line is that Benny from Whitestone—however harmless in his intent, and whether by nature or on account of his head injury—was abusive and inappropriate. It was the responsibility of the adults to make it known that his behavior was unacceptable, and to put a stop to it. They did no such thing. The blatant sexual and physical abuse by him was overlooked, despite its public performance. People have a knack of ignoring what they do not want to see or deal with.

This instance is just an illustration of the volitional blindness that was evident on that side of my family, the Dragna Family, allowing the most egregious and depraved activities to happen right under people's noses. Sadly, Aunt Chickie was the only one who could confirm any of my mother's remembrances, as she had witnessed Grandpa Lawlie's poor conduct (to speak mildly of it). A number of years ago, when Chickie's mind was still in good condition, my mother asked her about Lawlie's disposition, just touching on some of her abuse. Chickie said, simply, regarding her father: "He was not a nice man." She left it at that. Perhaps she, too, had witnessed some of what he may have done to her elder sister, Jeanne. Perhaps she, too, had undergone some of the same.

There were a variety of instances of abuse that my mother shared with me, too many and too numerous to enumerate here. But I will recount as many as I can in order to give the reader a better sense of what she suffered. I take no pleasure in this providing this testimony, but I feel it is my duty.

Lawlie and His Cronies

Grandpa Lawlie, whose real name was Giovanni (John) Dragna, was an immigrant from Sicily who came over from Corleone—the infamous town forever linked to the name La Cosa Nostra, and perhaps rightly so. He was called "Lawlie" as a family nickname from when my Uncle Arty (my mother, Barbara's older brother), as an infant, would mouth the baby sounds "law-law-law-law" while looking up at Grandpa Dragna from his crib. By extension, the family would call his wife, Grandma Lawlie as well. Giovanni was by all accounts a very handsome man when he was younger, and having unearthed several photos of him with his dashing handlebar mustache, I concur. He was a barber by trade and had served in the Italian Army during the late 1800s and played the piccolo in the marching band. He was a bit of a rascal, his wife would later recount, telling one particular story in which he had tried to seduce her while they were courting, by convincing her to reach into his pocket in a crowded movie theater on the pretense of looking for spare change; but in reality he had cut a hole in the pocket liner to expose his phallus to her searching hands. Her surprise and dismay still did not deter her from accepting his offers of marriage, his overwhelming charm being insuperable. She would cap this story off by saying, somewhat disapprovingly, yet resignedly, of his devilish nature, in her broken English, "Oh, he wass a deffu!"

When he was 22, he brought his young bride, who was named Gaetana, with him on his second trip to the U.S. in 1903, arriving in New York Harbor on the steamship Citta di Genova. He was a young man from a somewhat well-to-do family that owned a successful department store. As it turns out, some elements of his family evidently were "connected" to organized crime and there was good reason for him to leave Sicily when he did. Gaetana, whom I called Grandma Cookie when I was a little boy—and the name stuck, largely replacing the former monicker, Grandma Lawlie—was largely illiterate. Having come from a large family, an aunt and uncle who were a nun and a priest, respectively, took her in to live with them; since they lived together in private housing, they had funds to give the girl an education. So it was not due to lack of money that she lacked education, but out of her lack of interest in academic things. She had inherent abilities and interest in crafts, such as sewing, embroidery, knitting, and so forth. So her aunt and uncle paid to have tutors come and train her in these crafts. When her new husband brought her to the United States, she contributed to the upkeep of the family by working as a seamstress while he plied his trade as a barber. They lived in Astoria, Queens, and had five children—from eldest to youngest: Salvatrice (Tillie), Giacchina (Jeanne, my grandmother), Antonio (Tony), Giuseppi (Joey), and Vincenza (Chickie). Many of these children would make poor matrimonial decisions, some worse than others. Tillie and her husband fought constantly and mercilessly. Tony, a pacifist who served as a medic in the army during WWII, married a woman whose brothers bullied him with physical threats until he married their sister. She then forbade him from ever seeing his family after their marriage—he had not the will to defy her, and he saw his favorite sister only a few times before he died. Joey married a woman who had to be committed to an asylum after she chased her little daughter, Dorie, down a public street wielding a carving knife. Chickie, simply to escape the house, married a skin-flint named Frank, who had socked away more money than anyone ever knew, but convinced everyone that he didn't have enough money to even repair the holes in his shoes; she divorced him only after she awakened one night to find him holding a gun to her head, insisting that she had been having an affair. Grandma Jeanne was the only one who had married well, Arthur Merget—my "King Arthur", as I had once as a child played Lancelot to his King Arthur, forcing him to sit on a chair as his throne and hold a scepter (some kind of cane) while I knelt before him. But it was Grandma Jeanne, evidently, who brought the insanity to that family, as I am given to understand.

When I look at photos of Lawlie, it saddens me that he should be so foul and nefarious. Many people said that he had a certain charm about him—that he cried at parades, nostalgic for his youth spent playing the piccolo in the Italian Army marching band; that he carried a can opener tied to the end of a long rope attached to his belt; that he liked mint so much that he would surreptitiously plant mint in other people's gardens, surprising them and establishing a source of mint everywhere he went. As a very handsome young man, he transformed into such a sweet looking elderly man, often dressed nicely in a suit and hat. Would that the shame and villainy he came to embody was in someone else's family and not mine.

Great Grandpa Lawlie's dalliances included affairs with neighbors, and as he got older, his affections and advances—pinching women's bottoms and breasts at will—were no longer as welcome (or tolerable) by the neighbors as when he was younger and more handsome. His daughters' friends, when fully grown and often married, would sometimes report that he had paid unannounced and inappropriate visits to them; they would phone Chickie or Tilly and beg them to come and take their father home. Evidently, his sexual predilections also included the incestuous and the violent.

Grandpa Lawlie, allegedly, according to my mother's testimony, was the ringleader of a gang of adults who operated together as a mutually beneficial child abuse entertainment society. However these people found one another, they seem to have exercised their interests using children that one or another had provided. And in the cases that became known to me, it was always my mother who was the victim. Others may have followed or preceded her—perhaps some of Lawlie's own daughters were these forebears. I do not know. But in my mother, Barbara, they had found a tractable, obedient victim, one who had been trained by the pre-Vatican II Roman Catholic Church that the way to salvation was through suffering, and she had been given numerous examples of martyrs whose obedience won them salvation. It is this very same obedient code of silence that appears to have been a common strand woven through the many cases of child abuse with which the Catholic Church has been proven to be rife in recent years. I must note that I am very much a supporter of the modern Roman Catholic Church, having faithfully served as a faculty member at one of its finest universities. But I am under no misapprehension about the damage that has been done by pedophile priests who have brutalized perhaps hundreds of thousands of innocent children over the last century alone, and have been afforded impunity by a hierarchy which was eager to maintain this code of silence for its own self-preservation. It is this institutionalized child abuse that has caused further generations of abusers to run rampant and unchecked within our society. And it is this culture of blind obedience to authority that caused my mother to be the obedient victim of some of the most despicable humans to roam free.

It seems that while my grandmother, Jeanne, was running errands, either alone or with her sisters, she would leave my mother with her Grandpa Lawlie (Jeanne's father) at the house that he and his wife were renting in Queens. It was during these times, when he had a few hours of opportunity, that the friends would be called and they would have their often drunken orgies of pederasty and abuse. These activities had to be carefully planned out and orchestrated, or someone might find out. Whereas, Barbara's mother had access to her any time and just had to make sure that the injuries she inflicted on her daughter were not life-threatening. But it is apparent that at times, even Jeanne, when in an altered state of consciousness herself, would take part in the ritual abuse that was perpetrated and orchestrated by Grandpa Lawlie. Years later, therapist David Grand would indicate that Grandma Jeanne's dissociative identity disorder was undoubtedly caused by early sexual abuse of her own, informing me that many well-known psychiatric and psychological experts have argued that Dissociative Identity Disorder—or multiple personalities—is the direct result of early childhood sexual trauma. I am not expert enough to argue against them. The evidence that my family bears does not deny this.

One of the earliest memories my mother recounted of her abuse focused on being tied around her waist by a rope or a belt and suspended from the ceiling or a door—while still an infant of pre-verbal age, perhaps 12 to 18 months. She was experiencing difficulty breathing, and even crying out to announce her discomfort. She was not able to form real words, just grunts and groans. This was by far not the worst of her suffering, but neither was it an example of exemplary child rearing. In retrospect, I have found it noteworthy and also praiseworthy that my mother retrieved such vivid memories of her earliest experiences on earth. She has contrasted this experience, poignantly, with her remembrance of a slightly later experience of lying on her back on a carpet, drinking milk from a bottle, and recollecting that the windows were open, being able to smell the outdoor smells, being comfortable and happy.

In stark contrast to the idyllic scene above, Mom recounted another early experience, most likely a bit later—perhaps as a toddler—having been tied to a table and being vaginally stimulated by Grandpa Lawlie, using his hands or perhaps the handle of a hairbrush on the little child, while her mother, Grandma Jeanne, looked on, coaxing and facilitating him. It was possible that during this, Grandma Jeanne was in a dissociative state in order to compensate for the shock of what she was witnessing—and what may indeed have been done to her as well in earlier times. Finding that little Barbara had an involuntary reaction or response to the manual stimulation, Grandpa Lawlie was pleased. My mother found it noteworthy that a toddler, not knowing right from wrong, will sometimes react to such stimulation, the brain only perceiving a pleasurable feeling, and then later will realize a sense of violation, shame, or impropriety. I feel the need to reiterate that recounting these abuse memories shared with me by my mother gives me great discomfort; but providing testimony to her suffering serves the greater purpose of bringing to light and memorializing her abuse—ensuring that it is never forgotten.

The pedophilia and incest grew much worse. Groups of people would be invited in to do as they saw fit with the victim—with Barbara. She was forced to have both oral and anal sex with them at times. She does not remember any vaginal penetration, curiously. Most likely, the rupture of the hymen in a toddler would have caused significant bleeding and would have been difficult to disguise. The evidence for sexual abuse would have been, in this case, overwhelming. But it is still a mystery to me as to why he did not allow that kind of violation of her—considering everything else he had perpetrated. My mom attributed a high degree of calculation to him, and she suspected that he was also concerned about the possibility of impregnation of the child, as there have been cases of very young girls conceiving from rape, including the notorious and contemporary case of Lina Medina, a Peruvian child who had given birth at the age of five, following a precocious puberty. If Barbara became pregnant, people would start to look for the culprit. As such, Lawlie had to be careful. And he had to plan ahead carefully so as not to be found out. He would have to plan with his friends when he knew that little Barbara would be brought for a visit. The window of opportunity for them to convene would be necessarily brief, perhaps only a few hours, while his wife and daughter, Jeanne would be out.

Sometimes alcohol was used by those involved. Sometimes, they imbibed it in advance of arriving; sometimes while they were there. She could often smell it on the people. Sometimes it was even used to ply her, to make her more tractable and complacent. And it was almost always hard liquor. On one occasion she was on a table, perhaps in the kitchen. People held her down so that she could not resist. A big bottle of liquor was forced into her mouth, one person holding the bottle to her mouth while others held her body still. It made her sick and dizzy and nauseous. She felt herself choking because too much liquid was going in and she could not breathe properly. Some spilled on her, too. After this, they could do as they wanted with the inebriated child. Among these people, there was almost always the smell of alcohol. Throughout her life, she had maintained a persistent aversion to the use of alcohol and especially the smell or taste of hard liquor. No wonder.

There was one particular man among the group who stood out in her mind. He was a red-headed man, with very light orange eyelashes that made it look, from a distance, as if he had none at all. At first, he seemed very kindly and very sweet. The man had impeccable manners and wore gloves when he arrived. He was always well dressed. It seemed to little Barbara like he was the only nice one in the group. But then, as it turned out, he would do terrible things to her. He had seemed safe, trustworthy, but was not. For many years following, she had a persistent fear and distrust of red-headed people. The red-headed man came late one time, wearing a topcoat. He smelled of alcohol when he came close to her, contributing to her impression that sometimes the people came to the gathering already drunk. It was perhaps the drug that they used to numb their consciences to what they were doing to an innocent child—if they had any consciences left at all.

One particular incident involving this red-headed man stood out in my mother's mind, and when she would speak of it, she would be visibly affected. She recounted that while still very young, perhaps still pre-verbal and baby-talking, she was forced into a strange and unfamiliar posture by Grandpa Lawlie. She felt a choking feeling in her throat, even though no one was strangling her. And she felt pain in her anus. She was seemingly suspended from both ends of her body, like an animal impaled and roasted on a spit. Grandpa Lawlie had inserted his engorged phallus into her mouth and it was choking her. The red-headed man had penetrated her anus. She was in terrible pain from this. One of them, perhaps the red-headed man, had strings tied around his phallus. One can only surmise what purpose these strings played. She later tried to research this, as if it were a noted paraphilia, but with no success. Whatever depraved function they played, these hurt Barbara even more during the penetration of this rape. Up to this point, she had never been abused sexually by two people at once. Any kind of abuse, sexual or otherwise, had always been carried out by individuals, taking turns, one after another. Something about this particular experience disturbed and wounded her more than all else, she said. The utter violation and helplessness was particularly damaging to the psyche of the little child.

Among the other people, there was a nurse. She was not a terribly attractive woman, an older looking woman, with a very frumpy, plain-looking face. She didn't seem to be wearing makeup, a little chubby looking in the face, like the stereotypical Russian peasant, bearing a flat, wide countenance. Her hair was a kind of mousy light brown and was pulled back. She didn't wear a nurse's hat, but almost all the time she wore a one-piece nurse's dress with an emblem of some sort on the breast pocket. When she was there—and it was rare that she was ever absent—sometimes she would administer a hypodermic to the child. Usually, during these abuses, Barbara was placed on a kitchen or dining room table, to be brought up to the adults' level. After all, why should they have to kneel down to the child's level when they were abusing her? The nurse was talking to the gathered people about how to hold Barbara and what she was going to do; that they needed to hold her so she wouldn't squirm and break off the needle when it was inserted into her. The nurse was behind Barbara, who was seated at the end of the table with her legs dangling. In telling the story, my mother could not say whether there was anything in the needle or not; she did not see the syringe prior to its deployment. But she felt the sting of the needle. At the time, she didn't really know what it was. At first, it was deployed on her right side, injected in the hollow of the trapezius, straight downward and in, between the scapula and the clavicle. Then on the left side, repeated. Shortly after, she went unconscious, possibly given a sedative or anesthetic. This would make her, once again, even more complacent—an easy victim, who had no memory of her abuse. Sleeping children don't tattle.

But this was not the only source of hypodermic needles. Apparently, some of them had been brought by Grandma Jeanne, having been formerly retained by her husband, my Grandpa Arty, to give insulin treatments to his mother, Gabriella—my mother's paternal grandmother. Grandma Gabriella had died recently of complications of diabetes, on April 4, 1944, when my mother was only five; Gabriella no longer needed the hypodermics where she was. And so they sat around the house as either family heirlooms or clutter. But Barbara's mother, normally fanatic about throwing out clutter, had a use for these. And this hypodermic was the old fashioned kind, with thick steel needles, manufactured before the age of high strength surgical steel that could be formed in thinner gauges for the comfort of the patient. So, the hypodermic found its way into the hands of Jeanne and Grandpa Lawlie. What had been the instrument of salvation and preservation of the health of Barbara's paternal grandmother had become a new instrument of torture for little Barbara while she was in the care of her maternal Grandpa Lawlie at the house her grandparents were renting in Queens. It was still likely that it was the nurse who administered the hypodermic, but now there were other sources for the people to gain access to hypodermic needles. My mother recalled at least one other time that the needle was used on her. This time, she knew what to expect. It was painful and was the source of bad things. The people told her that there were poisonous liquids in the hypodermic and that they would inject her with them, demanding that she keep absolutely quiet and perfectly still. They threatened to kill her. She knew what to do and learned quickly. Many years later, I myself saw the remnants of one of these hypodermics in the house. My mother had evidently saved pieces of it as evidence of her torment, perhaps to help revive and disarm the memories she would one day undoubtedly uncover. Could one say that this was related to her hoarding? I cannot say.

These experiences hardened little Barbara to suffering. When she was bitten by a stray dog in the neighborhood in her pre-adolescence, a dog which could not be found in order to determine whether or not it was rabid, it was imperative to give her rabies shots. Prior to finding the dog and verifying its lack of infection by rabies, they injected little Barbara during several treatments with long, heavy gauge needles in to her abdomen. The doctor told her that it would hurt very much, but expressed how important it was for her to remain still. He was so surprised that she was so silent, so obedient. She hardly gave even a whimper and was totally still. He commented on it to her mother. Perhaps the doctor suspected something—that perhaps she had been through this level of pain before. Indeed, she had been.

The Kitten

Perhaps the most poignant of all of these stories, in my opinion, was one episode in which she was given kittens as a gift—a gift to the victim, to keep her quiet and compliant. She loved kittens, and they loved her. What child would not see itself in the pure innocence of kittens, and identify with their sense of curiosity and helplessly delicate playfulness? She played with them. And then Grandpa Lawlie took one of them, a grey tiger or a little black and white, and showing it to little Barbara, he simply broke its neck—emotionless, mechanical, its purpose being in its simplicity. She knew what this meant. If she did not keep her silence—the code of silence of the victim—she would be killed just the same as the kitten. And when they were done raping her—the helpless innocent child who had taken to heart what the priests and nuns at church had taught her, while they beat other little girls and boys who spoke too loudly or didn't listen to the religious instruction, the child who knew that suffering in silence yielded the best possible chance of her survival—they smeared her with cat feces and they wrapped her and the kitten together in newspapers and left her to lie there, stinking, pondering how long she had to remain still in order not to anger them even further, that they might do even worse to her.

She saw herself akin to that kitten, broken, destroyed, murdered, her innocence taken from her. She had seen too much. She had been through too much. She felt alone. Her mother, mentally unstable, was just as much her enemy as these strangers who flocked to her pedophile grandfather. Her mother, who was supposed to be her nurturing protector, was just as much a violator, at home and while away. Her only ally, her father, my Grandpa Arty, was away for long periods, working for the War effort during WWII, during the height of the Great Depression. He had to be away for long spells; that was where the work was. That was the only way to support his wife and two children. And besides, the abusers had threatened Barbara with killing her father if she told anyone. If she squealed to anyone, they said, her beloved father would be killed by them. Never mind that he was a big, strapping man; they were children of La Cosa Nostra. Who knows what they were capable of in moments of cowardly aggression, piercing the back of an ally with their concealed daggers? Or cutting his throat with a barber's straight razor. But even still, if he knew—if he only knew—he would have broken the neck of his pederast father-in-law, or struck him with a baseball bat as he once did to a snake in order to protect his family while camping in the woods. My mother had cried for him not to hurt the snake, but he killed it—for better or for worse—because he feared it would bite and kill his family members. If he only knew what kind of serpent—a snake in the grass—his own father-in-law was, he might have struck him down likewise and then spent the next several decades in jail, unable to protect his beloved daughter from his own wife, Jeanne. One can only speculate that things turned out as best as could be expected.

Years later, my mother and I speculated that it was the issue of being wrapped in the newspapers with the kitten that somehow contributed to the centrality of the symbolism of newspapers in her compulsive hoarding. And in addition, throughout her life, she has defended and fiercely championed cats, as well as other helpless animals—perhaps symbolic of her own helpless little girl self. She and I would often also speculate that if animals do reincarnate, the cat that appeared on our doorstep in November of 1992 and lived well into her early 20s as my mother's best friend—alternately known as Missy Tarot and Kittycat Rotten—may somehow embody the spirit of the kitten that was momentarily her companion seven decades ago, before its life was snuffed out by her abusers. She chooses to believe that this may be. And I have no evidence to deny it.

The Choice to Remain

One other experience that my mother relayed to me may compete for the title of being the most poignant and heart-wrenching, and that is the story of the nearly fatal head injury sustained by little Barbara in the midst of a debauched episode of abuse. This may have been, perhaps, the fourth or fifth time that she was abused by the crowd gathered by Great Grandpa Lawlie. The little victim was about three or four years of age at this time, having to make a tremendously grown-up decision.

She remembered having been in the care of Grandpa Lawlie once again, and being hit on the head with a hammer. It was deliberate, intentional, part of the torture regimen. Usually, he was much more careful. Usually, he and his friends took care not to harm the victim so much that there would be undeniable evidence that could incriminate them. Little bruises and cuts were commonplace with children, so clumsy, always getting hurt. It was easy to disguise the abuse in this fashion if they were careful. But something more like a serious injury, or even signs of sexual assault were more to be avoided.

In the situation at hand, regarding little Barbara, it was no different. People could be counted on to look the other way a large amount of the time; they simply didn't want to get involved or perhaps they were afraid to do so. I recall once being a silent bystander amidst a crowd of people at the Post Office, witnessing a young mother repeatedly hit her toddler so hard that the child began to vomit, still screaming obscenities at her while the rest of us looked on in shock, unable to move or protest. We didn't know what to do, or if there was anything to be done. The woman, still shouting, dragged the child out of the building, suspended by its shirt. I wanted desperately to intervene, but I along with everyone else could not figure out what to do before the woman was no longer in our midst, the whole episode taking no more than a few seconds. As such, even good people are often caught in a trap of inertia when they know cognitively that something must be done. But this tendency toward inertia, toward looking the other way, could not be consistently counted on, and so the abusers knew they needed to take precautions. And usually, their caution paid off. Their circumspection and their careful planning of the 'acceptable' levels of abuse which would not raise eyebrows or draw attention was indeed successful. But in this one case, they went too far. The situation had to be fixed or they would be in trouble. The death of a child was too hard to conceal.

It happened at the house in Rego Park—6361 80th Street. The house was at ground level, a bit raised, and the entry to the garage was below the ground level, below the house, with a steeply slanted driveway that led from the street to the level of the basement. At this point, little Barbara was lying on a table in the hallway. There were people around her. The side of her head started to ache. She couldn't remember being hit, but she felt warm liquid on the side of the head. When she put her hand up to touch it, she looked at her hand and saw red—it was covered in blood. At this point she realized that something bad had happened. She knew that this time it was serious.

She did not remember who actually wielded the hammer. But someone, in a blind fit of rage or lust for power—domination over a small, helpless child— had gone too far. And they knew it. In fact, all of them knew it. The child was severely injured. There was a cranial injury. She might die. Then what would they explain to Arthur, her father? As her mother, Jeanne, was often complicit in these affairs—her multiple personalities causing her to accede to her father's machinations in abusing little Barbara—she was there this time as well. She would have been hard pressed to explain her daughter's death or permanent disability, but she would have done what was necessary to conceal her guilt. Her husband, however, was not to be trifled with. He had been a boxer earlier on in life, lean and strapping, and he loved his so daughter dearly that he could have likely killed anyone who had harmed her—if he only knew. They had to keep it a secret; they had to rectify this, clean it up so that he would never know. And since he was gone for long periods of time, working in the shipyards during the war effort, it was not too difficult to conceal it from him.

Next, the most extraordinary thing occurred. I cannot say what things take place in the spiritual world and I cannot judge whether this was in my mother's imagination or if it was real. But suffice to say that—as she told it to me—the vision which little Barbara had was evidence of some kind of turning point—a decision that she had to make. While she was on the table, bleeding from the side of her head, she was aware of a being, standing to the side of her. It was a man with long, light colored hair and a pleasant face. Not like the red-headed man—one of the abusers—who was merely masking his inner ugliness with a pleasant demeanor. This being was truly good and he had a kindness about his face. He was wearing two colors of material. She couldn't see what was on the bottom of it, but it was made of a white fabric, with a different color, a sky blue, worked into the textile somehow. There was a looseness to his sleeves, and no cuff, just a large loosely hanging sleeve opening, about six inches wide. This man seemed to be on friendly terms with her; he was not one of the abusers.

It was strange that he was there, and he said to her, "You have the choice to stay here or if you want to, you can leave now." No one else seemed able to see him. Only she could hear his questions and she thought her answers to him rather than speaking them out loud. She was confused. She questioned him about what he meant. He said that he could take her away to safety if she wished. She replied that she wanted to stay. His reply was simple and definitive, soothing: "We're working to protect you…rest now, rest." She rested. She didn't remember seeing anyone else in the room, but she knew the abusers were still there. They were somewhere nearby, doing something while she was having this conversation with her unearthly visitor. Evidently, the strange man had been talking about her death; that if she wished, she could leave this earthly realm and be done with the suffering. Perhaps he was an angel, sent to guide her away if she wished. But she made the choice to stay. And he also had the ability to help protect her. After this, she must have lost consciousness. It is impossible for us to know, objectively speaking. Perhaps she may have already been unconscious during her experience of the vision.

So they put her into a taxicab, with her mother—my Grandma Jeanne—and her Grandpa Lawlie in the backseat. She could tell that they were driving a long way. She must have been taken to a hospital in a remote area, so that the abuse couldn't be traced to her family. She knew that they had gone over a body of water—possibly going toward Canarsie, Brooklyn, where the water was to the right of a car going into that area. They took her far away from Flushing, Queens, to a hospital where the family was not known. They took her to be treated by doctors who would not be able to identify the family in these days before mass media and the internet and the easy identification of people by checking databases and electronic records. Cash payment would ensure silence and a quick, discreet treatment to preserve her life and preserve their anonymity.

She felt like she was blacking out off and on and she didn't remember being brought into the hospital, but remembered being inside. There was somebody doing something to heal or stitch her or patch it up. That was all. She remembered being home later on in Rego Park. She didn't remember how she got back home. She just knew that an injury had been sustained and that she had been attended to.

She had been given a decision to make. And she knew that, on some level, this was different than all the other "close calls". She was closer to dying than she had ever been before. She had a choice. She could let go and let herself succumb to the onslaught of the damage caused by the injury. Or she could fight it and live. She had chosen the latter, and she had lived. The man in her vision, whether an angel or a manifestation of her own will to survive, expressed the choice succinctly. Did she want to stay or to go? Ultimately, she chose to stay. It was not an easy choice to pursue. There would be many more years of abuse, and of many different kinds. But this was a turning point, one in which her inner resolve and her love for her father—her desire to protect him from losing her—won out over the damage caused by the monsters. This sentiment would continue to guide her during several more years of torment.

At times, it seemed that Arty suspected that something was wrong, but he couldn't tell how or why. He just suspected that his beloved daughter was in danger somehow. So he used to caution her frequently, often clipping newspaper articles about children being kidnapped, trying to warn her about all the evil in the world that could happen to children if they were not careful, vigilant. Unfortunately, this attempt was futile. She knew her abusers. It was Lawlie, his friends, and her own mother. And she had been unable to do anything to protect herself. But perhaps by the time she was old enough to read these newspapers, the abuse had already ceased.

It was several years later that the physical and sexual abuse finally stopped. At about the age of six or seven, an episode occurred in which Grandma Jeanne without cause began once again to choke little Barbara. Something snapped within Barbara's normally tractable mind. Something made her fight back. Almost instinctively—an instinct which had been hidden, tricked into submission—she bit her mother's arm. Jeanne released Barbara, shocked at the child's act of retaliation, recoiling from the pain. The skin was not broken by the child's teeth, but it was painful. This was yet another turning point. Jeanne would never attempt to physically harm the child again. Emotional abuse would continue for many decades to come, but she would never again try to drown the child, scrape her skin, beat her or torture her in any physical or sexual manner. It was also around this time that the group of Lawlie's friends ceased abusing Barbara. She had become too old. She would remember. She could fight back. She could tell someone. They would be found out. She could recognize faces. So it had to stop. Their heyday was over. They had to find new victims. Lord only knows whom they moved on to next. But the damage had been done. Their sickness had been injected, like a serum, into my mother's psyche, and into the society at large. People's psyches had been compromised, altered. More negativity, the Devil's offspring, metaphorically speaking, had been infused into the world through their acts of abuse.

Six Bags

I feel the need to include an essay that I wrote in honor of my mother's sixty-fifth birthday, in 2004. Grandma Jeanne had passed away just a few months prior, in late 2003. I was visiting New York during this event. Grandma had been in a nursing home for several months, her phenomenal health having declined rather quickly after her son's untimely death just a few years prior at the age of 70. She had lived for many years after the death of Grandpa Arty in 1987. Mom and I both observed that she often seemed distant, unable to truly connect with people on a deeper level than the mundane. I often wondered what was inside her head. Perhaps the glimpses I got from my mother's stories of abuse were fairly accurate pictures of what lay inside.

When my mother and I delivered a joint eulogy at Grandma Jeanne's funeral, numerous relatives came out to honor her. During this eulogy, my mother noted that Jeanne's baby sister, Aunt Chickie, was still here among us; the aged woman interjected loudly in response, "Not for long!" in the most shrill Astoria, New York accent she could muster. Nearly a decade later, she was still alive, though somewhat delusional in her late 90s. She eventually passed around the age of 100, cared for by members of her family.

Jeanne was well-loved, but perhaps more for her deceased husband than for her own contributions to these relationships. She spent many years of her life hiding behind closed doors, afraid to go out, afraid to connect with people, afraid…just afraid. By this time, I had already learned much from my mother about her alleged abuse at the hands of Grandma Jeanne, and I had no reason to doubt my mother's testimony. Yet there was no way that I would incorporate this into a eulogy, which speaking etymologically, was supposed to be a "good word" for a person. I had to say something nice about her, so I focused on my grandmother's relationship with me. She was, by all accounts, a good grandmother. She fed me when I visited. She gave me gifts of money when she could spare it, carrying on a tradition of avuncular generosity that my grandfather had started. For years after Grandpa's passing, she would play a little game with me whenever I would visit from college or grad school. As I would end my visit and kiss her goodbye, she would feign that Grandpa was calling to her from the other room, and she would answer loudly, "What's that, Arty? You say I've forgotten something?" And she would rush quickly into the bedroom and come back with an envelope, and begin to dispense a monetary gift to me, sometimes in the form of a stack of 20 dollar bills, sometimes in 100 dollar bills. She would sometimes stop halfway through, and call back to Grandpa in the bedroom, saying, "What's that? You want me to give more?!" And she would continue until the stack had been depleted, leaving me with enough funds to cover books that semester, or take care of rent for a month, or the like. And my mom and I would chuckle the entire time, enjoying the spectacle of the gift-giving. On some level, this was a response to her guilty recognition that she had stifled my grandfather's generosity in his later years. He would feel the need to hide this from Grandma Jeanne, due to her cautiousness with money, and he would take me into the bedroom before my visits ended, and quickly, furtively empty out his pockets of change—whatever he had saved up since my last visit—being sure to not let my grandmother see, for fear that she would disapprove of his profligacy with funds. Occasionally, she would catch him with his hands in his pockets, handing me money, and he would look up, discovered, with a "shit-eating grin" on his face at having been caught. The two would laugh uncomfortably at the scene, but he knew he had been undone and would have to pay for his generosity with her shaming and disapproval. Years later, she knew that she had been wrong to stifle his great pleasure at giving, and she revived his tradition as her own. As a college student, and later a grad student, on a tight budget, I appreciated the magnanimity of this penitence.

It was through this game that she revealed to me her gift that helped me buy a good used truck when I was in grad school, to replace the 1977 Cadillac Eldorado that Grandpa had left me. Grandpa was a Cadillac man, growing up in a generation when owning a Cadillac signaled the pinnacle of financial achievement. Being more financially stable in his later years, he purchased a 1972 Cadillac, which was later replaced by a 1977 Cadillac. They were always yellow. Canary yellow. On his death bed, he required that my mother and uncle sign a codicil to the existent will, stating that I would receive the Caddy. I was 16 at the time, and just learning to drive. The idea of receiving his Caddy as an inheritance was a welcome surprise to mollify the loss of my beloved grandfather, one of my dearest friends in the world. It was this same Caddy that I would later drive cross country nine times throughout the '90s, going out and back to grad school in California, returning to New York to spend the Summers with my parents, working whatever job I could find at the time, then heading back in the fall on the 3,000 mile, grueling five and a half day drive. By 1997, the old Caddy had been having a lot of mechanical problems and was costing a lot to be fixed, more than its current value. Grandma asked me to sell it and take her new monetary gift of $5,000 to buy something more reliable. I kept the Caddy, nevertheless as a family heirloom, but I bought a restored old '68 Chevy pickup truck that I felt I could work on. The latter proved to be equally unreliable, but between the two vehicles I always had a ride.

I was always told that when I was born, Grandma was enthralled with me as a new baby in the family. When I was in the nursery shortly after my birth, she observed that I was lying on my stomach with my face down, and she was extremely concerned that I would suffocate. Eventually I turned to a more comfortable position and this also comforted Grandma. It was Grandma who gave me my first bath, as documented in a spate of embarrassing family photos and even a home movie. As a toddler, my mother and she, and my Great Grandma Cookie would fawn over me and, chuckling together over our Sicilian heritage, they would drape my little pale yellow flannel blanket over my head and tie it around my neck, to resemble an elderly Italian flower-seller woman, replete with kerchief, and they would ask me facetiously in an old-fashioned accent, "*Dona, how much are you roses today?*" to which we would all laugh, and I would laugh in concert with them, the jocular mood being contagious. Whatever relationship she had with my mother, Grandma loved me and it was obvious.

In the eulogy, I said simply that "she was an *excellent* grandmother," remembering a phrase that had come to my mind many years earlier as I sat in her kitchen eating her home made lentil soup. I had mulled that phrase over in my mind at the time, thinking how curious it was to say that. But that's what she was. In her role as my grandmother, she excelled. She treated me well, with respect and generosity. I had no complaints. I suppose I even loved her, in a way that you loved a relative that was somewhat inscrutable to you. But I still could not find a way to understand her on a deeper level, as a person. She was a mystery to me and to many other people. She had such a rich history of hiding from the world, and evidently for good reason. Perhaps this book will give a bit of a glimpse as to what she was and why. She, herself, was most likely abused—and severely. She suffered. It made her what she was, to her daughter and to the outside world. I unearthed and retained an old black and white photo of a family portrait which featured my grandmother as a young girl, perhaps 10 or 11 years old, amid a crowd of relatives gathered together in a photo studio to commemorate a family wedding—she had likely been a flower girl or a young bridesmaid. The year was possibly 1920 and she was dressed in a white flowing dress with a headdress or veil, innocent and pure, her southern Mediterranean skin visibly dusky, appearing like a mysterious dark-skinned sprite or nymph, or some beautiful Moorish princess from another time, giving voice to the travels of her Arab and Berber ancestors who stepped easily across the narrow waters between Carthage and Sicily. The innocence in her eyes is striking, but tinged with a certain fear or apprehension, confusion perhaps—like the face of Sharbat Gula, the iconic "Afghan Girl" of National Geographic fame—betraying her own terrifying experiences that compromised her naiveté, the product of generational abuse, a family secret, a family tradition. For her also, for that stunted child inside her, have I chosen to write this essay, including it here in its original and unedited form, to give the reader a better idea of what I was thinking at that time.

Six Bags

I recently found out that a 95 year old woman's belongings could feasibly fit into six bags. Six clear plastic garbage bags, the kind you use to put leaves in that you've raked up. A couple of months ago, my 95 year old grandmother died, just a few days short of her 95th birthday. She had been in a nursing home for several months, in and out of the hospital as well, with pulmonary fibrosis. I had wondered if it would hurt when she died. I had hoped that having the inability to breathe would not be like being under water and holding your breath for too long, the pressure in your chest building as you wish for the ability to breathe some air and yet you still hold your breath in order to accomplish whatever childish game or goal it is that drives you to hold your breath even further. You wonder what it would be like to die this way and if it would hurt more than this when you did, your chest about to implode for want of air. I was hoping that it would not be that way when she died. The doctors assured me that she would die painlessly, getting progressively sleepy from the lack of oxygen and that she would feel no pain. It concerned me, despite the fact that in recent years my mother had remembered submerged memories of having been severely abused by this woman. I was never particularly close to my grandmother; she was hard to get to know and hard to really communicate with. By all accounts, she was kind to me and very generous, but only with money and food. She was not forthcoming with her emotions or her words. But for that matter, she was not free with anybody with respect to these things. Perhaps even her own husband had died of a broken heart, having felt abandoned by her when he was ill in the hospital. She had been afraid to visit him, because she would have to be around sick people. Now she, herself, was the sick person, my own mother charged with the responsibility of being the dutiful daughter, visiting her incessantly, brushing her hair, washing her, feeding her, completing months and months of paperwork for reimbursement of the payment for her stay at the nursing home, and after all that, taking her annoyance and even verbal abuse here in the 95 year old's enfeeblement and dotage.

I was having a late dinner with a friend when I received a call from my mother, saying that my grandmother had died and my mother tentatively and almost imperceptibly suggested that she would appreciate my help in going over to the home to identify the body and begin to make arrangements, my mother not wanting to seem too needy. I immediately made the offer to do so, that she wouldn't have to make the request. She was grateful. After driving back to my parents' house, where I was staying during the holidays, my mother and father and I drove together over to the nursing home. The staff was very sympathetic, having gotten to know my parents fairly well over the last several months and holding my parents in high regard, seeing the love and devotion they showed for my grandmother. We entered her room, Grandma's roommate being sound asleep and having refused to leave the room when the staff told her that her roommate had passed away. She evidently was not bothered, judging by her sound sleep. Even she had sustained verbal abuse and contumely from my grandmother, who often regarded her as a soulless peon. She had been a very sweet roommate to my grandmother, who was always happy to see my parents when they would enter. She now was sound asleep in the same room as my grandmother; I prayed for her happiness and safety while she lay there nearby.

Upon entry, my parents and I viewed the body of my grandmother, frail and emaciated. She was always tiny, but she was now a mere shadow of her former self, having lost so much weight from being ill and bed-ridden. The first thing that I noticed, which shocked me, was that her mouth was open as she lay there. I was immediately concerned. It appeared to me as if she had been gasping for air. The gape of her mouth was open much wider than how one would normally think of a sleeping person. I would not have wanted to think of her in pain, even in light of how she had treated my mother at an early age, facilitating and even at times participating in the abuse of a two to seven year old child, allowing her own father (my mother's grandfather), who perhaps held an emotionally enthralling grip over my grandmother, due to his abuse of her, to sexually and physically and emotionally abuse my mother along with a group of his sick friends. While my own grandmother may have felt emotionally helpless to stop this through her own psychological illness, she herself at times initiated abuse of my mother. Still, it was the recognition of her psychological state that prevented me from holding a grudge against Grandma, as one might reasonably hold against a Hitler. Nevertheless, I did not want my grandmother to have suffered. I bore in mind her own, possible psychological abuse, herself having perhaps been a two to seven year old child, raped and tortured by her own sick father, producing a cycle of abuse that perhaps she herself—small and frail in every way—was psychologically unable to cease. And so my mother was the unwilling victim of the last stage of this family tradition, she herself having been so careful to disarm the time-bomb prior to and during my upbringing, attempting as best she could to shield me from the tradition that had been started so many generations before, the one that would insidiously creep into a parent's mindset and predispose them psychologically to abuse. I later asked my mother about the position of Grandma's lower jaw when she had died, and my mother assured me that Grandma had felt no pain when she died, and that she used to sleep that way, perhaps snoring or merely breathing through her mouth. It still was a disturbing image, despite this reassurance.

I held my mother's arm as we entered the room and viewed the body. I believe my father was holding my mother's other hand. We stood there for a short while, my mother only taking a moment to view the body initially. My father did not have much of a connection, perhaps even less than my own. He often felt slighted by her in recent years and he also resented the treatment that she had bestowed upon my mother, not only years ago but even in recent years. He and my mother almost immediately began to empty out her dresser drawers and her closet of all her belongings. In they went into those six plastic garbage bags. My mother wanted to clear the room out entirely that night, so that the room may be vacant for some other needy person to occupy it. I admired that. I am sure that she also did not want to let this be a protracted experience. Mom separated certain classes of items into different bags, none of them being filled entirely. Leftover unopened food went into one, cosmetic and toiletry items into another, clothes into yet another, and so forth. The bags could have been condensed further, but there was no time or need to be stingy with the bags. And so six bags were used and the entire collection of things belonging to this 95 year old woman, who had indeed done many good things in her life and had, along with her husband—now gone seventeen years before—raised a family and touched a lot of lives, along with having herself stood in the way of many more good things that her husband had hoped to do, was reduced to six bags.

As my parents worked away to fill those six bags, I sat quietly next to my grandmother's bed, staring in amazement and even basic visceral curiosity at her dead body. Her eyes were closed, mostly, I think. She appeared, in her extreme old age and decrepit condition, very similarly to other old persons I've seen in similar states. Just as infants often resemble one another (my mother used to say all babies looked like Winston Churchill), so too do those in extreme old age. I stared at that open mouth and tried not to think of her in pain. I began to cry. I had been afraid that, since I was not very close to her, I would not cry at her passing. Another grandfather who had died twenty years earlier (not her husband) had received no tears from me because I did not know him well. I had felt guilty about that. I felt sinful that I had not mourned or truly missed him. But I was not close to him and his loss did not affect me in the profound way that the loss of this woman's husband (seventeen years before) had. I was afraid that it would be the same with Grandma. It was not...at least not entirely. As I sat there, or perhaps knelt, on the floor next to her bed, saying goodbye to this ancestor, I could not help but think of my mother as a little child being abused by this woman. One scared little child (Grandma), abused and tortured, having grown up too fast, her innocence being stolen by her own father, abusing another scared little child (my mother), causing her to grow up too fast and think in tactical, grown-up ways to defend her life against a caregiver and her staff of occasional abusers (my mother's grandfather and friends). As I wept, I realized that I wept for my mother. I wept because my grandmother never got the opportunity to see my mother as she truly is—a remarkable, loving, giving, brilliant human being. And my mother never got the chance to feel the love and respect of her own mother. I sat there and wept over this. And I realized as such—that I was not really weeping over my grandmother, knowing that her loss would not affect my life in a profound, day-to-day sense, as did the loss of her husband (my grandfather) seventeen years before. But I was weeping for my mother's loss. I wept for her lost opportunities, her lost and irretrievable ability to feel her own mother's love and respect in the way that I had always felt from my own mother.

When my mother and father had finished packing six bags, they came back over to the curtained section of the room where my grandmother's bed was. While my dad stood back a bit to let my mother and me have our space to say goodbye, loving and supportive from behind, my mom came into the area and joined me, knowing that this would be her last farewell to her mother, her erstwhile caregiver, her former abuser, whom she loved, but from whom she did not receive a requisite and reciprocal amount of love. She was visibly reluctant, almost appearing to view this as a distasteful chore. She wanted to take a lock of my grandmother's hair as a keepsake, spiritually representing Grandma's energy and thoughts, as the hair springs from the area closest to the mind. She first brushed my grandmother's hair one last time, as she had done many times, both in the nursing home and well before, showing the love of a daughter for her mother. At this point, I felt remarkably honored to, as a man, be privy to the kind of dynamics that go on between mothers and daughters. In recent years, there has been much literature that addresses this class of sacred relationship—mothers and daughters. Unfortunately, most do not cover the not-so-positive examples of this. And most do not encourage male involvement or perception of this. I felt honored and grateful to see how my mother interacted in these last few moments with her mother. Hair was a big issue between these two. At an early age, my mother had been told by my grandmother how much she hated to cut and wash my mother's hair, initiating a certain negative bond between them over the issue of hair, and on one occasion slipping into a psychotic episode and trying to drown my mother, pushing her head into the basin that was used to wash her hair. In later years, my grandmother would often deride my mother over her hairstyle, as an adult, saying it was "too long—too long." My mother had grown her hair out to a beautiful, almost old-world, plait of such length that would make Rapunzel very envious. It had silvered in her late thirties and was so beautiful that one foreign-born friend of mine had remarked, in a very ingenuous way, that my mother "looked like royalty." My father has always loved my mother's hair as well, remarking on its sheen and its color and its health. My grandmother did not share this sentiment and would often tug on my mother's hair and deride her about it, saying that it made her look unkempt and unrefined. Perhaps my grandmother had been told the same about her own hair many years ago.

I watched my mother brush her abuser's hair one last time, and she then cut a few small locks of hair from different parts of my grandmother's head. I was amazed at having been privy to this incomparable moment. The amount of love and even forgiveness from my mother was beyond description. Like Christ saying from the cross his famous plea to his father for the forgiveness of his tormentors, my mother showed loyalty and compassion for this old woman—herself an abused child whose mind had been warped and disfigured by an earlier cog in the machinery of the family tradition—demonstrating to me once again just how incredible my own mother is. We said goodbye to my grandmother together and I continued to cry. My mother wept a little bit, but not uncontrollably. She was at peace with what had come to pass, I believe. She was ready to be free of her bondage to a not-so-kind master.

When the three of us left the room, and had finished thanking the nursing home staff, we went out to the car. I held my mother's hand. She suddenly realized that she had forgotten to tell my grandmother to "go to the light," something that they often say to the souls of the deceased these days in New Age circles. We looked up at the sky together and said it to Grandma, while my father warmed up the car in the cold December midnight air. The undertaker was on his way over, having been notified of Grandma's death, and would soon collect her body to begin the procedures for cremation and the other funeral customs we had previously arranged for.

At the funeral, several days later, I had the opportunity to say a eulogy for my grandmother alongside of my mother. We stood up at the lectern together and delivered dove-tailing speeches. I was very proud to speak alongside of this incredible human being who was able to arrange not only the funeral of my grandmother, but also to arrange the last few years of the woman's life in a way that would be as easy and painless as possible.

I write this in tribute not only to a deceased woman who had touched so many lives, in some good ways and also in bad ways, but also to a living woman whose 65th birthday is today, and for whom I have been composing this essay for the last couple of months, since the event itself happened over the Winter holidays, just before New Years, my grandmother's would be birthday. My mother is an incomparable human being, whom I love dearly and look up to and revere and even idolize. I am grateful for all that she has done for me in my life and also for having been able to take part in that event with her and to see her moment of forgiveness and bidding farewell to someone whom I wish had been able to know my mother the way I know her.

March 4, 2004

This was written five years prior to the Exile. Since that time, my respect for my mother only deepened, despite the fact that I have seen her at her worst and her most illogical. I have come to comprehend more of what made her what she is. In addition, I have come to a deeper understanding of Grandma Jeanne as well, which has also engendered in me a more compassionate view of her, a very complicated human being who had suffered much.

It is my conviction that nearly every abuser was once an abuse victim. I affirm that a person is likely to develop a chip on their shoulder when they are bullied into submission and silence, never to be able to defend themselves or to cry out in pain, affirming that they do not deserve such treatment. The Bible reminds us that "you shall not muzzle an ox", meaning that when an animal (or by extension, a human being) is worked or pain is caused, they must be able to express their pain. As such, a person who has been denied the ability to defend themselves or to express their indignation, being convinced that they deserve ill treatment, is often likely to subsequently seek to harm others as an expression of their own desire to dominate. That is to say, a bully is created. This is not to exonerate bullies, but to seek to understand how they are made and to show compassion for them. We can be angry at the bully in front of us, but we need to remember that they, too, were once helpless children being bullied by someone more powerful and more cruel than they. It is this realization that stops me in my tracks. A society of bullies is created very easily by one bully. A cycle of abuse is thus created. This realization can help disarm that cycle of abuse.

The End of Grandpa Lawlie

Around 1965, my mother, then a graduate student in Child Psychiatry, interning for her mentor, a New York therapist named Dr. Dalton, had to make a tough decision regarding the life of one of her former primary abusers. As Grandpa Lawlie aged, he became more and more of a loose cannon. As I mentioned above, he began to pay visits to women whom he hardly knew, making sexual advances toward them. He would visit his daughters' friends, married or not. He would visit women in the neighborhood whom he took a liking to. He would charm his way in and try to have sex with them. Perhaps when he was younger, and even perhaps a few times when he was older, his advances were successful. But as he aged and as he became more of the classic "dirty old man", he was no longer widely welcome, but was detested. The women upon whom he called would phone his daughters or other family members and beg them to come and pick up Grandpa Lawlie, stating that he was making a nuisance of himself. A pinch of a full bottom or a grope of an ample bosom might have been vaguely tolerated back in Sicily, but here in the U.S. his full-scale advances were just too much.

Whether or not his own aged wife was still willing to engage in sexual intercourse with him, he had made a nuisance of himself with her as well, pestering her for sex all the time. And finally, one day, he went too far. Grandma and Grandpa Lawlie were living in an apartment on the top floor of a house shared with my own grandparents, Jeanne and Artie. One day, Lawlie was running around after his wife, pestering her for sex, and in her attempt to escape him, she fell partially down a flight of stairs, saving herself from worse injury only by bracing herself against the railing. She was a portly woman, nearly eighty years of age, and she was not in any condition to be chased, unable to properly protect herself against a violent fall. So my mother, now grown and educated, a professional woman, was called upon (or rather the family just expected her to help somehow) to handle the situation. She consulted her mentor, Dr. Dalton, who advised that Lawlie was now a danger to himself and others and that he suffered from what was called satyriasis—a pathological excess of sexual drive. Dr. Dalton got Barbara in touch with the right psychiatrists who would examine Lawlie and make a proper diagnosis, and if appropriate could have him confined.

And this is what they did. He was examined. They questioned. He answered. I do not know the details of the questions, or how deranged his answers were. I do not know whether he was able to properly identify the month or year, or whether every other word out of his mouth was a request for sexual favors. But somehow, they knew he was a danger and could not be trusted to refrain from chasing his elderly wife down a flight of stairs or from wandering the neighborhood pestering strangers for sexual gratification. And so they had him confined to a mental hospital. This was my mother's initiative. It was not an easy thing to do. At the time, she did not even remember the abuse she had sustained at his hands, having repressed the memory of it until many years later. To her, he was the slightly creepy, and now totally deranged grandfather who was endangering her grandmother and who needed to be safeguarded against himself. So she allowed the authorities to make the judgment call and to confine him. He was remanded to Creedmoor State Mental Hospital in early 1965.

When Barbara came to visit him, he would cry and plead, begging her to arrange for his release. She found it pitiful, and if he were not a danger to himself and to others, it might have been a request worth considering. And with the revelation of his allegedly diabolical past, it seems less of a worthwhile request, and his confinement more of a just desert for a criminal whose past had caught up with him.

Lawlie remained there for a year and a half, crying for release each time someone came to visit. And then, by May of 1966, he had developed stomach cancer and had died. Perhaps it was the result of his years of smoking cigars, perhaps the result of his moderate but lengthy career of alcohol consumption. Or perhaps it was knowing that he was trapped, with no way of ever abusing children or helpless women ever again, left there to die. Either way, Barbara had made a decision according to her best information, for the greater good of the family. But ironically, it was her very abuser, still unbeknownst to her at that time, whom she had undone, putting him where he could no longer do anyone any harm. Later that year, she was married and on her way to having a family of her own. Lawlie's widow, Grandma Cookie, attended that wedding, escorted by family that loved and protected her, celebrating the new life that was inaugurated by the young girl—now grown—whose abuse happened unbeknownst to the former, under her very roof and perpetrated by her very husband.

And as much as the reader may see some justice in this end to the man, Lawlie, I find it important to remember that he, too, was a child once. He, too, was the son of two human beings, Antonio and Salvatrice, who later immigrated as well, and he too probably suffered abuse as a child. Abusers do not usually spring from thin air, like Athena from the side of Zeus' head. Abusers are made, as are hoarders. They are made, carefully crafted from the abuse and conditions that they undergo, that shape them, that mold or warp their minds. These people—and that is what they are, people—begin their lives like you and me. They need love, they seek their parent's approval, they grow, they think, they suffer, and they live. Twentieth century psychologist Alice Miller notes that when a child is abused or not given the love they inherently deserve, oft times they become deranged, their thinking distorted, carrying around a grudge against their abusers but unable to express it, they act out against any and all living things—helpless animals and people.[3] I am reminded of Vlad Tepec (the medieval Transylvanian warlord who inspired the myths about Dracula) who, when confined to a tower prison as a younger man, would catch mice and birds and torture them to express his rage. And when he found his freedom, he carried out this practice on every conceivable person inside and outside his dominion, leading to his moniker, "Vlad the Impaler". What made him seek to foist his rage upon innocent victims, when by comparison the Apostle Paul or Mahatma Gandhi or Nelson Mandela, all imprisoned at one point in their lives, did not seek anything of the sort, but sought instead to make peace? In the opinion of some, like Alice Miller, it is the early childhood abuse—unabated or mitigated by the validation of a sympathetic ear—that caused those like Hitler and Vlad the Impaler to make these violent choices, while others did not. While some may disagree, making the important observation that we cannot fully understand the part that the element of free will plays in these decisions to flourish and affirm life or to despair and choose the evil, it still must be noted that the chain of abuse in humankind has played a crucial role in the perpetuation of evil and abuse. It is the persistent abuse of people by other people that causes more abuse. When a society or village or a community suffers atrocities in warfare, a hardening of the spirit is often noted among its members, yielding higher levels of child abuse and domestic violence, as if the hardening of the spirit were a good thing, protecting one against further abuse. We thus see societies such as Ancient Rome and Sparta deliberately fostering forms of entertainment that would harden and inure the society against the sight of death. This in turn fosters a society that lusted after the blood of the conquered—for the Romans, often innocent Christians. These, in turn, fostered a society based on fear within the Christian orthodox hierarchy, ready with its racks and tortures to stamp out heresy and dissenting theological opinion. Then, a Christian Europe, fraught with fear of a brutal aristocracy, ready to torture its own citizens at the slightest offense against the total authority and divine right of kings, gave rise to some of the bloodiest revolutions, like that of the French which butchered countless innocent civilians on account of their employment as servants and lackeys of the aristocracy—an ethnic and social cleansing no different than that of the Khmer Rouge. And when the Sicilian Mafia—at times in many ways the only stable bastion of grass-roots authority to stand against foreign domination on an island that was perennially tossed from the control of one empire to another— presented its brutal fist to the local populace of Corleone, many generations were not spared the iron rod of child abuse. Lawlie was likely a product of that

---

[3] Alice Miller, *For Your Own Good: Hidden Cruelty in Child-Rearing and the Roots of Violence*. Hildegard and Hunter Hannum, translators. Fourth Edition (New York: Farrar Straus Giroux, 2002).

brutality, warping his mind so that the most helpless and innocent beings within his care—like that of his own daughter Jeanne, and later his granddaughter Barbara—were not safe from the explosive broadcast of his blind rage, inappropriately directed not at perpetrators, but at innocent children.

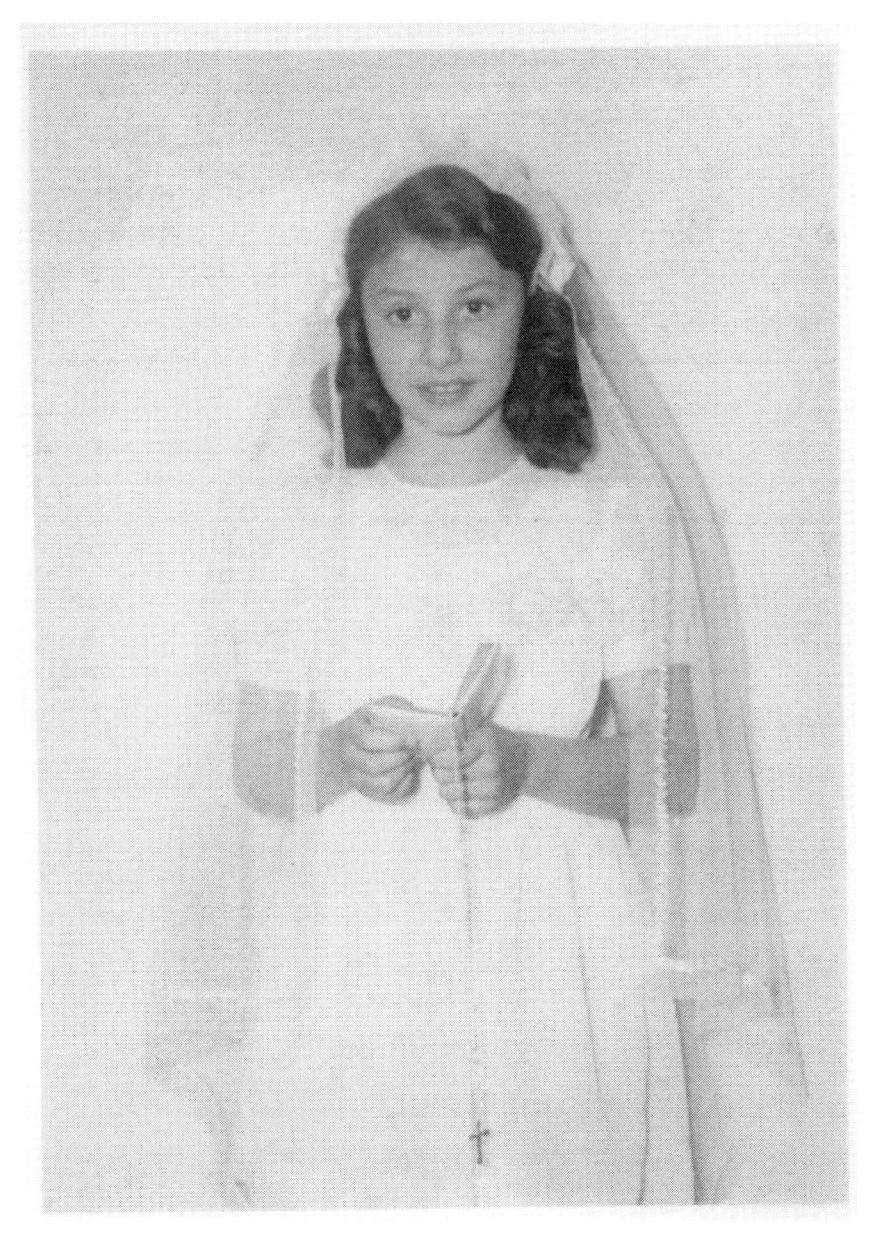

Barbara Merget, Communion, 1940s

THE EXILE

Barbara Merget, 1942, aged 3 1/2

CHAPTER FOUR:
THE PRE-EXILIC PERIOD

Sometime after my marriage in 2005, which immediately followed graduation from my Ph.D. program, my parents' relationship seriously and visibly deteriorated. Their interactions were marked by strife and difficulty. Never before had I seen them get along so poorly. They were almost always arguing. And of course, this was all while they lived 3,000 miles away on Long Island. I was still in Los Angeles, working a variety of part-time teaching and consulting jobs in higher education, unable to find steady full-time work in my field, due to the erosion of the tenure system in higher education, which I will address later. My ability to visit them was severely limited due to my decreased income and lack of steady employment. Subsequently, I saw them once a year, at best. But during my weekly phone conversations, I witnessed their decaying relationship.

I had last seen the house during my visit over the Winter holidays, 2004. I was without my then-fiancée, Melissa, during that visit and I stayed in my old room, which was more cramped than ever before, as my parents had continued to use it for storage while the rest of the house suffered from extreme clutter. And while I did enjoy my time with my parents, thinking that this might be my last chance to visit with them alone for quite some time, the visit was strained on account of the space factor.

Melissa and I had met at a Renaissance faire the year prior, and after reconnecting in late April, we were largely inseparable from the time of our first date in May, 2004, and it was rare for me to travel without her thereafter. I would describe Melissa as a curvaceous, blue-eyed blonde who only became more voluptuous with time, and whose fair complexion belied her mom's Ashkenazi Jewish heritage in favor of her dad's British heritage, and left her appearing more like the typical *shiksa* than a member of "The Tribe". In fact, an Irish priest had once somewhat dismissively expressed disbelief over her claim to be Jewish, repeating the phrase, "No you're not!" and insisting pleasantly, in his brogue, that she had Irish eyes. Also born under the sun sign of Libra, Melissa was born three days before me, my dad often joking that "she's too old for you." With very similar sensibilities, she has been my helpmeet and partner in crime since our second date, when we gained the sense that this relationship was marriage-bound.

Whenever I visited New York, after we were married, usually once a year during Summertime, I would have Melissa with me. And since there was no place to stay at my parents' house, we were invited to stay with the family of my dear friend, Aimee. When I first met Aimee, she still lived at her parents' home, very close to my own parents' house in Dix Hills, and was in her first few years of practice as an attorney. She was very diligent about helping raise her younger siblings and she was doing what many Long Island adults do, saving money while living at home with their parents until they, too, get married and then move out. It was part of the culture of my homeland. A few years later, she got her own apartment, about a mile away from her parents' house. A year or so later, she had an extension built onto her parents' house, with her own apartment and private entrance, and she moved back in. Aimee and I had dated for a short while, many years before in the mid-'90s, and we had maintained a close friendship. She was like a sister to me, and our families had become close as well. They would be integral, later, in the cleanout of the Exile. Without them, the results would never have been so good, as I will later recount.

The first time that Melissa and I were Aimee's guests, we stayed at her apartment while she was away on business. The next time, we stayed in one of her siblings' old bedrooms at her parents' place. We were honored, both times, to be so graciously taken into their home and treated like family. My parents would then visit with us, while at Aimee's, and then go the two or so miles back to their house at night. We were not invited, nor were we expected, to enter my parents' house. My mother was embarrassed about the condition of the house, and was unwilling to let her "daughter-in-love" (as she had affectionately termed Melissa) see the disaster that was our home. Melissa got to see the exterior once or twice, and while she saw the utter arboreal beauty of my suburban Long Island homeland, she was somewhat surprised by the wildness of the weeds and vines and haphazardly arranged potted plants outside. There was no rhyme or reason to the orientation of the narrow, winding pathway down the center of what had once been a bluestone, gravel driveway, now become a garden in its own right. It was covered in ground cover, ferns and ivy, with bags of cement or potting soil and other such garden accessories strewn about in half-finished projects. Outdoor tables were stationed here or there, children's plastic playground furniture was employed hither and thither, obviously having been salvaged from someone else's garbage. The scene was more than primordial. It was pathological.

And at this point, it began to be evident to me that it was no longer really "my house", but their house. Sometimes, I would instinctually refer to it as "my mother's house", indicating that in my mind I viewed her as the one in charge—that it was her decision to keep the house the way it was. Even though she would vehemently disagree, asserting that it was my father who was in charge and that it was his decision to keep the house this way, due to his lack of interest in cleaning up, I knew better. She would perennially claim that he had always been the one in charge and that it was he who made the house this way and that she had always been disempowered throughout their marriage; she, the shrinking violet to his dictatorship. She would often claim that she didn't want to live this way, that she wanted to live in a clean environment. If pressed or confronted about the illogic of these claims, she would answer that she was just now beginning to take back her power. But I knew that this was just a device, a tactic to justify why she hoarded. Of course, my father was involved; he was indeed an integral part of the problem. Their relationship was part of the problem, as also was the abuse she had gone through as a child. But it was not his decision to hoard. None of the items were brought into the house directly at his behest, nor did he ever proclaim that he didn't want things to be taken out or discarded. That was purely her decision. And her adamant assertion to the contrary was very much reminiscent of delusional thinking that I had seen in truly mentally ill people.

At times, when I confronted my mom about the mess, reminding her that I was here to help but that her insistence upon having me "dusting off books" was tantamount to a rejection of a clean house, she would say, "Maybe my idea of cleanliness is not the same as yours." She would sometimes claim, when I would reproach her about the deteriorated appearance of the exterior of the house and its surrounds, that she "liked things wild" and wanted to see things "growing wild, unmanicured". While I agreed that the excessively regimented manicuring of shrubs, reminiscent of late 18th century French imperial gardens, was absurd and unnatural, I also thought that our home had become too much like a derelict home. There was no logic to how things were organized and there was too much debris strewn about, never to be discarded. The concrete apron that covered the last third of the driveway leading up to the front door was largely covered with ivy that had crept up and over one full half of its breadth, leaving only a few feet of pathway next to my old 1971 Chevy Nova that I was still storing there, a classic that I one day hoped to transport to California for a full restoration. And moreover, that very automobile was decorated by plants and things that my mother had put there upon it, when I had asked her to merely keep it covered with the tarp I had provided. But most of all, the pathway up to the front door, leading from the concrete apron to the house's entrance, was severely encroached by yew shrubs that were left to their own devices. Many years before, when my grandmother was still living and able to visit us, she would sneakily prune these yews and cut them back in ways that would make trained arborists cringe, baring woody limbs to the elements where there formerly was greenery. It was evident to me that my mom's refusal to trim them at all was a conscious backlash against my grandmother's excessive attitudes about throwing things out and discarding everything. But this had become dangerous as well as unsightly. The yews' broad reach was not necessarily a sign of their good health. Despite the fact that my mom had deliberately let them grow to their hearts' content, they had large bare patches close to the center and there were large gaps closer to the house, where yews had originally been stationed but had now grown erratically away from their roots. The yews had extended tendrils overhead that caused the pathway to be covered by a canopy. And the canopy drooped lower and lower so that one had to duck down further and further each year, if one wanted to reach the front door. This surely annoyed any delivery people who had to drop things off. And the front stoop was half covered with debris and articles that had been salvaged, with or without any possible further usage. It was in the Summer of 2009 that I saw both the HBO film *Grey Gardens,* and the famous 1975 documentary by the same name, on which the feature film was based, chronicling the unconventional lifestyle and home of the Bouvier Beales. The state of disrepair that the grounds suffered from caused me to dub our family home, ironically, "Green Gardens", appropriately renamed for the Greenbergs. But the humor intended in this moniker quickly turned to sadness when the Exile was declared in August of that same Summer, and the similarities between our situation and that of the Bouvier Beales abounded.

The Car Accident

At some point in 2007, my parents had a car accident, in which my dad fell asleep at the wheel for a moment, late at night, and drove their minivan off the road and into a shallow ditch at the side of the Northern State Parkway. There were no injuries, but there were a few dollars of damage to the vehicle. My parents did not immediately tell me about this, for fear of scaring me. And their inclination was right. When I did finally hear about this a year or two later, I was scared out of my mind. It alerted me, all too abruptly, of my parents' fallibility, as well as their vulnerability, frailty, and ultimate mortality. When my dad had retired from his teaching job of thirty years, back in 1995, it was a big awakening for me. Prior to that, my identity was in some ways hinged upon the fact that "my daddy is a teacher," as I would later describe it. But for him to retire and no longer be currently described as a teacher, made me realize that I was now expected to be a grown up and that my father was aging. And when the aforementioned accident happened, it continued this awakening for me in that I was reminded that my parents are not immortal. No child likes to realize that his or her parents are mortal. It reminds a person of one's own mortality and the fragility of human life. That we, too, are getting older every moment. And this incident with my parents was only a harbinger of more things to come that awakened me to my need to turn the tables and take care of them.

My mom and dad consulted with their therapist at the time and somehow this incident was interpreted as a potential sign of my father's suicidal tendency. To this day, I am not sure whether there is any truth to this or whether it was more an indication of age. More and more, my father would need help with directions in the car. He would get lost frequently. My mother would have to guide him in areas where he had been driving for four decades and surely knew the way. He began to fall asleep when in the presence of company. He was more and more forgetful. This growing trend began to scare both my mother and me. But my father could still be smart as a whip when he wanted to. This suggested to Mom and me that it was more an emotional reaction than a permanent, biochemically driven one. This gave us hope, but it still was a frightening trend. And the car accident was the first major sign to me that my parents needed to be protected and that something more serious was wrong.

Cousin Marian's Death

When my mother's cousin Marian died in May of 2004, following her late husband's passing no more than a couple of years prior, a huge amount of volume was adopted into our house by my mom. Granted, there were indeed some family heirlooms, old family photo albums, tools used by my great grandfather, Andy (Grandpa Arty's father), and various other items whose salvation and preservation really did make sense. And many of these were initially discarded by the incompetent and duplicitous executors of the estate who were initially left in charge; they were neither blood nor legal relatives (merely family "friends" who later raided the inheritance and maintenance of Marian's surviving mentally disabled daughter, Amy) and saw no value in these things. My mother, very logically, went into the garbage cans out front—in full view of these executors—and saved what she could. But in addition, she took carloads of sewing materials, arts and crafts, little dollhouses, dioramas, and so forth, with the intention of donating them, but which were never brought over to Goodwill or the Salvation Army, and were now the possession of the great gaping maw that was my mother's addiction. They were nestled into the few remaining niches inside the garage, or piled on top of piles inside the house. These were things with no particular connection to family history, no direct personal sentimental value for my mother or any of us, but they on some level represented my mother's broken childhood. The one piece that stuck out in my mind and touched my own heart, was a small diorama dollhouse with small three or four-inch-tall figures of a family. I thought to myself when I saw these that I was glad they were saved—striking my own sense of pity and sentimentality which I speak of elsewhere in this book—but that I wish they would be given to someone who had room for them and a use for them. I feared that these charming little artifacts of Marian's life and creativity would be submerged under a pile of junk forever and forgotten, not at a dump, but in my mother's house. Little did I know that within a few years, during the Exile, they would indeed be sent to the dump after all.

I would editorialize that we do have a serious problem in our society, in which things that should be saved and given to charitable causes like Goodwill and the Salvation Army are instead trashed out of a misguided sense of pride, not wanting to sully our collective hands with used items whose reuse is below us. But this malady of excessive wastefulness becomes simultaneously a playground for the illness of hoarders, a breeding ground for their sickness.

The Kitchen Tile Incident

In 2007, I believe it was, when Melissa and I came to NY during a Summer, my mother had been talking with her friend Barbara Simmons, about putting down new tile in the kitchen of our house. The old linoleum tiles that had been there since the very beginning in 1972 had begun to delaminate and come loose. And as part of my mother's enthusiasm about restoring the house to its former glory, she had gone out and bought new vinyl tile in quantities sufficient to do the entire 10 by 15-foot kitchen. It was a wonderful idea. She had asked for my assistance in doing the installation, and I was more than happy to oblige. I wanted very much for the house to benefit from improvements. And I was happy to take some of my vacation time to help. But knowing how my mother tended to work, more haphazard than systematic—and her lacking any real construction experience—I knew what questions to ask her and how to prompt her from 3,000 miles away so that the area would be prepared for my labors. So I reiterated time and time again over the phone that the kitchen had to be entirely cleared out and that there could be **nothing** there on the floor, so that we could take consistent measurements, work quickly, and lay down the tile in a few hours' time. She reassured me several times that she understood and would comply; that she and Barbara were working to move things out of the kitchen and clean up enough of the dining room to handle any of the items from the kitchen that needed to be stored there temporarily. I was not so naïve as to think that the entire house would be cleaned by the time I arrived, but I was sufficiently assured that, simply put, the kitchen would be empty and prepared for my work. I was deluded and deceived.

When I arrived in the house during that trip, ready to work, I discovered that nearly nothing had been moved out of the kitchen. The old, white Formica dining room table that now sat in the center of the kitchen, topped with piles of plant seeds and half done projects, was still in place. Numerous potted plants still sat in place at the end of the kitchen where the sliding glass doors, once clear enough to look out of onto a set of evergreen shrubs, were now clouded by age and mildew. There was insufficient room for me to work. Having a fair amount of experience in construction and home renovation, working part-time in these trades while I was attending grad school, I knew how important it was to have enough space around you while doing these projects. You simply cannot get a proper idea of level and grid lines when you are working section by section, and the entire area to be tiled is unable to be viewed for measurements. And moreover, to have garbage and plants underfoot is not only inefficient, but also dangerous to work in those conditions.

So I flatly refused to work. I tried to make it as kind a statement as possible, but I was angry. I had been lied to. My mother, though not out of malice but delusion, had lied to me about the condition of the kitchen. She had stated shortly before that there were just a few small items to be moved aside prior to work commencing. What I saw was far from that. This was not only a gross exaggeration, it was a pathological, deranged untruth. I was simultaneously livid and frightened. This rude awakening to my mother's level of delusion was unsettling, to say the least.

She was hurt by my unwillingness to proceed as planned. I tried to explain to her that it could not be done. But she interpreted my unwillingness as a lack of desire to help her. I tried to convey to her that it was simply not possible to be done. This was not clear to her. She could not comprehend that while, yes, I *could* go ahead and begin, it was simply neither practical nor possible to be completed in a manner that would be free of major mistakes. If I wanted to, *could* I begin? Yes. *Should* I begin? No. No flooring subcontractor would have set foot in that house, let alone given her the assurance that he could do the job. I did not feel that I should do differently. And I felt trapped, as if I were entrapped by her delusional thinking in light of my love for her and desire to keep her happy.

So we argued. I was able to make her basically understand my concerns and my point of view. I asked if I could accompany her to her appointment with David Grand, the family therapist, the next day. She agreed. I secretly planned to enlighten David about the situation which involved not only my mother's compulsive addiction to collecting, but also to her level of delusion in the situation at hand. I was very frightened of her state of mind. The next day, as we drove in to see David with me at the wheel and my parents as passengers, my mother—from the back seat—began to press me about what I was going to talk with David about, claiming that she had a right to know prior to the session. I attempted to refuse, saying that I wanted to leave it until we got into the session. But my mother persistently pressed the issue and I became very irate. I said some things that were not very kind, delineating to her the level of delusion and even insanity that I saw in her inability to comprehend with any clarity the reality of the situation with the kitchen, or any part of the house. She was hurt and I was still very angry.

The session with David was somewhat tense, but civil; by the time we finished, I thought that things were somewhat settled. All three of us met with David and discussed the matter. I was under the impression that I had successfully conveyed my concerns to my mother and that she understood, believing that it was not capricious unwillingness to help that caused me to rescind my offer to do the job, but rather a concern about safety and feasibility. After the session, David spoke with me privately and reassured me that in many ways, my parents' problems were separate from mine and he encouraged me to continue to pursue my own destiny and allow them to pursue theirs. This did not seem helpful to me at the time. We were still a family. And as much as I respected David for all his work with my mother and for helping my family, and especially me over the years, I still disagreed with this approach. The situation in my family was getting worse and I could see the dangers poking their heads out. No one seemed willing to see what I saw.

After I exited, my mother was missing. I looked for her in the car. She was not there. My dad couldn't find her either. Finally, after about ten minutes of searching, we found her standing, fuming, at the bottom of the staircase in the lower level of David's building, in an area that was rarely trodden by those entering through the main entrance, only those entering through the parking area. She stated, despite my former belief that the situation had been settled amicably, that she had felt ganged up on, that she didn't think anyone understood her position, and that she just wanted to hide. She had displayed this kind of behavior before, as I have mentioned—running away for a short time, either to get away or to engender a fear reaction in the family that would send them running to her rescue or to accede to her wishes. It was no different here. We talked for another half hour perhaps, after I finally got her back to the car. Things were less tense. We didn't speak of the kitchen tiles again for a while. The several boxes of long vinyl tile were put away to be stored in the only vacant place my parents could find—the back of the unused 1987 Buick station wagon that was parked in their driveway, registration expired.

Dr. Pupusa

Somewhere in 2007 or 2008, my parents befriended and began to consult with some type of holistic medical doctor, Dr. Pupusa, who lived nearby. She was an older woman from the Philippines (perhaps in her late 70s at the time, about a decade older than my mother) who by all accounts was indeed a medical doctor, but I do not know her specialty or much about her credentials. I do not dispute these. They had found her by accident, having met her through some friend or vitamin store. There was no referral or formal start to their professional relationship. She invited them over to her house and had them as her guests numerous times. On some level, she began to mentor them, talking with them about a variety of holistic medical issues, spiritual practices, and so forth. They saw her approximately once a week and, if I am not mistaken, there was never any money that changed hands. By all accounts, she was charming with a lighthearted attitude, an extremely positive element in their lives. My parents raved about her to me in our weekly phone conversations.

Eventually, my mother began to have one of her mood swings again in which my father could do nothing right and the entire situation of the house was his fault—entirely caused by him and entirely solvable by him. Something would set her off and she would transform from her usual optimistic self into something much darker and pessimistically adversarial. I had seen it throughout my childhood. Surely it was a form of depression or bipolar reaction that was the result of her own childhood abuse. My mother would describe my father as having had these himself—"punitive sulks", as she called them—throughout their marriage, but I did not notice them in him until many years later, until just before the Exile. She was the one I observed having them.

But Dad had done something wrong, something insensitive or careless.

When I would hear from my parents, it was a crapshoot as to whether they were going to be fighting or getting along like pals. It was a matter of chance that something might have gotten knocked over in the house, either succumbing to gravity or being accidentally bumped into by my father as he tried to navigate the ubiquitous piles of junk. And more often than not, he left it where it lay, either out of exasperation or annoyed laziness. This enraged my mother who reasonably thought that he should have more respect for her things and try to pick them up, if not avoid knocking into them.

At around this time, my father had begun to develop a limp. We were never sure what the cause was, whether it was his knee or his hip. The chiropractor our family went to said that it was nothing more than sciatica, due to inactivity and that it was easily remedied by exercise. Dad began to use a cane and to allow himself to distort his body while walking, to resemble a hunched over old man. Prior to this, he was a fully ambulatory, relatively fit and capable man in his early 70s. But in an instant, he became an old man. While sitting, his head became hunched over, projected slightly forward like that of a turtle. He shuffled when he walked. He always required the cane. And when he walked in our house, he kept his hand out to brace himself on anything that was nearby. And as he passed, he would unthinkingly brush his hand along whatever was there, dragging it with him. This often became the source of things getting knocked over. When Melissa and I visited in 2007, we witnessed his newly acquired gait. At times, Mom and I would experiment and ask him to try to straighten up rather than hunch over his cane. Momentarily, he would comply, straightening up with slightly arched back, shoulders to the rear, arms almost akimbo, head looking up as if suddenly straining to see a distant object. Whenever he did this, he would say that he felt much better, as if surprised by the helpfulness of this suggestion, a Neanderthal who had all of a sudden become *Homo erectus*. Then he would soon after drop back into his old habit of hunching over. We tried numerous experiments, including taking away his cane. He always straightened up without it. He always felt better when standing upright. His limp always improved with his more vertical posture. But he always deteriorated, unconsciously, back into that slumped over posture, guarding his cane as if a vulture or a gargoyle on its perch. It was surely an emotionally generated, psycho-somatic ailment that would indeed have been improved by exercise, as Allan, the Chiropractor had said.

But my dad had become more and more oblivious of the world around him. He withdrew into himself, intensifying a reaction, a personality trait, that my mother reported was always there in him since the beginning of their marriage. He now began to forget simple things. His short-term memory began to suffer. As an Air Force veteran of the Korean War era, we had him checked out by medical doctors at the VA and they stated that there was no evidence of any kind of medical illness, such as Alzheimer's or Dementia. It was most likely emotional, we surmised. But it was dangerous and maddening, all the same.

Evidently, some kind of conflict or disturbance had occurred between my parents, and one morning, I received an unexpected call from my mother, saying that she had temporarily left my father and had moved into Dr. Pupusa's house. She had a tone in her voice that was almost robotic, artificially calm, the way a therapist would speak to a patient that was suffering from delusional thinking. Mom expressed to me that she was letting me know where she was so that I would not get concerned, but that she would be incommunicado for a while, during which she would be under Dr. Pupusa's care. She said that she had been in a dangerous environment and that she needed to undergo treatment at Dr. Pupusa's. Dr. Pupusa got on the phone and gently reassured me that my mother was alright but that she would be working with her to help get her back into proper condition. Mom would be encouraged to pursue her artwork and her writing while being fully under the care of the good doctor.

I was shocked. No actual diagnosis was given. No explanation of the cause, either. Just that she was taking a voluntary break from my father and was, in some ways, replicating the situation of a rest home or a sanitarium-resort. I agreed to give my mom her space, to allow her to initiate the phone calls to me. I arranged to call my dad at home to check in with him. It was him that I was worried about now. I was not sure how he would handle this. At times, he was oblivious, insensitive and sometimes reminiscent of the cartoon character Homer Simpson. But he was not at all a heartless or cruel man. He was, in fact, one of the most mild-mannered, gentle people I had ever known, whose passivity at times was the bane of my existence and whose lack of assertiveness, by example, had contributed to my own inability to defend myself throughout my life. I was not sure if this was the right decision that my mother had made.

I spoke to him by phone at least daily. He was in poor spirits. We had a lot of heart to heart talks during that time. I spoke openly with him about my mom's shortcomings. I was aware that in therapy—in which he had been for many decades and with many therapists—he was not really sharing with the therapists the extent of my mom's addiction to collecting, or the nature of her occasional rages, which were never physical, but at times were extremely hurtful and illogical in their unfolding. It was his lack of truthfulness, I am convinced, that caused David Grand—my parents' previous therapist—to "fire" my dad from their sessions at one point. My dad was making no progress. He was evidently not even being truthful with David, choosing "everything's fine" language over getting to the heart of the problems. I can never really be sure if David understood the full gravity of my mother's hoarding problems at this early stage, choosing to work more with her on the nature and roots of her abuse rather than the current outward manifestations of her illness. I do not know if I endorsed or entirely understood that decision to cease working with my dad. But it was not my decision to make. He later came to understand the gravity of the whole situation.

But I confronted my dad about this, reminding him that if he was untruthful with his therapist, then what was he paying him for? I reasserted that the therapist is the one person in the world you need to be truthful with—or how are they ever going to help you? So I convinced him to contact a new therapist—one which was recommended by Allan, the Chiropractor. Kim Catalano rented space from Allan and was, by all accounts, brilliant and came well-recommended. I convinced Dad to call him as soon as possible and set up an appointment to speak with him. I encouraged my dad to do what he could to clean up after himself in the house—something he rarely did. I told him to try to "date" my mother; bring her gifts or something when he was able; treat her to special occasions when she returned or when he was allowed to see her.

He did as much as possible of what I suggested. He contacted Kim and went for an appointment. He visited my mom at Dr. Pupusa's house about once a week, or whenever allowed. And his spirits improved as much as could be expected while not knowing whether his wife was going to leave him. When I spoke with my mother on the phone, she still had that decidedly dazed and dreamy quality to her voice, as if she had been hypnotized—brainwashed, almost—into believing in the rightness of this decision. She stated unequivocally, "This is the most healthy I have ever felt," maintaining that mesmerized quality, as if the next words out of her mouth were going to be something like "Yes, Master…" or "Destroy the humans", or some other phrase suitable for the antagonist in a horror film or a campy science fiction movie. She was there about ten to fourteen days, inclusive.

At the time, I was heartbroken, horrified that my parents might get a divorce. I listened to a lot of the music of pop singer Anastacia, with lyrics about heartbreak, which encapsulated what I thought was the mood between my parents and myself. On her website, a brief clip from a song was posted on a loop, and I listened to it again and again, the word, "Broken" ringing in my ears again and again, evocative of my parents' life with me. For many years, I believed that my parents were the paragons of wedded bliss and matrimonial success. Neither of them had ever had an affair. Growing up, my mother was proud to proclaim that she and my father were exemplars of good marital relationships. At times of arguments, when my father somewhat coyly and half-jesting, expressed fear that my mother would divorce him, her response was playfully menacing: "I'd sooner divorce your head from your shoulders." We all thought this was charmingly folksy in its implied violence. It was part of our New York gallows humor. And now, the prospect of an impending divorce struck me as the possible end of my world. The people whom I most counted on as exemplars of marital dignity were now on the verge of the unthinkable. To whom would I turn as a model for my own marital behavior?

About a week and a half to two weeks after my mother arrived at Dr. Pupusa's, she was done with the situation. It was all very quick for me to catch on, but I received a call from my mom or dad and they alerted me not to call at Dr. Pupusa's and that Barbara Simmons would be picking my mom up and having her stay at her house for a while. I expressed concern, believing that Barbara was not an impartial party, being first and foremost my mom's friend and fearing that Barbara's own lack of marital success would cause her to encourage my mom to leave my father for good. Mom assured me that Barbara liked my dad and was sufficiently impartial and would be a good influence on the situation. She also briefly and enigmatically explained that Dr. Pupusa was not what she thought she was, and became demanding and hard to deal with; that leaving was the best thing for her to do at this point. She would stay at Barbara's for as long as was necessary. Mom later explained that at some point when she and my father both went back to Dr. Pupusa's to pick up some of her belongings, the good doctor was alarmingly urgent in her manner, demanding that my mom return back to my father; that she was concerned about my dad's health, stating that if my mom did not return home immediately, my dad might have a heart attack. This was all too confusing for me: first, she wanted my mom to leave her husband and stay under her care indefinitely; now that she was no longer under her care, but staying with a friend, she wanted her to return to her husband? Something was not quite right, but that stage of things was now over, thankfully.

When I spoke to Barbara Simmons within a few days, she explained what she saw at Dr. Pupusa's. She relayed that Dr. Pupusa had her own problems with hoarding. She had cat food dishes everywhere and her yard was an indication of her own lack of order; that there was no sense in having my mom receiving "help" from someone who was not well herself. She had no business counseling my mom with regard to an illness that she herself suffered from. I was happy to hear this assessment from Barbara. It reassured me of her good sense and impartiality. Mom stayed at Barbara's for a few more days to a week, perhaps. Then, after a sufficient amount of negotiation and peace talks with my father, she returned home, optimistic that he would change his attitude and begin to help her make their home cleaner.

I was very relieved that she was home again, no longer even considering a divorce. But I was not so optimistic that anything would really change. They had gone through these kinds of patterns before, and the cycle continued over the years. They would argue; Mom would make demands on my father to change; he would make an effort; the effort would diminish; they would return to arguing; the cycle would then repeat. At times, I wondered how much was his lack, and how much was hers. He was oblivious. He lost things. He would lose the mail, Mom accusing him of hiding it. He lost bills and checks and cell phones. He would not finish anything he started. He would leave his clothes, dirty or clean, all over the place. He had even recently gotten my parents into financial jeopardy by opening excessive numbers of 0% balance transfer credit cards and forgetting to pay them, leaving my parents drastically in debt. But it was a two-way street.

My whole life, the adversarial pattern described above was largely directed at me, not at him. It was I who would go through these cycles with my mother; arguing, reconciling, arguing, reconciling. Our frequent arguments tainted what was otherwise a peaceable family life, causing me to always be off kilter, off balance, never sure when to expect the next argument to arise, beyond my control or ability to predict and preempt. I had come to compare our lives to those of "poignant movies," as I once called them during the aftermath of a heated discussion, like "Ordinary People" with Mary Tyler Moore, in which our dysfunctionality revealed that we were just like the families therein that served as the cautionary tales within these modern tragedies. And I never truly understood what my sin had been. It was this lack of certainty or clarity of the situation that caused me to somewhat facetiously and yet somewhat deliberately nickname my mother an "evil genius" while I was still a child, on account of her uncanny ability to twist the details of a situation to convince me that I had done something wrong, that I was a severely "inconsiderate" and "selfish", "narcissistic" human being and that I needed to repent. And yet, after these incidents, as I apologized and begged for forgiveness, I still never understood concretely what I had done wrong or what needed to change. I often prayed for clarity. During one particularly bad episode while I was home on break from college, I remember inscribing the words, "INADEQUATE SON" on my chest in blue felt-tip marker and sequestering myself in my room stripped to the waist, covered only in a blanket to keep myself warm, as if repenting with sackcloth and ashes. A little later, I recall prostrating myself on all fours, and repeatedly hitting my forehead against the concrete fire bricks that surrounded the woodburning stove in the main area of the house, as if this act of contrition would somehow make the yelling and the pain stop. Perhaps there was some element of accusation behind this act—as if to say, "YOU have called me an inadequate son". As if this subtle gesture of resistance were my own form of self-mutilation to control an out-of-control situation, all I could do to quell the pain.

It was only years later, as an adult, having undergone years of therapy, that I came to realize that I was never nearly as bad as my mother had convinced me I was in those early days; that I was merely a child who, perhaps somewhat emotionally immature just like any other child, had needed some time to grow up and recognize his affect on the world around him. In fact, I was a very good son. I never did drugs; I never drank; I never broke the law; I was an honor student and an athlete; I was the model child, by all accounts. I merely required reminders to do my chores, and I daydreamed a lot. At this point, I finally came to realize that it was more my mother's shortcomings that caused her to perpetually make a mountain out of a molehill. And that this "dance macabre", as David Grand once characterized it, that my mother and I engaged in, repeatedly entering into arguments that could not be solved, said more about her than me, and that on some level I had been "gaslighted" by her. David later playfully described my upbringing to Melissa, when he finally met her early on in our marriage, as a "feral childhood". The two of them chuckled knowingly, as did I, but the truth of it smarted a little bit. I had put up with a lot of dysfunction from my mother, not least of which was her hoarding—her middle-aged acting out through her addition to junk. She had chosen me as her adversary for whatever reason she needed to do so, counterpointing the generally positive interactions of the very close relationship we had. And I began to wonder if the same dynamics, now that I was gone and was unavailable for argument, had been transposed upon my dad.

My dad continued to go to Kim Catalano for treatment. By my estimation, he was an excellent therapist, much more confrontational and direct than David Grand or any previous therapist that the Greenbergs had gone to. My mother continued, at times, to go to David, who had expertly helped Mom unearth her repressed memories. But Dad made some initially good progress in his own therapy with Kim. My mother, on a few occasions, joined my dad in his therapy sessions. This, however, gave Dad the opportunity to slack off and rely upon my mom's superior memory to buttress his often lackadaisical attitude toward details and facts in conjunction with his deteriorating short term memory. At times, Kim could be brutally honest. I applauded that. He even at times confronted my mom about her excessively long-winded manner of conveying facts, forcing her to get to the point and not use her detailed nature to serve as an excuse or as an avoidance tactic. But one thing that my mom quoted Kim as saying was somewhat odd to me. She relayed that he had given her literature about domestic abuse and suggested that she get herself to a safe house for women. This, to me, was preposterous. My dad's contributions to the family problems—while they were many—had nothing to do with physical or sexual violence. He didn't have a violent bone in his body. I laughed at this and wondered how much of it was my mom's misinterpretation of Kim, or whether she had obscured the facts to him as well. I mused playfully to myself that if she did go to a "safe house", she would begin to clutter up their environment, too, with her incessant hoarding. And as they began to grow tired of her amassing junk, they would laugh her out the door after finding out that she was not in any way being physically or sexually abused. In fact, I began later to find out that while living at Barbara Simmons' apartment for those several weeks, she began to amass things in the same way that she did every time she had visited me in California. Wherever she went, she was followed by a growing mass of things that she had to collect. She had done it in the past when staying at my various places in California. A few newspapers here, a few unique rocks there, and shortly she had amassed a collection that needed to be shipped back to Long Island for her in a large box —usually costing $30 to $40 by UPS. Perhaps Kim had not yet recognized this.

It was during this time that Kim Catalano had suggested to my dad that he had been severely sexually and physically abused as a child, that he had repressed the memories, and that many of his memory problems—his limp, his oblivious and depressive behavior—were all symptoms of that. He suggested that it was taking a lot of unconscious energy on my dad's part to keep these memories submerged, so that the side effects were the acting out and the depressive episodes that he had. My dad then began to have a more open mind about this, my mother supporting and endorsing such an analysis. In fact, we all began to surmise that it may have had something to do with my father's Aunt Sadie, her name ironically suggesting the sadistic nature of this woman, who was his frequent babysitter as a child and was a very strange and perverse woman. It was possible that in addition to his father's (Grandpa Charlie) distant and emotionally abusive demeanor and conduct toward his son, that Sadie may have done some very destructive things to Dad. However, no concrete abuse memories ever surfaced at that time, just hunches, feelings and emotions. It was not until much later, after the Exile, that we truly were able to coax out of him some concrete memories of abuse, to which I will return later.

The Photos for the *Dr. Phil Show*

During my visit in the Summer of 2007, Melissa with me, I spent very little time inside the house, other than to look at the kitchen prior to proclaiming that I would not be able to do the tiling. But something told me to take a few photos of the interior, while my parents were outside, talking with Melissa on one particular day toward the end of our visit. So I brought my digital camera inside with me, spent a few moments and took some photos of strategic areas, careful to show the volume of clutter in perspective. But when I finally downloaded them to my computer back in Los Angeles, I realized that there would have been no way to showcase this without a wide-angle lens. The clutter was so all encompassing and so vast that all one saw was an undistinguished wall of mess. Clothing, socks, bags, books, nothing at all ordered—just an undistinguished, uncategorizable wall of junk.

But, having my photos in hand, I decided to contact Dr. Phil McGraw, of the *Dr. Phil Show* on television, whom I had always admired and respected. I thought that if I contacted his show, obviously being vetted by his production assistants, I could convince him to chronicle our case as a prime example of compulsive hoarding, perhaps helping us in the process. It was only now, through previous episodes of his show that I had finally learned a term, a diagnosis, for this illness: compulsive hoarding. So I wrote a letter:

August 2, 2007
Dr. Phil Show
5482 Wilshire Boulevard #1902
Los Angeles, CA 90036

Dear Dr. Phil:

You have been an inspiration to me and to so many people that you have never even met. Thank you for what you do. I am asking for your assistance on behalf of my aging parents. I hope that you or your staff will read this letter and be moved to give some advice or steer me toward a professional that can help.

I am a 36 year old man living in Los Angeles. My aging parents live in the home in which I grew up, on Long Island, NY. They are both retired. They have created an **unsafe, unsanitary condition** that I believe could be **potentially lethal**. There is junk everywhere and no place to eat, sit, walk, or live. It is a fire-hazard and a safety hazard on many levels. They are wonderful, brilliant, loving people who are helpful to everyone they know, but they are detrimental to themselves and to each other. They have both been in counseling for many years and are both currently in counseling. I have done everything I can to convince them to clean their environment, short of reporting them (out of tough love) to the health department or the fire marshal. They say that they want to change, but they seem unable to take the next step. My mother is a compulsive hoarder and my father is an enabler who sabotages things and makes things even more disorganized than they already are. They have experienced a lot of abuse in their lives and I feel as if they are continuing to act out toward themselves and each other on account of this abuse. But now it is becoming dangerous and unsanitary. I am very concerned.

I do not believe that they would be interested in appearing on television, but they need help. Perhaps if they are able to overcome their problems, they will see that they in turn could be an inspiration to others with similar problems. Could you please tell me if there are professionals who help to handle such hoarding disorders, or if you feel comfortable giving them a little bit of guidance yourself? Please help.

Thank you so much in advance for your time and attention. Please feel free to contact me.

Sincerely,

L. Arik Greenberg, Ph.D.

****

I provide the accompanying photos, which I sent along with my letter.

Front hallway looking west

Front hallway looking west, longer shot

Dining room looking toward back slider

THE EXILE

Front hallway looking east

Kitchen

THE PRE-EXILIC PERIOD

Master bathroom

Living room viewed from Dining Room

THE EXILE

Arik's bedroom

Closeup of Arik's bed and bedroom

My letter was received by his staff, but never answered. I can only assume that they receive far too many such letters to respond to all of them. But it was disappointing, nonetheless. So I began to research hoarding specialists and clinics myself. Any possible leads I found and shared with my mother were immediately dismissed as either too expensive or that they would take over and deny her the autonomy and self-determination that she needed. This, of course, was patently incorrect. All the information I have found on successful hoarding treatments focus on empowering the patient to make their own decisions, reinforcing the fact that they have control over the situation. Mom's reaction, most certainly, was a stalling tactic to avoid progress. She swore that she was already working very hard on cleaning up, getting rid of large amounts of newspapers. In the course of certain conversations, she even admitted that she hoarded, now knowing the term that readily described her addiction. But she wanted to handle things her way, citing that most of her life, people had taken control away from her and that she suffered under many dictators and that self-determination and the ability to govern her own belongings were of critical importance to her. So another year went by. We visited my parents in 2008, but never actually entered the house. There was simply no room to sit and chat, let alone stay there. If memory serves me, that was one of the years we stayed at my friend Aimee's apartment, while she stayed with her parents nearby. My parents would frequently visit us at the apartment, so we had joyful family time together in a clean and sanitary environment.

The Last Pre-Exilic Visit

On the last visit I made before the Exile, I barely had—or desired—a chance to look inside the house. When I did—a brief glimpse, if I recall—I discovered a horror worse than anything that I had imagined. To some degree, if I were honest with myself, allowing my mind to speculate and project what the interior of the house would look like if the clutter steadily advanced over the few years since I'd seen it past, I should not have been at all surprised. And so I dealt with both the recognition of the reality, as well as the shock from having been in blissful denial. My family was always so optimistic about things, particularly my mother. I chose to believe that, although I knew the house was getting worse, it would still be livable. But frankly, when I saw it, it was barely livable. I could not conceive how either of my parents safely got around in that home. The piles and walls of newspaper and utterly pointless clutter had become so high that one could not conceive of what was underneath them.

My parents' vehicles have always served as an indicator of what is going on inside the house. When I was a child, my mother usually kept diverse items of varying levels of usefulness in the car, including a few hair brushes, pens, maps, water bottles, emergency supplies, and a dictionary—always a dictionary, since we were avid readers! There was nothing really out of the ordinary here, as people tend to keep a variety of items in their car's glove box or in the trunk. When we would go on trips, we tended to take a lot of items with us, including the old style, portable (overhead) hairdryer, numerous suitcases, healthy home-cooked foods, and so forth. The sheer volume of it would usually be so much that items would have to be packed around our feet while sitting. That would annoy me to no end. And when I was an adult and began driving, my mom would keep a variety of items (including the dictionary and maps) between the front seats, where the armrests would be, and they would invariably shift and slide toward me when I would round a corner; the danger of my safe driving being distracted by this was a concern to me as well as a nuisance.

In the early 2000s, they bought a used 1999 Dodge minivan to replace their 1987 Buick station wagon which had begun to give them problems, but which they would still not get rid of. The station wagon was stored in the driveway, still fully registered and insured, and began to collect items of storage that were placed inside it. Subsequently, the drivable minivan began to be filled with bags of newspaper, magazines, cans of cat food to be delivered as a gift to Barbara Simmons for her cats, a variety of books, and any number of more or less useful items, such as flashlights, umbrellas, bags of sand (to put down in case of ice in Wintertime), and so forth. The vehicle suffered from overcrowding. A good number of canvas tote bags of schoolbooks belonged to my dad and stayed in there for usage with his students when he tutored. But I would say no more than about five to seven of these occupied the car. If they were the only nuisance items, the situation would be entirely manageable and largely negligible. However, augmenting these were the many duplicate items that were there because the first one had been broken or lost underneath piles of newspaper and magazines. Usually, five to six lantern flashlights resided therein, one or two of them actually working and containing fully charged batteries. The umbrellas and squeegees were also among the duplicate items, some broken, others lost under other items.

As time wore on, bags of fresh groceries would be left in the car, as there was less and less room inside the house to store these. The refrigerator was difficult to get to, and was invariably full. Finding room inside the house to store fresh fruit and vegetables was often a difficult matter. So, frequently bags of groceries would stay in the car; sometimes on purpose, sometimes by accident. Occasionally, my dad would forget to bring something in and it would stay and rot, only to be covered over by other things. Mail, freshly retrieved from the mailbox but forgotten to be brought inside the house, would be set down on the car seats and then covered over; sometimes, this included bills and checks and other important items. The situation was due to a combination of blamable parties. My mom simply would not let go of anything; my dad had no conception of urgency or import with respect to sorting mail or bringing perishables inside. Together, this was a recipe for squalor. People peering through the windows would see it and would cringe, strangers and family members alike.

In 2006, the year after I was married and had finished my Ph.D. program, I was looking for steady work in academia, my visiting position at LMU having ended in 2005. I had flown to Philadelphia where the annual conferences in my field were being held that year (the Society of Biblical Literature, paired with the American Academy of Religion), and stayed with an old grad school friend, Katy, and her husband, Rick. My parents and I hadn't seen each other in a while, now that I was engrossed in married life and trying to find work. Since it was within driving distance from New York, my parents took the opportunity to drive down and meet me there, which delighted me. We met at Katy and Rick's apartment and had some time alone there while the two were out. At first, things were bright and cheerful. We were overjoyed to see each other. During a heartfelt chat, I started a conversation with my parents about the car—at this time I believe it was still the Buick station wagon—which Rick had seen on the street when he went down to guide my parents in and help them find parking, and had made a passing, non-judgmental observation to me about the packed condition of their vehicle. The talk that evening rapidly declined into an interrogation of Dad, largely orchestrated by my mom, but in which I unwittingly participated, much to my regret. The focus of the session was that the condition of the car, as well as the house, was largely his doing, which was of course a false narrative, but Mom and I nonetheless urged Dad to pay more attention to his domestic responsibilities and help Mom clean so we could have a nice living environment again. Dad and I never had the fortitude to turn the tables on Mom and demand that she address *her* contribution to the problem—her hoarding. I was merely grateful no longer to be the focus of her anger. Dad wound up crying, and promising to do better, while my mother took no responsibility in this. Eventually, the mood turned brighter, as if some kind of safety valve had been sprung and Mom's anger was satiated, attention had been shifted away from her faults and she was convinced that somehow the situation in the house would change—if only Dad would buckle down and contribute. The outcome was that we had spent quality time together, working on a common problem—which was always our family's favorite pastime—but it took its toll on all of us and nothing pragmatic ever came out of it.

Several times, I had urged my parents to clean out the minivan. My dad was perfectly happy to let me do it. He had no emotional connection to the junk therein, even his own schoolbooks that he used for tutoring. He just had no interest in doing the work to clean and sort, or in risking crossing my mom and arousing her ire. My mom, however, was usually ready to blame my father for "messing it up" after the last time she cleaned it, claiming that she had it perfectly cleared out just prior to my arrival back home. Lies. When I would offer to help clean it out for them, she would flatly reject my offer, saying that it was a waste of time. What she really needed help with, or wanted to start on, was the inside of the house, she would claim. But of course, in response, I would remind her that 1) cleaning the van would be good positive reinforcement and would stand as a recognizable accomplishment, and 2) that it would provide open space where one could place items that needed to be discarded from the house and brought to Goodwill or the recycling center. But this logic did not matter. She knew better, she would say, and that I was just wasting her energy by arguing with her about it—a hot button issue since she suffered from low energy all throughout my childhood, due to her numerous health challenges. Most of the time, I would then give up out of frustration, feeling completely powerless—short of resorting to physically restraining her while I cleaned—to change a situation that was not in my control but exclusively in Mom's. A few times, however, I would forge ahead and empty the minivan against her will. The first time I did this was, I believe, in the Summer of 2007. I threw out huge amounts of newspaper and debris. The tote bags of lesson books that belonged to my father I put on the ground in the driveway behind the minivan and asked him to go through them the next day and cull out what he could discard and sort what he wanted to keep. Along with these were several black plastic bags full of magazines that I wanted my mom to sort and discard. Since I had run out of time and needed to return to CA the next day, I left a tarp over these to keep them from the rain, asking my parents to sort these as soon as possible and finish the job I had started. There was absolutely no room in either the house or the garage to store these. We had run out of any practicable room for storage. The small sixteen-square-foot area under the tarp was the only place I could find to store them other than putting them right back into the minivan. My mom expressed dismay that I had foisted this upon her; my dad promised me that he would go through them the next day and sort them. A year later, Summer, 2008, when I returned, the same damned bags were still there in the driveway, under the tarp, badly waterlogged despite their coverage. They were useless now. And the minivan had been filled full of junk, yet again. And despite my mother's vehement assertions that she would rather start working on cleaning the house, rather than cleaning the minivan, she never did either.

Earlier in my visit of the Summer of 2008, if I recall correctly, I did my mom a favor in order to help keep her spirits up. While the minivan was still as yet uncleaned that time, I used it to take a group of antique chairs from the dining room set to get reupholstered. This was obviously a drop in the bucket compared to what needed to be done in the house, but I knew that anything I did to help was always immensely appreciated by my mom; it was the effort that heartened and buoyed her spirits amidst her addiction. These chairs had been part of the beautiful, dark hardwood set that we had bought at a garage sale about twenty years prior and their seats were now very badly worn, the springs unsprung. So, I had to literally dig them out of the dining room, enmeshed as they were amidst the clutter around the dining room set. We loaded them into the minivan as best we could, placed atop the clutter inside it, and we took it over to a local upholstery shop that my mom had found. She was so grateful that someone was helping to make some kind of progress, but I knew it was just a formality. When they were done, a few weeks later, she told the upholsterer that she was redecorating and asked if she could store them there for a few months. He okayed this, and there they sat. He did not realize whom he was dealing with. A year later, they were still there at the upholsterer's shop and he had to ask her to pick them up. They went to Barbara Simmons' since there was no room at my parents' place. They sat there for several months more, only to be finally reunited with their table and redeposited inside the home during the cleanout period of the Exile, almost a year and a half after they had been sent to the upholsterer.

Interestingly and ironically, when I went back to California, Melissa and I had bought a few things for my parents that we thought would help the situation. One was a CD, created by a therapist of some sort, which had subliminal messages on it about becoming uncluttered. Listened to, it was designed to help reach the unconscious mind and encourage a person to be more organized. Once received by my parents in the mail, it was promptly lost in the mess. A few months later, around the time that we watched the movie, *Grey Gardens*, we came across a wonderful book called *Buried in Treasures*,[4] written by several professional therapists and experts in compulsive hoarding, but geared toward a lay audience. I thought the book was fascinating and brilliantly done, in some ways a self-help workbook for the hoarder that suffers, as well as their family. Even I felt I could benefit from it. So we bought a copy for my parents and sent it to them. This, too, was promptly lost.

When I left the house that final day of my visit, Summer, 2007, in disgust, I hoped that by having taken those photos of the house, I'd be able to show them to someone with some clout, someone in authority, someone who could help. God knows, I had done my part. I had tried to convince my parents to change their surroundings. I had many times tried to help clean, but with no results. I had tried to convince them to let someone come in and help them. They had spoken to the family therapist, David Grand, about the condition of the house. But my mom's presentation of it to him was undoubtedly one-sided. As she described to me, she even took her own photos of the mess to show David. She begged him to convince my dad to help her. There was nothing David felt he could do. Through my mom's lenses, she relayed that David was unable to convince my dad to change and to help her clean. But in my opinion, without being present at the time, David recognized that there was nothing that he could do to help either of them. I had informed him during my own previous work with him that my mom was the one doing the collecting. My wish would have been for him to be more direct with her and to arrange an intervention. As much as I love and respect David for his role in helping my family, and as a mentor to me, this was one place in which I disagreed with his traditional, hands-off methodology, allowing the patient to set the pace. In this situation, I believed an intervention was indicated. And considering the ultimate

---

[4] David F. Tolin, Randy O. Frost, Gail Steketee. *Buried in Treasures* (New York: Oxford University Press, 2007).

outcome, I was probably right.

In my opinion, the traditional, laissez-faire methodology of psychiatric and psychological counseling has tremendous limitations. When I began to talk more with my cousin Marty about the situation in my parents' home, I also witnessed this same ideology in his training. He had several years before given up his lucrative but unfulfilling job in the computer software industry to pursue a career in social work. I always applauded this choice. While he no doubt gave up much income in his immediate future, he also ensured that his life would have more meaning and more joy of accomplishment. And while to this day, the field of social work has treated him poorly, he might have also suffered in the information technology field when the eventual economic downturn began. One cannot know. But Marty, nonetheless, had gone to grad school and become trained as a certified social worker. And his excellent training allowed him to have a fairly good grasp on what was going on with my parents, their house, and their relationship. He was always close with my parents, particularly my mom. They strongly encouraged and supported his decision to change careers—much to his own father's pragmatic dismay, years earlier. They visited with Marty frequently, usually meeting with him at bookstores, and occasionally at their house. He saw the mess; he knew the situation.

So I began talking to him about it. I remember having called him on the phone one night to convey to him my concerns. He was very receptive and he shared my concerns. It gave us the opportunity to talk more with one another than we did up until that point. I had always looked up to him, like an older brother. He was exactly ten years older than I, born under the zodiac sign of Libra as well, and a shining example of carefully considered Libran analytical brilliance. I really admired him, and our frequent chats and check-ins about my parents' situation were very helpful to me. Marty and I grew closer as I called him more frequently. He became, on some level, my eyes and ears about my parents' condition. I needed that. It made me feel more in touch with what was going on. And it made me feel comfortable to know that a family member who cared was nearby. As an only child living 3,000 miles away, I feared what would happen if my parents needed help. Marty stepped willingly into the role of a sort of second son. I appreciated that greatly.

At some point, I divulged to my mom and dad that I had been talking to Marty. Initially, I was afraid that she would have a drastic reaction to the news that I was discussing the pathology of her situation with an outsider. But thankfully, she did not consider Marty an outsider. He was close family, her favorite nephew and a close confidant. He had seen the house more recently than I as well, so it was not a secret to him. She took it rather well, I thought, still honest about the embarrassment she felt when anyone saw or knew about the problem. She assured me that things were changing, still resorting to the handy excuse of my father's role in things, saying that she was forcing him to help her and to clean up after himself. I knew that this was just a drop in the bucket, if he even helped, that a few piles of newspaper might be discarded and that it would be he who was dusting old books this time instead of me. She even stated that she had decided she was finally able to part with the newspapers, having discussed with me at times in the past that her addiction was very closely focused on the newspapers. At times, my optimism got the best of me and I began to believe that she would be able to act on her own, without any outside help. At times I forced myself to believe that large quantities of newspapers were actually being carted out of the house at her behest, imagining it in my mind's eye. Optimism springs eternal.

One concern that Marty had was that my mom wanted to begin to burn newspapers again in the wood burning stove. My dad and I were both concerned about that as well. It was situated on a ten-by-ten concrete block platform in the hallway adjoining our dining room. It was now littered with vast amounts of debris and there was no safe area surrounding the stove, creating a very dangerous condition in which flammable things might have the tendency to combust. Marty and I prevailed upon my mom's sense of danger and we made her promise not to use the stove until such time as the surrounding area was clear. She had been adamant that she wanted to save money on heating oil and simultaneously get rid of newspapers. But she finally gave in and made the promise. I don't believe that she knew how dangerous it was. And having not seen the house in a while myself, even I did not know exactly how dangerous it was. Having this input from Marty may have saved us from a tragedy much worse than what we experienced during the Exile. God only knows, but the house might have gone up in flames with two elderly folks in it, as is known to have happened. An acquaintance's aunt lived in an apartment in New York City. She hoarded plastic bags. A fire tore through her apartment and the toxic fumes released from the melting bags permanently damaged her respiratory system. After several years of living, permanently disabled and reliant upon a respirator, she passed away. I deliberately recall that piece of information, and I relay it to those who would listen, as a cautionary tale.

Nevertheless, as I had mentioned, Marty's standard therapeutic training was still representative of the overly relativistic, hands-off philosophy that is pervasive in the psychiatric and psychological fields today. This was embodied within the response I received when I alerted one of the school counselors at my university about a student's potentially deleterious mental state, and the counselor responded that there really was nothing that they could do unless the student came to them seeking help. Thankfully, when I went above his head, the Dean of Students saw that my concerns were justified, and they went ahead and contacted the student. The outcome might have been less happy had they not done so. The Dean explained that the counselor was just following standard protocol, but that some situations indicate a more hands-on approach. Marty had also explained to me that current methodology suggests that no matter how outlandish a person's lifestyle may be, that as long as they are not a danger to themselves or others, it is their freedom to be that way. Laudable in its non-judgmentalism, this newer philosophy reverses earlier trends that saw everything that was barely off-center to be abnormal. But the problem is that people who are in real danger or would really benefit from some kind of treatment, and whose families are very concerned about their well-being, are often allowed to drop right through the cracks on account of this newfound reluctance to dictate morality or propriety to people—going in entirely the other direction, toward extreme non-judgmentalism. That is to say, "do what you like," "live and let live," and other such platitudes are programmatic of an unhealthy, almost irresponsible backlash against the earlier rigidity of fundamentalisms. I would surmise that the potential for lawsuits in our overly litigious society is also a factor mitigating the need for therapists to sometimes step in and get involved. How long before we restrain counselors from intervening in cases of deliberate self-harm and suicidal tendencies? After all, it's the individual's choice, isn't it? I speak ironically, of course.

Plastic "Piss-pots"

At some point in the year prior to the Exile, my mother brought to my attention what seemed to be a very dangerous trend that my father had been pursuing. This, of course, was brought up to me in the midst of one of their more and more frequent, knock-down, drag-out fights. In order not to have to go all the way to the bathroom in the middle of the night—or any other time of day that was inconvenient—my dad had begun to urinate in gallon sized plastic water bottles and occasionally quart sized yogurt containers. The main problem with this was not that he did so, but that he would frequently forget to empty them in the morning and would leave them under the dining room table for weeks on end, their liquid becoming discolored. When my mom found a small group of these clustered among the legs of the dining room table, hidden beneath the clutter that was there, she became enraged at my father and his laziness. One of the smaller containers did not have its lid properly capped on it and when my mother moved it to investigate it, some of the liquid contents spilled on her. This, of course, set off a chain of events that led to my getting involved to disarm the situation. When I was informed about this habit of my father's, I, too, was dismayed and alarmed. I spoke to him about it and charged him with never doing that again. It was my fear, and my mom's as well, that this was a sign of his growing delusional state and his diminishing mental acumen.

While I cannot entirely rule out the possibility that this was connected to his mental condition at the time, I was entirely unaware of the intolerable extent of the current pathology of the house itself. Having not seen it in a year, and having not investigated or lived in it for about two years, I did not know how horribly inaccessible the pathways were. I still believed it was somewhat negotiable, though difficult. It now has dawned on me that at the time, access to the bathroom was severely limited. It makes sense that an elderly man with a limp cannot get to the bathroom that quickly when he has to jump over piles of newspaper to gain access to it in the middle of the night. It was understandable, in retrospect, if you know what the house looked like at the time. But the matter of leaving the containers there for weeks on end was still an unanswered question. As I have said before and will say again, this was a problem in which both parties had equal claim to the blame. In retrospect, I am ashamed of my inability to help my dad as he became more enfeebled, both in deterioration of body and mind. It is a debt that I feel I can never repay, despite the counseling of other wiser people that I forgive myself for my limitations and fallibility. I still feel like I have failed in the discharge of my filial duties.

During this time, Mom continued to claim that after she cleans anything up, Dad just messes it up again. The rhetoric of this always went unchallenged, but in my mind, there was still too much that was unexplained. It was too much like the rhetoric that I had heard from mentally ill people who were out of touch with reality, like the young homeless guy that I mentioned in an earlier chapter who desired the discarded blinds. I had already learned to remain doubtful any time I came home and my mom warned me that the house had been cleaned up until the week prior, but that my father had "messed it up again." Frankly, I began to doubt that it ever really was clean in the first place. Maybe small sections of it were clean—a counter here or there—but whatever had been cleaned had no permanently sustainable method of keeping it clean. Where were things supposed to go? There was always a long, complicated system of discarding things, as I had mentioned earlier, that involved dissecting elements and throwing them in different containers and such. To the claim that Dad always messed up the areas my mother had cleaned, Barbara Simmons would challenge, "where is he supposed to put the stuff?" She and I had begun to agree about my parents' situation, noting that it seemed to be a very convenient combination of illnesses that my parents had forged together. In answer to my mother's complaint that my dad would go throughout the house and knock things over as he walked by them, holding his hand out and bracing himself against things to prevent himself from falling, Barbara noted that the issue was compounded by the fact that nothing was where it should be, and that if things were better placed and more organized and less cluttered, the things would not be so easily knocked over. She and I agreed that both of my parents had problems which dovetailed with one another, producing an impasse. This was the beginning of our excellent rapport that would be so important to my emotional survival during the Exile.

Intervention?

One might reasonably ask why we didn't just stop my mom from hoarding. We couldn't very well physically restrain her. And when opposed, she could become this yelling, angry woman, completely unreasonable and uncontrollable, lashing out and making you feel two feet tall. She had that ability, just as easily as she could, in better times, build you up to feel like you were the greatest person in the world. But in short, looking back on this situation, I believe that some kind of intervention was necessary, indicated, and timely. At the time, I knew it, but I was too much of a coward to do anything about it and I regret it. On some level, I feared what my mom's reaction would be to having her house taken from her control by inspecting authorities. I feared that she would have a dissociative episode in front of them, causing her to be hospitalized. For this very reason, I refrained from contacting the authorities up till that point. When all was said and done, and the Exile was initiated by the Town of Huntington Department of Public Safety, her reaction wasn't as bad as I had feared it would be. In fact, I was pleasantly surprised and relieved.

But at the time, I was also still fairly afraid of her anger, formidable as she was throughout my life. And her ire and disapproval felt to me a little bit too much like abandonment. It slightly smacked of the kind of "poisonous pedagogy" that Alice Miller repudiated and criticized within the pre-World War II German educational system. Of course, I am sure this was not on a conscious level that my mother created this dynamic. All of her educational training was opposed to this. But her early childhood abuse left her sometimes at a loss for appropriate responses when she could not recognize and comprehend normal childhood behavior of acting out. She had been the perfect child; her life often depended upon it. My normal childhood disobedience and individuation—testing the limits of what was acceptable—was inconceivable to her. To her, it seemed more like a lack of love and respect on my part, when in reality, it was just a kid being a kid. And her response to my simple exploration of childhood individuation was less than ideal or dispassionate, lacking the distance necessary for a parent to make clear decisions.

So I began, at the time, to investigate whether I should contact the Suffolk County Department of Health. It felt like I was thinking of "ratting" on my parents. It didn't feel good. But knowing what my parents' house was like, and fearing that it was getting worse, I really believed that something had to be done. So when speaking candidly with my parents and finally coming clean about my conversations with Marty about their house—having initially not told them out of respect for their sense of privacy—I began to threaten them with the possibility that I would call the authorities to step in. They begged me not to. In particular, my father's impassioned pleas got to me, expressing a deep sense of shame that he was not able to control his household the way a traditional patriarch and father should. "Lee, *please* don't call them," he implored, "I'm asking you, *please* don't do it!" And so I told them that I would consider putting off my plan to make the call. But I attempted to employ it as a scare tactic to get them to begin to take seriously that their conditions were extremely dangerous and were ripe for a tragedy—either a fall, a fire, or some kind of pestilence. I did not know at the time how correct I was. Nevertheless, they were unable to make the necessary changes. It was a sickness that they had, and only outside intervention was able to make a difference. But I promised them that if they conversely promised me to begin to get help and clean the house up, I would promise to put off contacting the authorities. I was the only one that kept his promise.

The File Cabinet

At some point in 2008 or so, the filing cabinet in the master bedroom fell over, blocking entrance into the bedroom. Evidently, my mother or father had left several drawers open while filing, the weight shifted due to the altered center of gravity, and it fell completely over. It had been positioned catty-corner, nearest to the door hinge, in a little alcove behind the door's direction of swing. When it fell forward, it presented an obstacle that was reminiscent of barricading oneself into a room. But in this situation, they were both barricaded out. The symbolism of this is quite telling. The bedroom, which as any drugstore psychotherapy handbook will tell you, represents the heart of the marriage. In ancient Greek and Roman times, as well as in the Bible, the "bridal chamber" was a symbol of the marriage itself. And my parents' marriage, as represented by the master bedroom, was closed off to them; it was in trouble. This was very true and had been for some time, but now it was beginning to take its full toll, as I would begin to discover.

It was later revealed to me, first by Kim Catalano, then later by my mother herself, that it had been over 25 years since my parents had had sexual intercourse. This, of course, was a shock to me. Being a married man myself, the thought of being in love with my wife, being generally on good terms with her, considering her my best friend, yet not having sex with her for two and a half decades, seemed absurdly and direly disjointed. Obviously, there was some kind of emotional issue there that was causing this. What came as even more of a shock was that it was decided by my father, rather than my mother. This was confirmed by both Kim and my mother. Traditionally, one hears of aging women not wanting the continued sexual attentions of their husbands. And perhaps this is more of a vestige of earlier times when women were not as in touch with their sexuality and men were less educated or even interested in the giving of mutual pleasure to their wives; the result being a wife who is no longer sexually interested, and in certain cultures even helps find a suitable concubine for her aging, yet still sexually functional husband. Had I ever suspected that my parents were in such a predicament—as particular and sensitive as I knew my mother to be, and given her history of health challenges—I would have assumed that such a decision would have come primarily from her. It had not.

When I was a child, as is common with many children, I found it shocking to think of my parents having sex. It was uncomfortable for me to think of them in a physically intimate manner—as if the idea were preposterous and abnormal. It was an extremely disturbing imagery to me to conceive (pun not intended) of them as sexual beings, having sexual relations. And at this early age, I found solace in the thought that maybe my parents no longer had sex. It gave me comfort to think of them as a chaste, sexless couple—a Josephite marriage. But I am sure that it was not so much the remnants of infantile Oedipal jealousy that caused me to think this way, well into my pre- and post-pubescent years, but rather it was due to some kind of stilted lack of comprehension about the sex life of two healthy adults. What allows me to make this claim was the disturbance, or even jealousy, that I felt when I discovered that my father had not been a virgin when he married my mother. It became an important justification for my own growing sense of sexual morality during my adolescence and early adulthood to know that my mother was a virgin when she married my father (at least in relation to acts of consensual sex as a post-pubescent individual; her childhood experiences of sexual assault notwithstanding, as I have discussed elsewhere). However, conversely, it disturbed me to find out that my father was not. My desire to affirm their mutual chastity was directed toward both of them. But this was merely a child's self-absorbed and deluded notions of propriety and jealousy of his parents' attentions. One could devote volumes to the discussion of the psychological principles governing this type of valuation.

Nevertheless, as an adult, realizing the necessity for a healthy sexual relationship between two adults that love each other, it saddened me deeply to know that my parents had ceased their physical intimacy at around the same time that I most keenly felt my deluded childish whims about their being in a "chaste", sexless marriage. At some point in my early adulthood, I began to suspect that this might actually be the case between them, noticing the dynamics between them, but I just assumed that this was still my deluded childhood lack of sense about his parents' humanity. Most children one day realize that their parents simply were very good about keeping their private moments private. But all in all, I never realized that the decision to cease sexual congress would have been initiated by my father. Knowing my mother's temperament, fraught with psychological issues, it was natural for me to assume that such a decision would have originated with her, but I was thoroughly incorrect. And it eventually made sense to me that it was my father's decision. However, it is impossible for me to say that it was not a two-way interaction between them that created a deadly combination of pathologies, leaving them chaste. Nevertheless, knowing what I now know about his early childhood and the loss of his mother, it now appears that his lack of interest in continuing the sexual intimacy with my mother—and of course, I do not know the details of this decision—may stem from his desire to turn my mother into a facsimile of his own mother, replacing Ethel with Barbara, his new mother.

At times, it appeared to me that my father thrived on the dissatisfaction of my mother, as if she were being entreated, even trapped, into acting like a disapproving mother figure to him. It was a role that she fell into. Perhaps he chose her for that reason, seeing early on that she had this potential in her personality to satisfy that unconscious, sadomasochistic need in his personality. As they grew further apart and as their relationship suffered, the pattern played out by them was one in which I had been part of while growing up—the dissatisfied mother and the incorrigibly naughty boy. It was this pattern which our family therapist David Grand had pointed out to me as the "dance macabre" that my mother and I often engaged in and really needed to be free of. My father now occupied the role of the naughty boy, replacing me. He forgot things, he refused to do his chores or take care of himself. As he aged, he became more and more dependent upon my mother for simple things. And she willingly and lovingly gave them: all his meals prepared, his laundry, and later on, even all the bills and finances became her responsibility. It was as if he could—or would—no longer handle the things of adulthood, leaving them to his new mother, Barbara.

The thing about the file cabinet was that neither of my parents could open that door. They physically could not get past the barricaded door. Anything inside was no longer really that crucial to their daily lives, evidently. They began to live without a closet. For years, clothing had been hung on the shower curtain rods in the master bathroom, having to be moved every time someone needed to take a shower. I suspected that the trouble involved in this caused my parents to bathe less than they should have, preferring to spot wash daily and shower far less frequently. They began to sleep on the couches in the living room instead of their bed in the bedroom. My mother relayed that this was not as much of a problem since my father had "kicked her out of the bedroom" a while before. She stated that he would put things on her side of the bed and then fall asleep earlier than she retired to the bedroom, leaving her to deal with the mess. This happened often enough that she began to suspect something was behind it. Confronting him about it, he admitted that he no longer was comfortable with her in the bed. As I said above, I do not know the details of this interaction, but I am merely relaying what I have been told. I do recollect that she would pile things on top of the bed during daylight hours, in the guise of cleaning, or doing a project, and these cluttered items would have to be moved by nighttime in order to sleep there. Perhaps Dad had grown tired of this and just moved everything to her side, leaving her to tell the story from her own perspective. I cannot say.

Regardless of who was at fault, little difference was made by the loss of access to the bedroom, sadly. Occasionally, one of them would sleep on my old bed, but even this room was becoming less and less accessible, my dad shifting amounts of junk from the living room to there anytime my mother cajoled him into "cleaning", and my mother spending large amounts of time in there writing and drawing, and subsequently leaving her own trail of debris there. With my mother now sleeping on one of the couches in the living room, my father now slept on the opposite couch therein, perhaps to maintain some semblance of closeness. They adapted. Plans to have cousin Marty or Phil, my dad's former student who occasionally helped out with chores for my parents, dismantle or remove the bedroom door were always suspiciously postponed.

As my parents began to fight more and more, my mother spent more and more time apart from my dad. She, in the Arthur Merget Reading Room / the "Den", and he in the living room. She slept less than comfortably on one of the couches in the Den. He slept sitting up, on the living room couch, with his neck and head bent over. Numerous times, I would see him snoozing like this when I would visit; I could never understand how he was able to sleep or even breathe like this. My mom would sleep sitting up as well, usually with her head tilted back. They both assured me that they had no problem with this. But I knew there was something dreadfully wrong with two adults sleeping on couches when there was a perfectly good bedroom a few yards away. Yet I tried desperately to ignore the obvious pathology of this, knowing that there was simply nothing I could do to solve this for them.

Mom at times had speculated that the addiction to hoarding took the form, initially and primarily, of newspapers, perhaps due to her unconsciously desiring to build a wall around her, both to the abuse that she had suffered in her childhood as well as to the difficulties in her relationship with my father. Also, she was a "knowledge-chaser" as I had called her, perhaps one of her most admirable qualities, and the newspapers served to distract her from her daily troubles, as she readily admitted. For myself, I also had speculated that the focus on newspapers was additionally connected to the aforementioned horrifying experience as a child, being literally wrapped up in newspapers with the dead kitten that had been murdered to silence little Barbara during the abuse. And somehow the newspaper in that incident took on symbolic meaning and center stage in her acting out and medicating her addiction.

Regardless of the exact symbolism behind the newspapers, she admitted that the collecting and hoarding had become for her, over the years, a sort of self-medicating activity (as twelve-steppers often call their addictions). It momentarily made her feel better. If she had no control over the rest of her life, she at least could feel in control or satisfied by collecting items and saving them from being junked. Sometimes, she linked it to her relationship with my father, noting that he had a tendency to be very cold in their marriage, that he was very distant, unwilling to meet her gaze (perhaps it was as a response to her constantly blaming him?), and that as they grew apart, the newspapers emotionally filled a gap for her. I speculated that even more so, the newspapers made the house smaller so that there was less distance he could go to evade her when he became distant. That there was nowhere for him to go. That on some level, the decreased living area would draw him back to her—her husband and former true love. On some level, perhaps, the empty nest syndrome that must have fallen into place in a very final manner when I got married and got my Ph.D. (two very final events that solidified my status as no longer a resident in their home, even though I had already not really lived there in years) served to make the house even lonelier, so that it was that much more urgent that my father be brought close to her again. Knowing now what I know about their relationship and their lack of intimacy for over two decades, I have a much more forgiving and sympathetic attitude toward at least the source of my mother's addiction, if not the method of expression.

The Dog, Sonny Boy

My father having given up control of the finances, my mother now realized that he had opened up a variety of credit cards and ceased paying them. Their carefully won financial stability, built up over forty years, was now compromised. They owed about $75,000 in credit card debt and other related bank debts. They had to open up a line of homeowner's credit—having already paid off the original mortgage—in order to get rid of a large number of the high interest credit cards. When a close family friend was dying, and the executors of his estate were preemptively searching for someone to adopt his beloved pets, even offering a sizeable allowance for their maintenance, my mother volunteered to assist. She loved animals. She already had one cat, a beloved family pet who had come to our doorstep as an abandoned kitten in 1992 and was still spry and active at 16. But she felt that the several cats and one dog that this friend, Mark, had left were not a problem for her to handle. My mother claimed to have talked this over with Kim Catalano, now at times acting as the family therapist and not only my dad's, and that she received his approval. I later found out to the contrary, that this was merely her interpretation of his stance of professional detachment. I had vehemently opposed it, knowing only what the house had looked like a year prior and knowing already that there simply was not enough room for a dog and several more cats. My mom assured me that with the allowance, they intended to build a small pen in the back yard for the dog and that the cats were largely outside cats. I still protested, knowing in my heart that this was a very, very bad idea and nothing good could come from this.

The pen was built of cyclone fencing, occupying the original 10-by-15-foot patio that was immediately outside our sliding glass door behind the dining room and kitchen. A local contractor named James Hancock, who had helped clean my parents' gutters a few months prior, was entrusted with the job. He seemed nice enough and even initially reminded my mother of her father, my Grandpa Arty. So James was paid from the maintenance fee provided to care for the dog. On some level, given my parents' growing level of inertia and dysfunction, I was surprised that this task was ever completed. But this demonstrated my mom's resolve when it came to something she felt was urgent. And so, the dog arrived. The cats, however, were withheld by the executors, for whatever reason, and would be scheduled to be brought over at such time that seemed convenient. I am grateful that they never did come. The dog was work enough.

The dog's name was Sonny Boy, and he was an extremely active Australian Shepherd with different colored eyes, who always did tricks for people according to a set routine when Mark had visitors. He would run around, as that breed of dog does, often trying to corral people as if they were sheep or some other herd animal; then tired out, he would go to sleep. So, my mother knew the dog and his energy level, but never knew that he would react in such an unruly and vehement manner when taken from his usual environs. Almost immediately after his arrival at the house, he began to express signs of mourning for his deceased master as well as for his former home. He attempted numerous times to get out of the house and he succeeded. He got out of the fenced-in pen numerous times as well, causing my parents to have James come back to restructure parts of the pen, lowering the bottom of the fence to the ground, removing the gap between the gate and the next panel, and so forth. His escapes required my elderly parents to run down their street numerous times, trying to recapture him.

As I did not know how much worse the house had become only one year after my 2008 visit, I did not fully comprehend just how little room there was for the dog to move around when indoors. It was already nearly unnavigable the last time I had seen it the year prior. But now, there simply wasn't enough room for him to move at all. He was usually kept in a cage, positioned right in the middle of the already narrow hallway near my parents' formerly usable bedroom. It was near to the master bathroom, and the presence of that cage made the area almost completely impassable. It is no wonder he desperately wanted to get out of the house. On two separate occasions—I was later informed—he jumped through the mesh screen of an open window and escaped to the outdoors. On the first such occasion, he was picked up by a kind woman who saw his tags, and was ultimately able to contact my parents. The second time, he was hit by a car and did not survive. The discovery of his body was in part the catalyst for the subsequent involvement of town authorities.

Ultimately, I was correct that it was a very poor idea to adopt the dog. It was unconscionable that he was ever brought into that environment. It is understandable that the dog, feeling imprisoned in such a confining environment would yearn to escape through any egress he could find. The executors failed in their responsibility to ensure the safety and suitability of the environment he was going to. My well-meaning parents were incapable of caring for that dog and they should have known better, had they been in their right minds. I even felt partly responsible for not even more strenuously objecting to my mother's ill-conceived plans—absolutely forbidding it. Would she have even listened? Probably not.

I wish that has all turned out otherwise. I never got the chance to meet Sonny. He seemed like a sweet and beautiful dog. But I had to deal with the aftermath.

THE PRE-EXILIC PERIOD

Doctoral graduation, Claremont, California, 2005

Wedding, Malibu, California, 2005

Wedding, Malibu, California, 2005

CHAPTER FIVE:
THE EXILE

On Wednesday, August 19th, 2009, at around 10 or 11 AM, I received a call from Kim Catalano. It was the first of several calls I would receive from him that day that would forever change my life. I saw his name on the caller ID of my phone and immediately knew that this was not a social call. I had spoken to him on several occasions before, having established contact with him to make sure that he had me as an emergency contact for my parents, and also to make sure that he knew there was a close family member who cared about my parents' condition. I had also alerted him in the past to my parents' living conditions, making it known that I found this to be a very real concern. And on at least one previous occasion the prior year, I had accompanied my parents to a family session with him while I was visiting them. We knew each other.

Kim calmly said that he wanted to keep me informed, since an emergency situation had occurred. He explained that he was with my mom and was taking her to an urgent care center to get medical attention for a severe nasal hemorrhage, and that my father had had a violent episode and had gone missing. They could not find him. This was all very shocking, and I could not comprehend my father having a violent episode, as he did not have a violent bone in his body. I knew there must be some mistake. It just did not seem like him. Surely this must be some kind of exaggeration on my mom's part. But considering my father's recent episodic memory loss, the worrisome fact remained that he had gone missing.

I asked Kim if I should make arrangements to fly out there and help out, but he suggested that I just sit tight until we knew better what was going on. I had begun to fear the deterioration of my father's mental state; that something like this might happen. I also feared the worst about my parents, as I had earlier noted; that something might happen to them: a more serious car accident, a fire, a robbery, something tragic that I simply had no control over.

About an hour or so went by and finally Kim called me back to say that my father had been found and my mother had been stabilized and released from the urgent care center; that he had spoken with them both for a short while and they were on their way home and would call me when they got there. I was grateful to him for keeping me in the loop.

I would later come to learn the truth of the matter.

The day prior, while my mom was out of the house somewhere, my father was home alone and had become trapped inside the house. Once again, the details were still foggy to me, having been filtered through two parents who were, at the time, still highly out of touch with reality. Some of the following, I had to piece together through carefully inspecting the damage done. The doorknob had become worn with age and lack of upkeep and the internal elements no longer operated properly; mainly the spindle was not retracting the latch bolt from the strike plate to allow the door to open when the knob was turned. The door simply would not open. So my dad began to panic. The interior of the house was filled with the stench of animal dung, heavy with flies. The air had become heavy with mold and must and mildew. He was unable to breathe, to think. He felt the need to get out, gasping for air, and didn't feel able to wait until my mom returned from wherever she had gone, probably in a fit of exasperation at the situation that both of these intelligent but sick adults had created.

The entryway was comprised of two beautiful, solidly heavy, stained brown hardwood doors that we once re-stained and varnished in the mid-'80s, removing the doors from their hinges and completing the task on saw horses in the driveway one warm afternoon. Now, they were quite a bit worn and dull, the varnish coming off in thin strips and flakes. The left one (when viewed from outside) was always left closed, dead bolted at both top and bottom. The right was the one that we used for entry.

Many times, I have tried to imagine what it must have been like for my dad in this predicament, as this became a seminal moment in our family's history, in my personal journey. I imagined him at the door, feeling the walls of newspaper closing in on him, short of fresh air, short of breath, struggling to get out, the doorknob not properly turning. My dad got a few tools from the utility drawer down the hallway—not an easy task in itself, with all the hoarded clutter in the way—and began to endeavor to get the door open somehow.

First, Dad went to work trying to twist the knob open with a pair of pliers. No result. The teeth of the pliers deeply scored the brass of the knob, but didn't bite enough to make it turn. They merely scraped over the surface of the intractable knob while he attempted to twist it.

I could see him in my mind's eye beginning to lose focus and to panic. Exhausted, dehydrated, and thinking poorly, he began to hit the doorknob with a hammer he had close at hand. I could see him beginning to pummel the knob, at first with angry, powerful blows, but then losing steam, losing energy. Finally, as if with lazy and aimless blows, the efforts of a man whose air and life were both waning from his body, the knob came off, exposing the internals of the lock. He tried to turn the exposed spindle with the pliers but still could not get himself free. Still no ability to exit, as the doorknob spindle was hindered in some other way.

Exasperated, he took a different tack and tried to pry the door open at the centerline between the two doors, either with a screwdriver or the claw of the hammer; still with no result. Then in a desperate attempt, he began to chip out wood with the hammer and screwdriver to enlarge the space between the doors, so that he might get at the latch bolt of the doorknob assembly and open it that way.

Seeing progress, he continued to chip away at the wood of the door body, near to the latch, exposing it and allowing him to pry it open with the hammer's claws, so that finally the door gave way and slowly opened, inward, permitting a rush of fresh, cool air. Even in the humid August sun, it was cooler than the stuffy, mold-filled air that lay stale and stagnant inside the house, deathtrap that it had become due to neglect and active hoarding of useless matter.

My mom later blamed him, decrying the lack of necessity of destroying the door like that, suggesting in all seriousness that if he really wanted to leave so urgently, he should have climbed out the window of the Den. She said that it was not that high, and that she had done it before. The absurdity of this struck me like a slap in the face. Even if she had done it before—and why should any person, let alone an elderly woman, be forced to exit her own house that way—I am certain that with his bum knee and limp, my dad would not have been able to do so himself. The window was about four-and-a-half feet off the ground and before it was a ton of bushes; it could not really be navigated by an elderly man. My mom's thinking was evidently unsound at that time. Despite my dad's obvious participation in making the house this way—refusing to call plumbers or repairmen, leaving the house in a state of limbo between his inability to handle the repairs himself anymore and being too depressed to call someone to do the job for him—I could not fault him for panicking. I might have done the same. Though with my prior experience as a handyman during grad school, I would like to think that I would have simply dismantled the doorknob assembly more methodically, first unscrewing the integral screws that held it together. But a frightened old man, stuck in a hovel, cannot be faulted for panicking. There was nothing "violent" about this. It was the result of years of living like this, unable to get past his own demons, let alone handle his wife's demons as well.

And so, my dad was free. But because of this, the security of the door was compromised and the dog, Sonny, would soon be free, too.

At about 5:30 AM the next morning, August 19th, my mother awakened with a severe nose bleed in both nostrils and had difficulty breathing. Knowing that the family chiropractor and wellness center owner Allan started his day early, about 6 AM, and would be able to examine her, she called him as soon as she could, explaining what had happened. He told her to come right in. She awakened my father and asked him to take her to Allan's. They drove over there and Allan took her in immediately. Her blood pressure was through the roof, which was exceedingly uncharacteristic for her; she was not known for high blood pressure or any kind of ill health—at least in recent years—being a health-foodist. He told her that this was a severe nasal hemorrhage, most likely due to the extreme stress she had been under, and that she needed to go to a hospital. Immediately she protested, stubbornly concerned that they would give her all sorts of medications and treatments that her alternative health lifestyle would not permit. Allan rightly proclaimed, "Barbara, if you don't get to a hospital, you're going to die!" He was succinct and forceful. He immediately had my mother's nose packed with some bandages and urged her to get to a nearby urgent care center. So she and my father went driving, looking for an urgent care center, avoiding the emergency room which would likely have been too crowded and less than personal. But at 7 in the morning, even the urgent care centers in the area were all closed. So they came back to Allan's.

Allan's receptionist helped Mom find a listing for a place nearby that was a holistic doctor's office. The woman had gone there a few years ago herself. They called the place to see if they were open, but there was no answer. She suggested that my mom go over there anyway to wait for them to open, as it was now nearly 8 AM. So, my parents got back into their minivan and drove a mile or so down the street to the address and my father dropped my mom off to wait in the parking lot for the clinic to open. My father then drove away with the intention of quickly dropping off some paperwork at the school where he taught night classes in his retirement, in order to ensure proper processing of his paycheck. More complications to their daily lives. This, first and foremost, indicates to me that neither of them was thinking correctly. An elderly woman with a nasal hemorrhage does not belong sitting in the parking lot, alone, while her elderly husband drives away to do chores, even chores that are of a time sensitive nature and having to do with sorely needed income. And more so, an elderly man who is already having memory problems and getting lost in places he has driven for nearly four decades.

So, the clinic opened and the office manager found my 70 year old mother sitting on the curb in the parking lot with a double nasal hemorrhage and took her inside to speak with her. They consulted the appointment book and the woman said that unfortunately, the doctor was exceedingly busy and fully booked for the day. In fact, they would not be able to fit in a new patient until December 12th, nearly four months away. My mother stood there flabbergasted, no doubt while her nose kept bleeding. The woman politely but coldly asked my mother to get someone to drive her somewhere else. Not even an attempt to offer first aid or stabilize a patient while calling an ambulance to take her to an emergency room. In my opinion, that should have been grounds for a lawsuit against the entire practice, for refusal to treat an urgent medical case, as well as endangerment of an elderly person.

But my dad had not yet returned. He was lost. So Mom called Allan's office again to see if Dad had gone back there. He had not. But since my parents were supposed to have an appointment with Kim a short while after and he shared the same staff, being in the same wellness center, he was contacted to let him know that my mother and father would be late on account of extenuating circumstances. When Kim found out about this, he immediately offered to go and pick my mom up, as it was close by, and to bring her to the nearest urgent care center, since they were likely open by now. That is what happened. He drove over, and after waiting with her for just a few moments to see if my father would return, he got her into his car and was set to take her over. Coincidentally, they saw my father drive in the entirely opposite direction, lost and probably heading back to Allan's wellness center. My mom was tempted to try to flag him down and have him follow them, but Kim knew he needed to get my mom some medical attention as quickly as possible. It was around this time that Kim called me on the phone the first time, alerting me to the situation.

The insistence upon going to the holistic doctors' office appeared to me as another symptom of my mother's hoarding personality, much like the "alcoholic personality" or "addict personality" that is talked about in twelve step circles; nothing could be simple, there was an obstacle placed in front of every task. Nothing was as easy as just taking her to the urgent care. She felt she had to have the attention of a holistic doctor, who would not use various medications or drugs—all in an attempt to control her environment. Nonetheless, fate forced her to go to the more orthodox urgent care anyway, while my father remained lost in the process.

So Kim had driven her to an urgent care center about a mile and a half away from there, which he knew of since it was next to his dentist's office. He waited there for her while they treated her, packing her nose with bandages. They stabilized and released her. Kim drove her back to his office, where they would wait for my dad, hoping that he remembered their impending counseling appointment, and that he could even find his way back. Dad was still nowhere to be found. A little while later, about the time that the appointment was supposed to begin, Kim went to get something from his car and he noticed that my dad had indeed arrived and was asleep in the minivan, with his head upon the steering wheel. Kim didn't want to startle my dad in attempting to awaken him, so he went back upstairs to tell my mom and hopefully my dad would awaken and come up. About ten to fifteen minutes later, and that much into the appointment time, my dad came walking in. When asked where he was, he said that he had fallen asleep in the car while waiting for the appointment to begin and just realized that it was late. He had evidently forgotten where he had dropped my mother off, not even realizing how urgent the situation was. His mental state was evidently compromised. He was not getting enough sleep, what with the constant trouble with the dog escaping and causing my parents to run down the street after him, and cleaning up the destruction that he brought to the house. And the constant stress that both my parents were under was causing him to have tremendous lapses in judgment.

So, with only a little bit of time left on the clock for their appointment, they spoke for a bit and Kim ended the appointment. My parents went home, having no idea that while they were gone, Sonny Boy had gotten out of his cage, as he was often wont to do—exceedingly smart animal that he was—and began to work at throwing himself at the front door. Evidently, he had jostled the turn-bolt latch on the middle deadbolt lock, which was about mid-chest level on a human and not out of reach for a jumping dog, and continuing to throw himself against the front door—the knob of which had been destroyed by my dad in the prior day's incident—he bounced the door open and was free. Mom remembered very clearly having deliberately made sure the door was fully closed and the middle turn-bolt actuated prior to leaving, knowing Sonny Boy's tendency to get loose inside the house. But no amount of precaution was enough this time. He was free.

When they got home after my mom's treatment, the bleeding having been stopped, they were greeted by the assembled authorities—police, public safety, and adult protective services. The dog had been struck by a car and killed while my parents were gone, and they had been identified as the owners. The door had been left ajar by the dog's repeatedly throwing himself against it and getting loose. I often wonder, years later, out of masochistic morbid curiosity, how exactly he died. Was he killed quickly? Did he suffer? Did bone crunch under moving tires, unable to stop, rolling over the still living body of the dog, crushing his internal organs? Or did it merely propel him out of the way, rendering him unconscious in the process, at which point he died of shock? Or did he suffer from traumatic avulsion of some part, like his cranium, or a limb, and bleed to death? I still harbor some sense of guilt for my inability to convince my parents that they were unfit and unable to care for the dog, who deserved more space than they could provide him. He had deserved freedom. He now had it, but not the way he should have.

The police had been alerted about the dog's death. So the interior of the house was now open and visible and the police initially thought there had been a burglary. The police, peering inside the open door that had been left ajar by the dog's escape, saw the condition of the house. When viewed by them, they realized that there were more serious problems afoot than a mere breaking and entering. They felt it necessary to alert the Town Public Safety office, and subsequently Suffolk County Adult Protective Services. When my parents arrived, the house was in the process of being "placarded", or declared unsafe for human habitation until further notice on account of multiple safety violations. The jig was up. Now, everyone knew. There was no longer any way to avoid the consequences. While my mom facilely and futilely tried to provide an overly convoluted explanation of the mess as a product of mold which was caused by a water main break last month that flooded our driveway and ultimately our basement, causing my parents to turn everything topsy-turvy to repair the water damage, yielding the visible results that the public safety officers witnessed—and so forth—public safety did not buy it. She was panicking, realizing that she was in danger of losing her house. Her highly successful defense mechanism—her brilliant ability to concoct believable stories, gained through years of dodging life-threatening abuse—was now no longer effective. The authorities knew that what they saw was the product of years of hoarding which had now reached lethally dangerous proportions and it was their legal and moral responsibility to step in. And thus began the period that I later concisely termed "The Exile".

My family had become "one of those families". For so many years we had been the quiet ones, never drawing any attention to ourselves, never playing radios too loudly, always beyond reproach. Gradually, as the property became more and more densely overgrown with trees and plants that my mother insisted on allowing to grow wild, it became reminiscent of the aforementioned *Grey Gardens*. Numerous times, I had had arguments with my mother about the condition of the property, urging her to leave more room in the driveway for vehicles to pull in and for additional walk space. She would get angry with me and resist making any changes. Now it was all coming to a head—all at once.

At some point during all this, cousin Marty had been contacted. He was with my parents at the house when they finally called to alert me of the second round of tragedies that day. Yes, my parents were safe, but they no longer had a home available to them and the dog had been killed while in their care. I spoke to my mom on the phone briefly. She was dazed. I tried to reassure her that everything would be okay and that I would come out immediately to help ameliorate everything. She acceded, sounding too tired to even produce words. Marty would take my parents to Barbara Simmons' house to stay there while they were barred from residing in their house and he also agreed that he would take their cat into his care. I would get the next flight I could to New York and would begin to play the role of the responsible son, spearheading this impossible job, cleaning what should have been done over the course of nearly twenty years.

I was completely overwhelmed. I cannot begin to describe how frightened I was. It was like being a little boy, asked to do a man's job. I felt as if my almighty parents, so competent and powerful and self-reliant for so many years, were now the children and I was expected to act like an adult. But thankfully, I did not have to do everything all alone. People stepped in to help. People loved my parents, and they loved me as well. I was able to rely upon people for their assistance and I was grateful. When I called Dave Feuerstein to ask him for his help in securing a good flight, he went ahead and used his frequent flyer air miles and got me a roundtrip ticket to NY, arriving early the next morning.

No money ever exchanged hands. His kindness was always what made him stand out, head and shoulders above most other people and made me want to keep in touch with him over most other friends that I first knew from my junior high school years. And now, he was coming through for me once again.

That day, while trying to arrange my flight to NY, I called the officer in charge of the affair at the town Public Safety office, people who handled building and safety concerns along with other issues. Officer Barry Dibelius—who had the same surname as Martin Dibelius, a famous scholar within my academic field, surely a good omen—along with his partner, Lisa Ann Wallace, were the ones who had been called to the scene and were currently overseeing the investigation and the necessary remedies. When I reached Barry on the phone, I immediately tried to make him aware that we, as a family, intended to cooperate fully, that we had no intention of giving him trouble or contesting his decisions, and that I was flying out the next morning to help bring things up to code. He was very kind and my attempts to assure him of my cooperation were not lost on him. He evidently had a lot of compassion and was truly concerned for these two elderly people that were my parents. I expressed that I was aware of their living conditions but had so far been unable to make any material changes to them, aside from getting them into counseling. So, we agreed to meet the very morning I arrived on Long Island, in approximately 24 hours. I made arrangements with my friend Aimee to let me stay at her family's place, in one of the spare bedrooms. The Dressler family's kindness was unparalleled and without their moral support—and even the hands and backs of several of them—I would not have made it through this ordeal.

I packed what I could as quickly as I could. I left from LAX at 10:40 PM the very same night. The flight would arrive at 6:56 AM the next day. After a long "red-eye" flight, the next morning arrived and I deplaned to find a moderately hot, but muggy New York Summer. I always hated the humidity of Long Island Summers; it was my least favorite part of the climate of my beloved homeland. This time, the heat was that much more distasteful to me on account of the situation. Marty picked me up from LaGuardia in his car and drove me the 45 minute ride back to Aimee's house, saying a quick greeting at the door to Aimee's father and mother, whom he had met before, and then proceeding on his way to work. I had slept very little, if at all, on the plane and was simultaneously very tired and fully awake from adrenaline and worry. When I arrived, Charlie, Aimee's father, helped me settle my belongings in the room that I'd be staying in, gave me a key to the house and a spare car I could use temporarily. Aimee's mom, Suzanne, was just getting ready for work herself, and offered me a quick bite to eat. All I could stomach in the midst of this (quite literally) disgusting affair was a few morsels of toast and a cup of green tea to calm my nerves. I truly had no appetite at all, but I forced myself to eat something, knowing that I would need my strength.

I had been in contact with my parents briefly by phone before I left L.A.

and told them that I would speak to them later the next morning after I had had my meeting with Barry, the inspector. They were not intending to be there, and frankly, I didn't want them there. It would have complicated things. I wanted to speak directly to Barry, being the adult son coming to take charge. We had hoped Kim could make it as well, but he had other engagements. My parents and I would later check in with him at our afternoon appointment that day.

I got to the house that morning at around 10 o'clock and I made my first entry into the house. It would be an understatement to say that I was in no way mentally or emotionally prepared for what I saw.

First Entry

When I arrived at my parents' house, I was greeted with some of the most horrible filth that I had ever seen. Even the driveway was strewn with plastic flower pots, many broken, a shopping cart, baby carriages, a rocking horse, bottles, cans, leaves, all manner of debris and refuse, all placed very carefully according to the careless plans of an ill mind, seeking to make sense of the pain in her world and in the world we shared as a family.

When I approached the front door, I saw the usual debris and junk that was on the front stoop, obscuring the now faded, heavy double doors that were once a signal of our welcoming intent. And when I saw the large, 11 ½ by 14 inch rectangular yellow poster board sign that had been thumb-tacked to the right hand door of the once beautiful brown hardwood double doors, it gave a sense of numbing realism to an otherwise surrealistic situation. I was disappointed, as if there was still a chance that this may have been a dream, or a simple misunderstanding. I quickly read the code.

**DO NOT REMOVE
DEFACE OR MARK THIS PLACARD
UNDER PENALTY OF LAW**

This Building is hereby declared unsafe and unfit for human habitation pursuant to the Code of the Town of Huntington.

The occupancy of this dwelling or any part thereof is unlawful.

Violators are subject to a fine in the maximum sum of $15000.00 or 6 months imprisonment or both.

Telephone—351-2813/351-3167/351-3234
DATED: Aug 19. 2009
TIME: 1:30 pm
ADDRESS: ### DeForest rd.
POSTED BY: L. Wallace

Richard Bruce
Department of Engineering Services
Department of Public Safety

It was now a reality. I could not deny it.

I still had my key to the house, stored usually in a drawer back in L.A. and only retrieved when I visited Long Island. The doorknob that had been damaged turned from the exterior, contrary to what I had expected. The middle lock—a side motion, key operated deadbolt—opened easily. The top deadbolt—a vertical heavy brass bar that slid into a slot in the door jamb, above—had been actuated and applied from inside, as my mother had told me the night prior on the phone. I had figured it would be a good idea to check first either way. I would have to enter by the rear of the house after all. I was full of emotions at this point: fear, anger, sadness, even shock—and certainly the denial that this could happen to our kind and compassionate family. We were special, weren't we? Or so I thought.

So I bushwhacked my way around the right side of the house, through many, many vines and thickets, noticing that the northeast face of the house was still fully covered in ivy, to the point where even many of the windows were fully obscured. It has been said that this ivy, covering many of the Ivy League buildings, even those of stone, is slowly destructive to their edifices. Lord knows what it was doing to the 1972 vintage T1-11 plywood exterior siding panels beneath it. I continued around the back, seeing for the first time the pen that my parents had commissioned to be built for Sonny Boy to stay in. I squirmed past it, dodging more vines and young but vehement sapling trees, some yews and euonymus, continuing a few more feet to the rear sliding glass doors that opened out on to the back yard, once a vibrant vegetable garden, but now a site of nearly impenetrable weeds and brush. I crawled through the yews that were obscuring the first slider. Its bottom was about two feet off the ground, its purpose being more decorative than intended as entry or egress. I slowly slid the screen away, to the right, exposing the glass door. My mother had left it unlocked for me to enter, trusting that no prowlers would even want to go back here, let alone know that this was the only remaining viable entry to the house.

I pulled the heavy metal framed, glass door to the right, with great difficulty as its tracks were loaded with dirt and plant matter from years of neglect. It rumbled and resisted as I pulled it open until I exposed the interior of the house for the first time in two years. The feeling that I had in the pit of my stomach—knowing that this was undeniable evidence of my parents' sickness and also the moment in which I was required to become an adult—I cannot describe in words. My viscera, the entire front of my body, all ached with a cold groan, a diabolical, icy tingle in my chest and solar plexus. From the damp and muddy summer soil below, I stepped up upon the ledge and climbed in; dark, moist Long Island loam clinging to the tread of my black motorcycle boots.

Antithetically reminiscent of Howard Carter's declaration to Lord Carnarvon as he peered into the antechamber of Tutankhamun's tomb, stating that he saw "wonderful things", when I peered into the living room of my parents' house, all I saw was *horrible things*. Evidence of a beautiful life turned very wrong.

I had to climb over a huge pile, nay a platform, of newspapers and magazines, atop furniture and stereo cabinet speakers and whatnot. I was concerned that this five-foot-tall structure, blocking the cabinets at the left wall and the couches to my immediate right, would not hold my nearly 200 pound body. But it did. And I crawled up on top of it, on my belly, then swung my legs up on top so as to sit atop it. I shimmied forward to navigate past it. I wondered how my mother was able to get over this the night before in order to exit this way. She was surprisingly agile and always amazed me. I finally found some floor to set my feet down upon. There wasn't much. I had to clamber over piles of things in order to continue to move forward. What had been the living room of the house was now a junkyard, filled with anything that one could think of, and with small spaces carved out for human occupation, and barely enough room to move. No wonder that both my parents were exceedingly quarrelsome with one another. Similar conditions, providing little space for movement, have caused laboratory animals to go to war with one another.

I was astonished by the utter volume of material in that room. Not only were the two original 1972 chocolate-brown and cream striped tweed couches—now exceedingly worn and their surfaces stiff and crackling with mildew—still in place where they had been for nearly forty years, but also several other large sections of a newer couch that had been bought second hand about two years prior were stood upended in the room, covered with various things, and never having been put into a usable position. Surrounding them were piles and piles of newspaper, old phonograph records, furniture, potted plants, and every manner of detritus, so that I had to literally climb on top of everything, perched flat on my belly approximately four to five feet off the ground, squirming forward like an eel in order to be able to move to the dining room and then toward the front door. This younger sofa, in several sections, was brought in to replace the older ones a year or so prior, when my mother noticed that rats had entered into the house through one of the minute holes in the floorboards where heating pipes were directed in from the basement, and then had subsequently begun to make a nest in one or both of the older sofas. Unfortunately, even though Phil, my dad's adult education student, had helped bring the sectional sofa in, the older matching sofa and loveseat had never been brought out. Evidently, the sentimental connection to them was too strong for my mother to overcome the need to expel rat droppings from the house.

I moved toward the dining room, once the heart of my family's home, and location of many happy dinners, holidays, adolescent sleep-overs with my childhood friends. It was now a place that would have horrified even Ms. Havisham, the vendetta-driven, elderly, jilted bride from Dickens' *Great*

Expectations. It was she whose table was adorned by the petrified and spider web encrusted erstwhile wedding cake from decades prior, now attacked by rats—perhaps the archetypal forebears of the rats we would eventually find.

I had to move very carefully, so as not to fall over. There were many pitfalls and places where there were simply not more than a few inches of floor space to safely stand upon and balance before bounding to the next location. I moved through the dining room as quickly as I could, rounding the head of the great hardwood table, which was completely covered with junk, sheets to cover the junk, and then even more junk, resting about chest height, preventing it from being usable. All of the chairs were covered with bags of unidentifiable items, almost completely obscured as to their identity as chairs. The kitchen—also completely full of material both kitchen-like and not—which adjoined the dining room, was now to my left. With great difficulty, I moved past that and into the short entryway leading to the front hall.

The front hallway was now also full of junk. As I moved toward the front door in order to unbolt the deadbolt and begin to air out the house from the intolerable stench of decay and mold, I had to step over more and more things to navigate. There was not a single space in the house that was able to be called clean or clear or livable. I can say, categorically, that the house was worse than ever before. I had seen it briefly during each of the two years prior and it was terrible, but you could still get inside. To this day, I cannot believe that my parents lived like this—in the worst of conditions—for over a year. Prior to that, it was barely livable. Now, I would not have considered it livable at all. One could barely move around without jumping or clambering over piles and stacks. The term "goat paths" has been bandied about in these situations of extreme hoarding; none such existed in the house anymore. The house was filled inside with many years' worth of newspapers, books, old clothing, chairs, assorted furniture and knick-knacks, in addition to what can only be called refuse and garbage. In previous years, I had seen the mess growing, and when I came in 2007 and 2008 (during the latter year I only caught a glimpse through the front door), it was already shocking. But at least there were still pathways during that previous year. Pathways of about a foot wide, between tall piles of junk, as tall as the height of a human in places. In other places, they were just piles chest high that were precariously balanced so as not to fall into the pathways unless jostled. And my father's rebellion was that he jostled them (semi-unconsciously, perhaps somewhat deliberately) and they often fell into the pathways. And this would cause more trouble between my parents, as my mother was hurt if my dad made no effort to pick it up. He was angry that there was even the need to pick anything up. It was an impasse. Neither party would budge.

But now, you had to jump or climb over short piles of newspaper and magazines and refuse in order to get to the next square foot oasis of floor space. There were no longer any clear pathways. They were strewn with shorter piles every foot or so, in order that one would have to step over each pile into a small clearing, steady oneself, and then jump to the next clearing between piles. And with my father's walking problem, I don't know how he did it. That explains his inability to make it to the bathroom at times, which my mother described to me as a function of his laziness or his emotional deterioration. Regardless of the attendant emotional issues, there were serious physical hindrances between him and the bathroom. And this time, the stench was terrible. Previously, the home had begun to present a smell of mustiness and even mold. But this time, there was the smell that I dreaded ever smelling in my parents' house. It was the smell of fecal matter. It was the smell of two people finally being "over the edge." Continuing to explore, I saw large, fat flies buzzing around, spawned and gorged on the animal feces that was distributed surreptitiously around the house by both rodents and by the dog that had come to stay, ill-begotten decision by my mother to help a dying friend. The flies were not only located where the feces was, but also around various piles of squalor and pestilence. The air was oppressive, unrelentingly stuffy, without circulation, dead.

When I approached the front door, I saw the evident results of the incident that I had been informed of, that my father had been unable to exit the house two days prior, due to the doorknob refusing to turn and allow egress. Through careful inspection of the damage and the tools still scattered around the crime scene, as well as piecing together how my father later described his actions, I came to ascertain that he had used the pair of pliers and hammer to demolish the doorknob in a state of panic, and I could see how he had pried large chunks of wood out of the door body on the interior side, to try to gain access to the tongue of the doorknob, allowing him to exit. It was as if a burglar had approached it and made a mess of it—but from the inside. In my opinion, I could have easily dismantled the doorknob with a screwdriver and gained egress, in a manner in which nothing would have been damaged, but saved for repair. But this was the handiwork of a troubled mind, that of a man who could not breathe sufficiently in a house that was full of garbage and fecal matter, and began to panic as he realized that he could not open the door to gain egress. In this compromised mental state, he chopped it apart from the inside to get out, and subsequently, he unknowingly let out the dog that my parents had committed to care for, a promise to a dying friend but a promise that they could not honor. They, themselves, were in need of caretaking. They misjudged who was actually in need of greater assistance, the dog or they.

When I first attempted to open the front door and exit the house, I had great difficulty getting the front door to open any more than about a foot. In recent years, my parents had begun to pile more and more near the front door, behind its pathway, making it harder to open completely. One would have to sidle in, and then close the door in order to pass by it and enter further into the house. If there were multiple people entering, it was that much more of a hassle, requiring the first person to move further into the entry in order to allow the second person to enter next. Often, we had to move things from behind the door in order to allow entrance. But it was never this bad. Now, one had to literally force one's way in. It was almost completely blocked so that one would have to push one's weight against the door just to enter. In the end, I had to squeeze past the door to get outside.

When I went toward the bathroom, to the left of the front hallway, I was met with more and more flies. These were flies that I had never seen inside a human dwelling. Large, bloated flies, like those encountered in a barnyard, fed on animal excrement, much larger than the common black housefly. I remember looking at these, swarming around a 38-year-old bathroom light fixture whose bezel had been lost nearly 20 years before, and being amazed by their size, enthralled by them. Their source was, indeed, the excrement of animals. With nowhere else to keep the dog, Sonny Boy, my parents had placed a small steel cage for him in the hallway leading from the bathroom to my old room. It totally blocked the hallway. No one could move past it. But with me no longer in the house, there was really no need to get to that part of the house. So, there Sonny Boy slept, when indoors. Needless to say, he was no longer there, nor did he have any further need of it. That would be one of the first things we took outside when we began to clean house. The bottom of it was filled with his excrement, the obvious source of the majority of the flies. Once this cage was taken out, the fly population would start to dwindle.

I considered the couches in the living room as a symbol of our deterioration as a family. I recalled a photo that my father had taken of the three of us in late 1972 or early 1973, having just moved into the house. He had set up the timer on the Canon camera he had bought just after I was born, and snapped a portrait of a happy couple and their two-year-old child nestled comfortably between them on a Winter morning, holding several stuffed animals as family members in their own right. All three were the image of happiness, sanguinary sanity and suburban success: a public school teacher and a stay at home mom raising a bright, healthy little boy, curiosity shining within his brown eyes. This picture was now sullied by the reality of deterioration, of decrepitude and mental illness, compounded over the next four decades. That image was now supplanted by the reality of the increasing filth and squalor they had been living in for years.

This was the hell that my parents had created for themselves and for everyone who loved them. And at this moment, we could no longer deny our sickness—be it as enablers or the primary party who suffered—we were hoarders. As the only child, I felt it was my responsibility to save them. I had vowed to take care of my parents in their dotage, to be there for them as they aged, as a good son should—but I had failed.

The Official Inspection

Later in the morning, Inspectors Barry and Lisa showed up there at the house—the home I had grown up in, but was really no longer in my hands. Barbara Simmons had just arrived and I was greatly comforted to know that she was there, a good family friend who knew us and accepted us as we were. I had arranged this meeting by phone with all the parties. I was glad to get things started. I signed a waiver allowing Barry and Lisa to enter into the house and inspect it formally. Even though they had already seen it the other day, this was a necessary formality in order to involve me. The front door of the house bore the aforementioned large, yellow, thin oaktag placard on it, stating that the house had been rendered unfit for human habitation until various building and safety violations had been rectified. The word "condemned" was never used, but to me it seemed as shocking as if it had been. Condemnation would have been more permanent, irreversible, pertaining to the structure or foundation. The term that they kept using was the verb "placarded", indicating a temporary state that could be lifted once specific conditions were met. Nevertheless, this term stuck in my mind and in my heart, a stain on our reputations.

Barry and I walked around the exterior of the house. He pointed out a variety of places where the brush had overgrown so much that it violated several codes. Then, we transitioned to the interior. I was glad that I had previously entered on my own, so that it was not as much of a shock. It was, nevertheless, indescribably embarrassing to show it to them—a shameful blight upon the family that I loved. Barbara stayed outside while I took Barry and Lisa inside. Both officers concurred that it was probably the worst case of hoarding that they had ever seen. I could not conceive of any worse case myself. They could not even gain access to all the rooms, as many areas were blocked off by large stacks of debris. They primarily were confined to the two major hallways that met, L-shaped, following the plan of the house. They left fairly specific instructions on what had to be cleaned. They were very kind and compassionate toward me, and no time limit was given, though they said that the sooner we got it done, the sooner my parents could move back in. I told them that my hope was to get the job done within a few weeks at most, but that I would have to fly back to California within 10 days due to my own work commitments at my university. I mentioned, with James in mind, that there was a handyman my parents were working with and that we would talk with him about doing the outdoor cleanup, and that simultaneously, I would try to get a cleanup company to handle the interior.

After the inspection was over, Officer Barry (as I somewhat erroneously continued to refer to the inspector) informed me that the County Adult Protective Services (APS) had been notified about my parents' living conditions and that they would be sending an officer to check on my parents, interview them, make sure that they were mentally competent, and would generally make sure that their safety was not compromised. Having been given the name and number of Pamela McManus, the APS officer in charge of the case, I gave her a call and left a message for her, proactively to make sure that we got off on the right foot. Meanwhile, I had a job to do. I had to get my family home back to condition so that we could remove the placard and allow my parents to live in their house once more.

Chores

Later that day, when I finally linked up with my parents, I took them to an appointment with the therapist, Kim so we could try to debrief a bit about what had happened. It helped my parents' morale a bit and allowed us to reconnect as a family, reasserting our intentions of working through this ordeal together. After that, I took my parents to the urgent care center at which my mother had been seen the day prior for her nasal hemorrhage, and they changed her bandages and packing. During this jaunt around town, we also stopped at the local electronics supply store to get my parents' cell phones (which were on a pay per usage plan) topped up with minutes, so I could be sure to stay in touch with them while they were not at their home number. It was reassuringly comforting to have some time with my parents, doing mundane chores that normal families do together. But I was quickly reminded of the lack of normalcy when confronted with the state of their minivan.

During this whole time, while driving my parents around town, my mother had to crawl into and out of the minivan from the back hatch, as there were only the driver and passenger's seats available. My father's legs would only permit him to sit in the front seat and I insisted on driving. That left my mother as the "odd-man-out". But she could not simply clear out a back seat for herself in the sufficiently large, seven passenger Doge minivan—a seat which was accessible by the large right side sliding passenger door. In order to open the side door, we would have had to remove large amounts of papers and debris that were precariously placed against it, teetering and ready to fall out if exposed. So she insisted upon burrowing out a small hole for herself in one of the rearmost seats that were at this point only accessible by entering through the rear hatch and climbing over the rearmost seat. She had to enter and exit the vehicle this way every time. A 70 year old woman insisting upon crawling over the seat back into this little hidey hole! And it was no quick matter either. We had to wait. At times like that, I practically wanted to throttle her or just take the piles of junk out and leave them in the trash where they belonged. A quick trip to the grocery store right after this had my mom thinking twice about whether she wanted to exit the vehicle at all, and my dad and I just decided to go in and get a few items and come back out shortly while she waited in the minivan. We recognized the need to leave some of the back windows open for her, like a pet left in the car on a hot day.

The Car

On the second full day that I was there, I oversaw the removal of one of the two unregistered vehicles on the property. Officer Barry noted in his requirements that there were two unregistered vehicles on the property and that one of them had to be either registered or removed, according to code. One of them was my old 1971 Chevy Nova, our first new family car, bought in the Summer of 1971 when the '72 models were coming in and the '71s had to make way for the new. It was the first vehicle that I owned, saved and given to me by my parents on my 15th birthday, before I could even drive it. It was my first love, really, and I had built two engines for it, souped it up, hotrodded it, and drove it all around Long Island as my trusty red steed. I ran out of money to continue to restore it in November of 1989, and it sat, winterized and officially unregistered for "planned non-operation" since that time. I never had the funds or the wherewithal to finish the restoration. So it sat with a tarp over it that gradually became more and more ratty while my mother put plant pots on top of it and wasps made their nests inside the door hinges and the rust I had thought I took care of when I learned automotive bodywork back in 1988 slowly returned, cancer that it was to vintage automobiles. But, I had planned that, one day, I would either have it transported to California or I would restore it right on the spot when I had the money. I vowed that I would never get rid of that car, as long as I lived.

Meanwhile, there was the 1987 Buick Electra Station Wagon that my parents had bought second hand while I was in College and it gradually fell into disuse when they bought the 1999 Dodge Caravan—also used—the minivan that they currently used. As I described elsewhere, it became a storage spot for runoff from other areas. Potting soil and rock dust for soil repair in the garden, large bags of it, were placed in the back for storage to keep them dry. After the fiasco about the vinyl tile in the kitchen, many of the large boxes of tile that my mother had already bought from the home supply warehouse were stored in there as well. The tires had deflated and sunk deeply into the earth of the driveway. It was covered with leaves and acorns. It was likely undriveable, yet by all accounts, there was nothing really wrong with it other than a dead battery and maybe an alternator needing repair. But other than that, it was mechanically sound and could be used by someone willing to invest the time and funds to repair it. Nevertheless, it would have taken a lot of money to go over it and ensure that it was safe to drive. My parents had considered giving it to their friend Phil, one of my dad's adult students who occasionally came over to help out with yard work and repairs. He was down on his luck, having lost his job and having trouble finding a new one due to health problems and some learning disabilities. He was a good soul with a lot of heart and could have used that car. But it would have taken too much money to fix it up and get it driveable. Neither my parents nor Phil had that money. So, Charlie Dressler had called a local charity, as a favor to me, and arranged to have it picked up and towed away while I was there. In order to get the large dumpsters into the driveway later that day, the car had to be gone. I was already under pressure, trying to make all these arrangements dovetail so that we could get started on the cleanup. Not a moment was spared in the schedule I had constructed. I had less than nine days before having to return to L.A.

After a few hours of waiting and delays, the tow truck driver finally showed. I was so afraid, by the token of how things were going so far, that he was going to reject it. The main problem was that we did not have access to the title. It had been lost. More things that my father had lost track of in the house that they could not live in. The photocopy of the registration was going to have to do. Thankfully, the driver accepted it. I waved goodbye as he drove down the street with it, out of my life. I was, I must admit, a little bit saddened. We had had that car for about sixteen years or more. It had been a good car and, as I am the first to admit, I am more than a bit sentimental. That is the source of my own little bit of hoarding tendency. I wished that my parents had taken better care of it and used it or sold it to someone that could use it. But that was one of the basic *modi operandi* of my family: my mother would keep a hold of something for fear of giving it up (either from sentimentality or fear of lack), then my father would be unwilling to put the necessary amount of energy into upkeep. And now, a good automobile was being towed down the street in front of our house—hopefully to benefit some charity that accepted cars. Obstacle number one was down, the driveway unobstructed by a vehicle. Now, the dumpster could be brought in later that day.

After playing phone tag with Pamela McManus from the APS for about a day, she visited me at the house the second full day I was there. We had a nice conversation in the driveway of the house. She was very sweet and extremely sympathetic toward our situation. She and I both commiserated a bit about the issue of parents aging and needing more of our attention to keep them safe. Over the course of the conversation, Pamela informed me of what APS was responsible for in terms of ensuring the safety and well-being of disabled and elderly adults. She wanted to have a meeting with my parents, particularly my mother—who had readily been identified as the active hoarder in the matter—and would be happy to do it either at the house or at Barbara Simmons' place. I suggested, and later my mother agreed, that it should be conducted at Barbara's place, a more peaceful and comfortable setting. Pamela gave me reassurances that they would do their best to get us the help we needed, in terms of assistance with the cleanout and possibly some funds to help with the cost, as well as to ensure my parents' general safety in the matter. Mainly, she wanted to verify that my parents were indeed competent to take care of themselves, and to rule out the possibility of having to assign them a guardian or such. I sincerely hoped that my parents would be deemed competent, but I still hoped for some level of assistance in getting them the help they needed and convincing them that this situation could not abide. As kind as Pamela was—and I am sure her heart was in the right place and that she did her best—nevertheless County APS never gave us any of the long promised assistance at all. I would eventually come to consider their involvement a big disappointment.

James

By this time, I had already contracted with James—the handyman that my parents had paid to clean their gutters the year prior, and whom they had brought in to fence the pen for Sonny Boy earlier that year—to begin to work on the exterior of the house, particularly clearing away brush and debris to bring the house up to code and satisfy Officer Barry's specifications. There needed to be space between the bushes and the house, all windows and doors and originally designed methods of egress had to be clear, and so forth. James had been around the house, finishing up a previous job my parents paid him to do, when I arrived. When I first met him, he really impressed me as an honest and hardworking guy. My mother had told me, months prior, that James reminded her of my Grandpa Arty, a "rough around the edges" old fashioned, working class guy with a heart of gold. And for all intents and purposes, he was. It wasn't till later that we began to notice the extent of his rough edges.

Meanwhile, he was very eager to take on the job of cleaning up the yard for us. He had already established a rapport with my parents and he liked them. Initially, I was under the impression that I should shop around for price comparisons, and in my hyper-fearful state—seeing my childhood home effectively condemned and seeing my parents turned out—I was not thinking of James' feelings and was ignoring the sheer convenience of just getting him started. His feelings had gotten a bit hurt when I said that I was still shopping for price comparisons when we spoke by phone late in the first day I was there. I had to backpedal and apologize, reminding him that I had never had to do this sort of thing before, especially not with such urgency. We patched things up in a moment's time and I hired him to do the yard—with my mom's blessing, incidentally, as she had turned the whole affair over to me while she was still reeling from the shock of the situation. He told me he would begin the next day and he helped me make arrangements with a trash carting company to have a 20 yard roll-off dumpster delivered the next day. I had no money of my own to handle these considerations, and my mother did not have sufficient liquid cash either, but Barbara Simmons, our longtime savior, did have it and was willing to lend it to us, interest free, just to see my parents safely back home.

So, the day that the Buick wagon was towed, Day Two of the Exile, the roll-off dumpster was supposed to arrive. When it did, brought by a huge truck and lifted by enormous hydraulic arms into place, it made a great hollow crash of steel against the dirt and gravel driveway. I never thought such a huge dumpster would fit in our driveway. It was placed so we could just squeeze past it, and James could throw all his trimmings into it from the yard work. It would also be shared with the interior cleanout refuse. James began his work that day as well, the first thing in the morning, even before the dumpster was onsite. He got going immediately and did his best to win my trust as well. Interestingly, each time he arrived, he was always on foot. I began to wonder where he parked his car. He said that a friend would usually drop him off, since his truck was in the shop. Subsequently, he asked if I minded if he stored his landscaping tools here so that he didn't have to cart them with him each day, preferring to store them in the back yard, safely inside the pen that he had built for Sonny Boy. I had no problem with that. So there were a few power tools, mainly weed whackers, leaf blowers, chainsaws, rakes, and other such landscaping equipment. And every day, he would get dropped off and would picked up—usually by a sporty red car, it seemed. It was only later on that his transportation situation became somewhat suspicious.

James and I began to have a good rapport between us over the next week or so of working together. He showed me photo albums of his work, as he was a contractor who enjoyed doing interesting and unique renovation jobs using scrap materials, particularly slate and other stone work. That must have been the sentiment that my mom saw in him and liked. I began to dream about later on having him help to renovate the house, fixing it up to its former glory, and as inexpensively as all the other jobs he was doing or had done for us; his prices were very reasonable.

James had the yard cleared up in no time. Officer Barry came over during the second day of work, if I remember correctly, and spoke directly to James to give him the guidelines of exactly what needed to be done to bring things up to code. And really, he finished quite quickly, in about five days total, and very satisfactorily. On account of this, I overlooked what was an obvious smell of alcohol on his breath toward the latter half of each day. He never appeared to be drunk. But he did have the tell-tale "alky breath". There was also a slew of tall cans of juice-flavored drinks strewn about the yard when he was done each day. At first I did not know what they were, thinking they were just some kind of fruit juice based energy drink. It wasn't till later that my mom and I discovered that it was a fairly new brand of malt beverage, with fruit flavoring. He was drinking on the job and we were just ignoring it. This would only later come to affect us more extensively.

Sammon Pays a Visit

On one of the first days we began to work, the neighbor to our west came over to speak with me and express some concerns, having seen the commotion and work going on. Jerry Sammon was an attorney by trade, a somewhat diminutive man of a few inches shorter than I, bearing a bit of a Napoleon complex, and a bit older than I, roughly about 45 years old. He exuded an attitude that I had seen in a lot of other Long Island Jews whom I had grown up around; that they had finally "arrived" and that all that mattered was their comfort, and the solidarity of their community was a vehicle for this—the rest of the world be damned. So much for the altruism and *tzedakah*, or charitable giving, that was seen as a moral obligation by generations of Jews over the last few millennia, a sentiment that was central to the Jewish identity; that it was our duty to fix the world—*tikkun olam*. This no longer applied to them, in their estimation. The world had treated them poorly, and they no longer cared about the world, in my observation.

The Sammons had moved in sometime in the late 1980s, a young family with a child or two and a dog, and they had bought their home from the Fishers, who had replaced the original owners, the Higgins Family, who had lived there for decades prior to our arrival. The Sammons added on a section of house with decorative glass brick windows, looking into our yard; I found these attractive, even though it was a shift from the familiar appearance of the old Higgins house. The Sammons kept to themselves, polite, cordial, a little bit stand-offish, as if they couldn't be bothered with our kind—whatever that kind was, perhaps not sufficiently upwardly mobile. Afterall, an attorney trumps a schoolteacher. At some point, my parents had noted a strong odor of natural gas coming from their property and called the town Public Safety department to report it. It turned out that while most of our houses in the area were heated by fuel oil, a liquid petroleum heating oil that was used in residential furnaces around the Northeast U.S., a few homes on Long Island were recently getting supplied by natural gas. Evidently the Sammons were among them. And now there was a leak. At some point, they confirmed this with my parents, during a conversation, and a stingy thank you was proffered for my parents' vigilance. Mom observed to me later on that our actions had "probably saved their lives." This softened the Sammons' demeanor toward my parents just a little bit, but there was still a somewhat condescending attitude toward us, tinged with curiosity, as if we were the neighborhood freaks.

This one particular day, we had just had a visit from one town official or another and I was not in a mood for prying visitors. Sammon approached me with a relatively decent demeanor, polite enough as he was the one visiting our land. He walked over to our side of the property, crossing a little pathway between the yards in an area that was not covered by the long wooden picket fence that he had put up a few years before to delineate the line of demarcation between our yards—that only covered the back yard and stopped short of the front yard. The Fishers had only had a thin wire fence between our yards, to ensure that their dog didn't get loose. There was more neighborly feeling between the Fishers and us; their son Matthew, though a few years younger than me had been a childhood friend, and the border crossings between our yards were frequent and friendly during our youth. But now, the border crossing was a political endeavor which had to be navigated diplomatically.

The conversation began cordially, as I answered Sammon's basic questions of what was going on. It was obvious that we were doing major yard work. Brush, trees, weeds, and overgrown hedge bushes were being dramatically cut back, with some of the yews—with their distinctive, inedible red berries—having grown to over 8 to 10 feet tall, with their branches shooting wildly in all different directions, the perfect illustration of my mom's scattered and disorganized thinking. Sammon's request was simple, but odd. He asked that as we were doing our work, that I give him my assurance that I wouldn't send any of our wild animals over to his yard.

"Last week, our dog got sprayed by some kind of wild animal. I don't know what kind it was, maybe a skunk, but it took us forever to get the smell off of him. I don't know where it came from, but I just want your reassurance that you won't send any of your wild animals over to our yard," he explained, presenting his request like an attorney presenting his terms as he negotiated a contract. I was befuddled.

"Well, they're wild animals. I don't have any control over them. They're not pets. I don't know what's here, mostly squirrels and some raccoons, maybe. I didn't know there were skunks here," I replied.

"Well, I just want your assurance that you won't send any of them over to our yard," he pressed.

Still befuddled, I wanted this conversation over. "Well, I really don't have any control over them if they are wild animals, but I will be careful not to actively send them in your direction as we are clearing brush."

"Thank you. That's all I ask," he finished. Satisfied, he left and went back to his property and I continued my work. But this absurd request always stuck out in my mind as an example of his lack of common sense and experience with the mundane, as well as an indication of his interpersonal skills. This would not be the last time we had a disagreement.

A day or so later, while I was cleaning outside, Sue Sammon, the wife, came over with her mother, a woman in her early 70s, under the guise of just checking to see if we were okay, as they had seen so much commotion over here. I cannot be sure that their intentions were not noble and neighborly, but there seemed to be a certain gleeful, leering quality to their visit, as if they were snooping around for juicy gossip about the odd neighbors who were curiosities, scandalous side-show freaks, excited that there was some novelty to find out. I was as polite as possible externally, but really I just wanted to be left alone and get back to work.

The Accommodations

While I stayed at the Dresslers' house, they couldn't have been more helpful, accommodating, and hospitable. They gave me access to everything I needed while I was working on the house. Aimee helped me rent a van from UHaul and put it on her credit card. Out of the kindness of her heart, she never asked me to pay her back, even though I offered. The van served both as my primary form of transportation while there, and also as a method of taking things over to the storage unit that my parents and Marty eventually rented. And every morning, when Mrs. Dressler—Suzanne—rose to prepare to go to work, I met her in the kitchen and she made some type of nutritive breakfast for me. Of course, while I was overloaded with anxiety and fear about my parents' situation, I could hardly eat. But I knew that I needed to get some kind of food into me. Usually, two hard boiled eggs did the trick, along with some mint tea. She was happy to make it for me. I felt a little guilty that I wasn't making it for myself, being a fully capable adult who knew how to cook for himself. But it was just so much that I could do to fend off severe and crippling depression and muster the strength to even move and accomplish something. So having a little bit of help from the Dresslers really did the trick. Aimee usually got up around 5 AM to go to work at her law firm. Occasionally, she and I would have a little time to chat in the mornings if I got up that early. Those conversations helped keep me afloat as well. This old friend had truly been a life saver to me, and her thoughts and sympathy were of great comfort in my time of need.

In the afternoons, when Barbara and I were done with a day of labor—she worked with me every day, trooper that she was—I would go back to the Dresslers' house, take off my mud-laden motorcycle boots that had been my perennial choice of footwear but had now become work boots, take a shower and unwind with what I counted as a "normal" family. Of course, all families have their problems—and Aimee certainly counted her family among them—but the Dresslers seemed to be more normal to me than most, since they were not only a truly loving family that helped each other out, but they didn't have a hoarding problem. At the time, that was to me the most important indicator of normalcy—the lack of a hoarding problem. I suppose that I could have stayed with the family of Hermann Göring at that time and found them to be normal, simply on account of their typical Germanic orderliness. I jest, of course. But the sentiment is very telling. And overall, I felt a great amount of warmth from the Dressler family.

Occasionally, the Dresslers would have my parents and me over for a little dinner. It gave some level of normalcy to things and they could help keep my parents stimulated with some conversation, which they needed at this point to keep them grounded. For several years, the Dresslers knew that there was something amiss regarding my parents' home. Out of the many times that my parents had been over to the Dresslers' house for dinner, dessert, conversation and whatnot, even holidays, the Dresslers had never once been invited to my home. Aimee had been over once in the distant past, during the few months in the mid-'90s when we were still dating. She knew that it was a mess. Back in those days, it was not nearly as pathological as it was now. But no one asked questions. It was an unspoken matter, mainly out of compassion for my parents. Everyone knew it was a touchy subject and that socializing was for the purpose of increasing joy.

I had an upstairs bedroom to myself, which had formerly belonged to Aimee's youngest sister many years prior. It still had a number of stuffed animals in it and still bore the sentiment of a young girl's style and taste. I was happy to have a room to myself that was neat and comfortable. It had an in-wall air conditioner as well, something that my family hadn't had in years. The two A/Cs at my parents' house had been in disuse since the 1980s, their annual servicing ceased and their use deliberately discontinued on account of both the cost of electricity, as well as my mother's dislike of the ionized air that they emitted—Mom asserted that they emitted positive ions, which made her feel tired. But it was always a sore point with me that the one in my bedroom had been covered over, against my will, by a huge and unmovable cabinet, and that I no longer had the comfortable feel of cool A/C air during the hot and muggy New York Summers. Growing up, we spent long summer days at Aunt Bobbie and Uncle Artie's, where Grandma and Grandpa also lived, and which Mom playfully called Mergetland on account of the family name. Uncle Artie kept the A/C in the house cranked up to the point where Aunt Bobbie and others complained about how cold it was; but I enjoyed it. Even coming inside the chilled house after swimming in their backyard pool, it felt like luxury to me, filling a gap I experienced in my own house. I came to associate air conditioning with a sense of comfort and family time and carefree happiness of youth. But this one at the Dresslers' house was always available to me, blowing air as cold as I could get it, right across the bed, keeping me cool as I slept. It was at that point in time that I coined the phrase: "There are few situations in life that could not be improved by the addition of a little air conditioning." And I was right. This situation, hellish as it was, had been markedly improved.

I tried to keep my own items as neatly as possible, while I was in that bedroom—all my notebooks, clothing and accoutrements for helping organize one's elderly parents. I kept everything either in or next to my bags, clothing neatly folded, books neatly stacked, as if somehow my own deliberate neatness would offset the lack thereof in my parents, or perhaps would be a sign to the world that I was not like them; it was a desperate cry to be heard and believed—that I was normal and not like them.

While I was there, Aimee's middle younger sister and her new husband were there in town, visiting from Upstate New York. I was very happy to see them, a joyful extension of the perennially loving Dressler family, but I could not help feel that I was somehow a miasma in the midst of a joyful occasion, my depressive and anxious mood bringing down a pall over everything. I believe that Jenny and Aaron knew what was going on in my family and they, too, kept respectfully quiet about it. I remember saying to them, at one point, how nice it was to see them and that I was sorry not to be in a better frame of mind to be able to converse and socialize with them. Once again, as with other times in my life, I felt as if my presence brought the element of "the Different". My family was the oddity and I too was a part of it. But the nice thing about the

Dressler family was that they always did their best to make one feel welcome; my feeling of being an outsider was purely in my own mind, it was never engendered by them.

A few years prior, I had developed heart palpitations, related no doubt to the overall stress in my life. They invariably occurred in episodes which began in the middle of the night, usually while sleeping, and they would awaken me, last about an hour or two, and then subside. They were always intense and arrhythmic, sometimes causing minor dizziness, but always accompanied by oppressive, pounding discomfort in the chest. I had had them checked in 2008 by a cardiologist, who provisionally diagnosed them to be nothing more than PVCs—Premature Ventricular Contractions—and were likely the result of stress mixed with certain mineral deficiencies. As if right on schedule, the third night I was there, a severe bout of palpitations began right after midnight and lasted till after 6 in the morning. Needless to say, I got virtually no sleep that night. I tried to calm myself by talking to my wife, Melissa, on my cell phone, but nothing worked and the irregular elevated heartbeat lasted until it decided it had had enough and just went away. I had never had such a long or intense episode before, and it shocked and dismayed me.

The Cleanout

While James was cleaning the exterior of the house, I was interviewing firms to handle the cleanout of the interior of the house. Barbara had gotten a few advertisements and coupons from local newspapers, advertising companies that did such services and focused on recycling or donating old goods where possible, which was what my mom would want, and I felt that was important, too. We called several. Two came and gave estimates. One was fairly low, around a few thousand dollars, while the other was initially low and then was revised as they saw more of the house on the second occasion that they stopped by. During the second visit, they did not seem to want to handle the job, never actually giving a firm estimate, just saying that it would probably exceed ten thousand dollars. During that second visit, Barbara and I had already begun to clean large swaths of hallway, likely to cause an estimate to decrease; however, it had increased. They seemed more interested in buying my old Chevy Nova than making a deal to clean the house. Nice as they may have been, I chose not to commit to paying thousands of dollars that we did not have.

Meanwhile, I began to make calls to various agencies and follow up on various leads that might help me out. Initially, Pamela McManus, from Adult Protective Services, had made wonderful promises indicating that they might be able to come up with some funds or at least workers to help with the cleanout. I continued to follow up on this, but with no results. As I noted, she was very sweet, but the promises were made on behalf of an agency that simply could not produce. We were left to our own devices. All possible leads had led in circles. Officer Barry had made some calls to see if there were some avenues within the town that might be able to come up with funds for my parents since they were aged and in financial hardship. The problem was that they would have to demonstrate that hardship with all manner of documents that they did not currently have access to, such as copies of taxes and deeds and such. Even still, their raw income was considered too high to qualify for any of the town sponsored hardship programs, since they did not take into account my parents' fairly high debt, just gross income. This was the same problem that I encountered when dealing with some of the avenues that Kim Catalano had suggested. He had worked with various agencies within the town in the past, which had been able to help in such situations. Still, the same problems applied. The cutoff of income, about $40,000 per household, was a bit lower than my parents' gross income. There was no wiggle room. So, we still were out of luck. Interestingly, that amount for a married couple on Long Island did not go very far at that time, in terms of buying power.

It was a quandary for me. How do we get this done? We could not afford the amounts that the various cleanup companies were estimating. Two other possible solutions presented themselves simultaneously. James had made an offer to do the job himself, with the help of a co-worker named Mike. He had seen the garage and had briefly viewed the interior of the house. He knew what he was dealing with. He speculated that he would have to invest in some environmental suits and masks in order to shield himself from the filth and pathogens. Also, I could tell that he had a bit of trouble with the smell inside the house, leaving him queasy when he had gone in to inspect.

Ah, yes, the smell. The smell, as I had previously described, was largely the combination of years of mold, mildew and must. But it also included decaying animal fecal matter, possibly a few rat carcasses hidden under piles of newspaper and other debris, and also some rotting plant matter from various bits of fruit and vegetable matter that had gotten misplaced and forgotten. It was certainly an unpleasant smell to anyone who had not become inured and desensitized to it over the course of several years of living inside the house. Even to me, it was pretty bad, despite being the son of the people who had created it.

When I was growing up, I remember noticing the different smells of people's houses. It was a curiosity of mine. I remembered my friend Tom Schmidt, with whom I went to elementary school, lived in a house that always smelled like bologna or some other luncheon meats. It was not at all unpleasant, just a bit odd to me, having grown up with very different smells in my home. And I remember another little girl with whom I grew up, Amy—who came from a decidedly anti-health food family, which was common in the junk-food ridden '70s—had noted that my family and I smelled like vitamins. She noted that all health-food oriented families smelled like vitamins. Perhaps she was right, but our scent was not anything noxious. I do agree, having grown up around health food stores and still considering them my primary food source, that there is a certain "natural" smell to health food stores. It seems to be identifiable only as "grainy" or "wholesome," an admixture of bulk-bin grains with an infusion of herbs and spices—with some B Vitamins thrown in. But I didn't remember our house smelling like anything at all, while I was growing up. Of course, I was probably inured to our own particular scents, but I am sure it was never as bad as it was at this point, emitting a stench from the piles of refuse we had collected indoors. We didn't have mold and rotting animal or plant matter in my house when I was growing up. The odor I smelled here in 2009 was new. It hadn't been there in 2008 or before. I was sure of it. And over the course of the next few years, after the Exile, each time I went back, I could smell the same bitter, musty sort of smell (with a hint of overly sweet, rotten peaches or apricots) as when I entered the house, but in far diminished quantities. It was not as if I had become inured to it on account of my propinquity to it as family—since I did not live there anymore. It had definitely diminished since the moment I entered at the beginning of the Exile. It was trapped between layers of debris in the house and as these layers were gradually and systematically cleared away, the smell left with it, like shadows exposed to the light. Interestingly, even over the next few years, anytime I would smell something that my parents had mailed or shipped to me, it would bear the scent of that house, but in very diminished quantities. Even Melissa would take note of it and playfully term it "a Greenborg smell," evoking the Borg Collective of Star Trek, as if our family were a villainous galactic empire that had assimilated her.

And James, just like Officer Barry and others who came to inspect or to begin to help, could readily detect the smell of the house. It was embarrassing beyond description that this belonged to my family. It was ours, our doing. But I had to move past it, like a failed marriage. James suggested that he could do the job, and for cheap. He was eager for income and eager to help us. Barbara and I discussed it. My mother and I discussed it as well. Barbara suggested that we just have James begin on the garage while we try to do as much of the cleaning inside the house as we could ourselves. We had people willing to help. Marty was available. Charlie, Aimee's father, was in semi-permanent retirement, and was always eager to help my parents, having struck up a very good friendship with them. Barbara herself was willing to take some vacation time to help me spearhead the project. Others would possibly be able to help from time to time, their own work schedules permitting. Aimee, her mom, my friend Dave Feuerstein, Phil, and so forth. Numerous others were willing to lend a hand, out of love for my family. Barbara deemed it appropriate that I would have ultimate control, and that she would act as my second in charge. I felt comfortable with this arrangement.

My mother, while she was arguably the mistress of the household, was no longer really fit to make the necessary decisions about the house. My father had ceded his control over the family long before, though my mom would claim otherwise, citing his passive-aggressive actions as evidence of ultimate control. And in recent years, he had formally and deliberately ceded the control over the finances and taxes to my mom, as a result of his decreased ability to handle figures and such. An example of this was when someone asked what my parents were paying in property taxes. I wanted to test my dad's level of coherency; he could not remember. He speculated "$50,000?" asking quizzically. I said to him, "No, Dad, that's far too much. I believe it's around $11,000," trying to sound helpful and not belittling. What he speculated was their property taxes, already some of the highest in the country, was much closer to their overall annual income from his pension and social security. It was as if he had lost complete contact with levels of pricing and costs of living, like the original President Bush when he went shopping as a publicity stunt to demonstrate that he was in touch with the common man, and yet did not even know what a barcode was, prominently displayed on the underside of the groceries that he feigned purchase of.

My mom's participation in the cleanup was very slow. When she finally did show up on the third day of cleaning, she voiced her concern that she had been kept out of the house deliberately, restating that all her life she had been prevented from making her own decisions. Frankly, Barbara and I were very happy that my mom was not around, knowing that she would be largely under foot, like a family cat, and would probably hinder our progress by protesting the discarding of every little item. I had made my mom promise not to do that, making her fully aware of the gravity of this situation. She had promised that she trusted my judgment in the matter of cleaning the house, and yet she still would find numerous occasions to rummage through the dumpsters, justified or not. In my mind, she had lost the right to protest about this affair, having gotten us to this point in the first place. Her judgment was faulty and it was now my responsibility to guide the family back to health and safety. But Barbara and I had not deliberately kept my mom out of anything, as part of some grand plan to take away her power and autonomy. We had work to do, and we were not going to let anyone or anything stand in our way.

Barbara and I began work as soon as possible and worked as quickly as possible, and we were satisfied that Suffolk County Adult Protective Services had met with my parents at her house, where they were staying temporarily while barred from occupying the house; this kept my parents occupied for one more day and away from our worksite. And thus, Pamela McManus wanted to make sure that my parents were mentally competent and able to take care of themselves, which they were, for all intents and purposes. It was that they had an emotionally driven addiction to compulsive hoarding (active hoarder and enabler alike) and needed assistance. I had hoped that APS would help get them the help they needed. But in reality, they could not provide the resources that they claimed. It was an aspirin or a bandage for a diagnosis of cancer.

But when Mom finally began cleaning, it was the same as always. She was only able to pick up one piece of paper at a time, moving dreadfully slowly, carefully pondering each piece of paper as if it were a court case being deliberated over. She went into the den, where she had largely resided for the last several months with the family cat, avoiding my dad and his moods; there, she claimed to focus on finding tax papers that were needed for the upcoming October filing deadline for the extension they had been granted from the usual April 15th date. She spent a week going through that room with no luck. It was months later, even after the Exile was over, that she was able to find only a portion of these tax papers elsewhere in the house.

While team members were cleaning—usually Barbara and I, occasionally accompanied by someone else—my dad sat outside chit-chatting pleasantly with people that passed by, as if nothing were going on. He truly seemed oblivious of the gravity of the matter. While I kept reminding my dad that I was trying to save their house, he didn't seem to have full recognition of the matter. When asked, he would respond that he knew what was going on—and cognitively, he could demonstrate this. But emotionally, he seemed calm to the point of it worrying both Barbara and me. Then, as if out of the blue, from time to time, he would begin to cry, asking why this was happening to us. He seemed largely oblivious of the situation that he had helped to create but then would sometimes come to his senses and see how elaborately desperate the situation was. One time, when James had already begun the outdoor cleanup and was in the midst of it, Officer Barry had come over to inspect the progress, as he was wont to do (much to my gratitude). Dad was walking around to the backyard and suddenly addressed the fenced in pen where the dog had been kept prior to his escape and death, proclaiming, "Hello, Sonny-boy!" I asked him pointedly—probing his cognition—if he realized that the dog was no longer there. He responded that he knew; and while it appeared as if he were just ironically expressing his grief and sorrow to the spirit of the deceased dog, there was also a sense of disconnect, delusion. Then, a while later, after Officer Barry left, my dad walked back toward the front yard on the pathway that had formerly been impassable due to brush coverage, but now was torn apart by James' work. And while he approached me and my mother, he broke down, crying that everything looked like it was falling apart. The odd thing was that this was the best that the yard had looked in years. No, it was not yet perfectly trimmed and manicured. But just because there were brush and branches cut away and lying on the ground didn't mean that things were horrible. If anything, this was the very beginning of progress. The absurdity of this struck both Mom and me. It was just that he had gotten used to the matted thickets and brush and to see things shaken up and taken out of his hands exposed the powerlessness he had felt all along—powerlessness over my mother's hoarding, but also powerlessness over his own depression and his inability to lead, act, or guide the family in the capacity of head of household. And it was moments like this that I believe the gravity of the situation truly dawned on him and broke through the thick layer of fog that clouded his perception of reality. It was this fog that I believe enabled my parents to live in that horror and squalor for so many years. It was only barely able to cover the dramatic and depressive stupor that would come over them whenever they would reenter the house after being away for any length of time. It was this fog that then would re-settle and allow them to remain oblivious of the absurdity of the whole affair—that two intelligent, compassionate adults should not, and need not, live like this.

And so Barbara and I continued to clean every day. We would usually arrive around 9 AM, work steadily, and then knock off around 4:00 to 4:30 PM. We had Marty and Charlie with us most days, at least for part of the time we were there. Barbara and I dredged out objects, made quick decisions: keep, discard, or give-away. One would hold the garbage bag open for the other while one pulled out items from the archaeological dig-site that was our house. We would change off frequently to avoid exhaustion. I would often slow down, since I was so emotionally close to the affair and had my own desires to save as much as possible. Barbara kept me honest and urged me to make quick decisions for the greater good of the whole house. Marty and Charlie would also be there with boxes and bags into which the save and sort items would go. Marty would carry garbage bags out of the house so that we would not trip over them when full. These went into the dumpster. Charlie, as much as his aging back would permit—as he was in his mid- to late 60s at the time—would drag bags out of the house as well. The "keep" boxes and bags would then go outside to be sent to a storage unit that we would rent soon after. We continued this way for days on end. Only once, did Barbara and I, for the sake of our mental health and avoiding exhaustion, take a day off.

We knew that in lieu of having the garage bays available to us (still loaded with junk at the time), we would have to rent a storage unit to temporarily put all the items that were being pulled out of the house to be saved. As time wore on, we began to take large portions of savables (much of which was preposterous but was done to keep my mother happy) over to storage. The ten foot by 20-foot storage unit should have been enough for any family, but it quickly began to fill up with more items that my mother simply could not let go of from the house, either having a vague level of sentimental value or being something that she intended to fix or make into a project. After a while, we simply could not argue with her, and we just let her have her way on these small things while we threw away large amounts of material and volume from inside the house. It gave her some sense of control while she was very clearly no longer in control—either of her addiction or of the matter of the house cleaning project. So Marty and I did our best to organize the mess that was being put into the storage unit. My mother insisted on using black plastic garbage bags to store things, even though we had invested in hundreds of cardboard boxes. She insisted that since she could not lift many of the heavy boxes and since she would not always have people there to help her move things—especially after I left to go back to L.A.—she wanted to put things in these bags so that she could drag them. The problem was that one cannot stack bags very well. And bags quickly become unwieldy—and slippery like wet fish being stacked at a fish market. That was a major obstacle as well. It often felt as if we were fighting a losing battle on account of having to placate my mother's senseless requests, even though she had already conceded that I was in charge and that her methods no longer worked.

More Cleaning

We had taken to securing the front door from the inside every night with the slide action deadbolt bar at the top of the door jamb, since the front doorknob had been damaged beyond repair, otherwise leaving only the key operated side-action dead bolt lock to keep out prowlers. My mom had arranged this method when they left the house on the first night of the Exile. On account of having the security bolt on the front door locked from the inside, I had to climb in through one of the rear sliding glass doors of the house. As I described earlier, there was a bay of three of these in the living room, looking out upon the backyard, which at this early state was still overgrown with brush. The bottom of the jamb was elevated about two feet above ground level and was flush with the floor inside the house. One of these would be left unlocked and could, with a bit of bushwhacking and muscle, be opened to gain daily entry to the house. This persisted until we could replace the front doorknob and lock.

On this particular day, Kim had come to visit the property, being there for moral support during one of Officer Barry's visits. While he was there, he also gave me some contacts of tree trimmers and workers that he knew, in case I wanted more options than just James. Later on, Kim and I took a little walk into the back yard to chat privately. He was very sympathetic to me and to the situation. I appreciated his reassuring presence there, like an adult among children. With him there, I felt a little less alone and a little less like a little boy. Kim explained a few things about my parents and their situation, most of which I already knew. But this was when he clued me in about my parents' lack of physical intimacy, which I had never before known. He wanted me to know that about them, believing that it might give me some insight into the situation. He informed me that it had been my dad's decision and not my mom's, as I have elsewhere noted. It wasn't until a year later that my mom shared this knowledge with me of her own accord, over the course of a conversation about my parents' relationship. Kim was also of the opinion that my parents would now need someone to watch over them, to take care of them. Just hearing this frightened me. I did not want to think of my parents as helpless, or invalids. I had known in my heart that there were real problems and that things were going in this direction. But I had hoped that my parents still had some semblance of self-reliance and self-sufficiency so that they would not need a caretaker. But Kim seemed to think otherwise. He asked about the possibility of my moving back to New York to take care of them. I told him that many times I had tried to get employment back on the East Coast, but that the job market in my field was dismal and I had been unable to find work here. We chatted a little while longer, but this notion stuck in my head for quite some time. As I began to write this book, just a few months after the incidents of the Exile, I acknowledged in my heart that my parents' self-sufficiency would not last forever. And I was well aware that as they grow older, I would be unable to see them or spend the time with them that we all desired if we remained on opposite coasts. I resolved to attempt to convince them to come and live with me in California, when I would be able to rent or buy a larger house that would accommodate them along with Melissa and me. Until that intention could become a reality, their condition would continue to worry me every day.

Just looking at the sheer volume that was in the house was thoroughly disorienting and disheartening. I could not conceive of how I was going to get that much volume out of the house in such a short period of time. If it were just a matter of dumping everything, it would not have been a problem. For many years, Dave Feuerstein used to joke about me getting a 20-yard dumpster, sending my parents away on vacation and just emptying out the house. It turned out, ultimately, that four such dumpsters of that size weren't even enough. But the problem indeed was that mixed in with the refuse were valuable things, items that not only my mother, but also I, would want to save. Useful clothing was mixed in with usable stereo equipment as well as less useful boxes of old magazines and piles of newspaper. The lack of organization was what made it such a daunting task. Like separating gold ore from the layers of rock that enshrouded it within a mine, extreme care and attention was needed to separate the family heirlooms and valuables from the junk. Barbara's method was to just begin, picking up a handful of papers and quickly sorting and making decisions about the disposition of the items therein—toss or keep, toss or keep. We had to work quickly. I had to force myself, even more so than Barbara, because I was emotionally involved in the situation and therefore to the house and its contents. Sometimes, if I faltered or hesitated, Barbara would look me squarely in the face and in her stern British voice, she would give a sort of low, monotonic, slow growl, "Get rid of it!" And I would comply, reminded of the logic of her admonishment. And in a short period of time, almost magically, a space would appear; bare floor would materialize where it had just been covered with piles of junk. The rate at which we proceeded was phenomenal and I owe a great debt of gratitude to Barbara.

And so, those who were with us helped as best they could. Charlie and Marty being the two most frequent participants, they carried bag after bag—black plastic garbage bags—to the dumpster, and alternately carried box after box of items to save to the UHaul van for transportation to the storage unit at the end of each workday. In fact, that was our usual schedule. When there was no more energy or daylight, Marty and I would take the van over to storage and empty it of all the salvageable items, leaving the vehicle empty to refill the next day. Sometimes, members of the crew would switch off, working in different rooms in various pairs. Other times, we would all work together. It would change as necessary. But it was amazing that we could blaze so quickly down one hallway and around a corner and then down the next hallway in a matter of several hours. It gave me hope.

The entire time we were cleaning, the smell was overwhelming. Many people were unable to even enter the house or stay inside for more than a short time. I, however, had to force myself to get accustomed to it. It belonged to my family and it was partly my fault for not stepping in sooner. I had to deal with it. As mentioned above, the smell seemed to be comprised partly of old, putrefying fruit and vegetable matter, along with mold and must. It is unmistakable to me when I smell it still, nested inside the pages of books that were rescued from the house, or among clothes that I wore there during that time. It permeated everything. And it persisted strongly for nearly a year after the cleanout, only subtly transforming into a less offensive and more unexceptional smell of must and mold commonly found in old houses. I would often wonder if we would ever be able to get the smell out. But it would stay until the majority of the old newspapers, magazines, and junk were thrown out.

My Room

As I have said before, Barbara was in many ways my guide and savior. And in this situation, I felt very much like a little boy who was asked to do a man's job. But with Barbara's decidedly can-do attitude and almost military bearing, we tore through room after room, discarding things that simply did not need to be there. She had in past years, however, shown herself to be a bit careless about throwing things out. In previous times during the previous decade when she helped my mother clean house, she had thrown things away that should not have been—family recipes, brand new kitchen items, and so forth. Her enthusiasm for cleanliness was sometimes unchecked by her circumspection and conscientiousness. But her generosity with her time and support were, to me, well worth the risk of losing a few things. And afterall, one might argue, what business did my mother have in keeping any items of value in such poorly organized condition, hidden under piles of junk? Truly, it was me who was the casualty in this. Although I will continue to blame myself for not being tougher on my mother, it was objectively through no fault of my own that this situation had occurred, that the mess had piled up. I had long ago cleaned my room and my living space to a satisfactory level before leaving to live in California. But as time wore on, having offered my clean bedroom to my parents as a safe haven, or a place of refuge from the junk, they both began to pile things into my room and make it as jam-packed as any other room in the house. In recent years, there were times in which my mother or father would stay in my room—sleep, eat, and relax there—to get away from the constant arguing and the marriage that they could not fix. But my room was the casualty. My few remaining belongings were at risk.

THE EXILE

I remember that every time I would come home for a visit, up to a few years prior to the Exile, my mother would store things in my room and blame it on my dad. My dad would store things in my room and blame it on my mom. Prior to arriving each time, my mother and father would make excuses and state that they just hadn't had enough time to finish cleaning the room and that they asked for my understanding and leniency, also requesting that I would not chide my mother for leaving my room in that condition. And it got worse every year. So, that the final time I visited for any length of time and stayed at the house—just prior to getting engaged to Melissa in 2004—I truly could not feel comfortable in my own room. There was clutter and newspapers and books and projects everywhere, covering every surface and chair. None of these were mine. Many of my own belongings were covered and unreachable. I only hoped that at some point, I would gain the courage to force my parents to clean their garbage out of my room so that I could retrieve things like my drum set or other things, such as my books.

But year by year, that room got worse. Having started out as a safe haven offered to my parents, they gradually filled it up. My father would take things from elsewhere in the house and would shift them to my room to make a few meager inches of space elsewhere. But he did not dare to throw anything out. My gravest resentment was that he did not handle these things in therapy. He had been in therapy for fifty years, with over half a dozen therapists. And over the last two decades while the mess and the hoarding grew, he had not put more than an ounce of effort into this problem. In my eyes, he—as the man, in the man's traditional roles—should have laid down the law to my mother and refused to support any more hoarding—not because she was a woman, but because she was dysfunctional and was putting our family in danger. But the problem was not that simple. He was part of the problem. His lack of involvement, his lack of attention to the affairs of the house, his unwillingness to fix or take responsibility for anything, all of these contributed to a situation in which he was not willing to play the man's role. Neither could he defend me from my mother's periodic rages over the years, nor could he defend our family from her hoarding. By her accounts, he was part of the reason that she did hoard—to defend herself against his coldness, or perhaps to fill the empty space in order to bring him closer, as I have elsewhere discussed.

Whatever the reasons, this time, my room was utterly wrecked. When Barbara and I finally broke into my room, having blazed a path through the hallway leading there, I was struck by the oddly familiar smell of fish- and plant-based oils. Almost immediately, I recognized the smell from vitamins I had taken over the years, things like Vitamin E, or EPA oils, or Oil of Evening Primrose. The smell was overpowering in the room, as if I were in a vitamin factory. As we gradually cleared out the junk that both my parents had placed there—newspapers, pen caps, paper clips, all manner of things that my mother could not bear to throw out and which my father did not know how to address—I finally came to the source of the overwhelming smell. On one of the formerly comfortable plush, blue velour-covered chairs that were in my room, some rodents had eaten into several bottles of vitamins that were incongruously stored there. I recollected that we had purchased these twin chairs around 1985 at a local tag sale, as a matched set, my mother planning to put them in my bedroom. When we went back on a later evening to pick up the chairs, we spoke briefly in the front hallway with the mother, a divorcee who was selling her home, and we saw her beautiful blonde daughter, Lisa, for the first time, who made a brief appearance as she was preparing to go out with friends. As I stood there prepared to move the chairs, I had become enrapt, her hair piled high with hairspray in typical '80s fashion, as she came skipping down the staircase before us, oblivious of my existence—or at least too shy to acknowledge otherwise—skinny fourteen year old nebbish that I was. And now, regaining my conscious presence in the room, I realized that the rats had literally gnawed through the plastic container and begun to eat the contents. I thought to myself, ironically, that they must be the healthiest rats in the neighborhood.

I found several bottles opened like this. And even after the room was fully emptied over the next day or so, the smell persisted. It had permeated the cushions and fabric of those chairs. It sank into the nearly 40-year-old, now matted, shag carpet as well. This smell would persist in that room, fading ever so slowly, over the next year.

When Barbara Simmons and I were cleaning my room, I found all sorts of items that my mother had deliberately saved. I knew this because they showed some semblance of organization. She had saved pen caps, strips of perforated paper removed from the connected paper sheets designated for the old dot-matrix style printers, decal backings, and all manner of things that otherwise would be thrown out by any sensible person. These items had absolutely no intrinsic value—though some of these were probably intended for use as bookmarks, my mother's favorite task to reassign to small slips of paper. They could not be redeemed, sold, kept for sentimental value, or anything of the sort. The only sense behind this was that one would want to dispose of them properly, as in recycling them. But why had they not been recycled? Huntington had a recycling program. In fact, even though figuring out and remembering which categories were picked up on which days was somewhat confusing at times, there were indeed multiple days for garbage pickup and at least one day every week when recycling was picked up.

But the bottom line was that I was enraged. Enraged that my room had been treated thusly. I left this room immaculate when I last lived there. And every year when I returned to visit, the room would get more and more cluttered with *their* things. In earlier times, when I was the learner and my mother the teacher, if I left my personal belongings in the pathways in my room, blocking movement, my mother would playfully proclaim that there were "rocks in the river", and we would chuckle as I would take her hint and move them elsewhere. Now, it was she who had placed the rocks in the river. My mother would blame my father for bringing things into the room to get them out of other rooms in the house, and I believed her. This was probably true. But in addition, she was saving things and leaving them in my room herself. The two of them were abusing me and my personal space. It was violating. I had no say in it. Except for now. But it gave me no real respite. I threw these things away with gusto, even anger. But I often felt the pangs of guilt that go with an animistic belief, to which I am unlucky enough to subscribe. While I was angry with my parents for doing this to themselves and to me, I could not help but feel that I was holding anger at the spirits or animistic essences of the items themselves, and these were innocent. This made me feel guilty. And I knew that on some level, this was the same kind of animistic thinking that helped facilitate my mother saving everything—the fear of harming what was being thrown out. I know that this might shock and befuddle some readers. But I hope to convey the marginal sensibility that is embodied by hoarders, to the point of convincing themselves of the correctness and necessity of their hoarding. And as a burgeoning and marginal hoarder myself, with many of the same traits and predilections, carefully held at bay, embattled on a daily basis, I can convey these sensibilities to the reader in a more or less coherent manner and hopefully help one understand.

Slogging Through the Mud

Barbara and I worked, as the two leaders of the operation. We operated like two Roman consuls—she with the greater sense of aggression toward the junk, deferring to me to make split-second decisions as to whether to save any particular item or not, and I with final say over everything that came across my path. Sometimes I suffered from despair and had to lean heavily upon her sense of drive and determination to save this house. Charlie Dressler, cousin Marty, and a few other people helped to carry boxes and bags as we filled them. Barbara and I worked generally 8 hour days. We couldn't take much more, as the work was both physically and emotionally exhausting.

Initially, my mother was not with us at the house, as I said earlier. We encouraged her to stay away at the beginning, and it worked well with her doctor's appointments and various appointments with the social workers and such. Barbara and I did not want her to be nearby to slow us down, constantly insisting upon saving this item or that. When she finally did come to the house, on the third day of cleaning, she was annoyed that she had been kept from the house and that things she would have saved were thrown out. In all fairness, it was a difficult decision whether to include her early on or not. In my eyes, she had had her way for long enough. It was her best thinking that got her here— to quote Twelve Step adages once again. When she did finally arrive to help, she would spend hours in one room—Barbara and I kept her as far as possible away from us so that she could not comment on everything we did and slow us down. We were concerned mainly with getting my parents back into the house and committed to preventing it from being condemned permanently. We felt that we would deal later with my mother's issues about feeling left out or not being consulted. The emergency at hand was more important. But when we occasionally observed my mother working in one particular room by herself, she was like a child attempting to clean, satisfying herself with her conception of the task. She would belabor every piece of paper, convincing herself that she was actually throwing away a lot of volume and was making progress. In all fairness, maybe she truly believed she was. But in actuality, that room never did get cleaned by the end of the Exile. It would be quite some time before it ever would be, as it was the least of our worries.

So Barbara and I worked tirelessly for nearly two weeks. By the time that my flight departure date came, about half of the house was cleaned. It was truly better. But I knew that Barbara would have trouble dealing with my mother's persistent attitude of hoarding which was absurdly contradictory with her outward insistence upon getting the house cleaned. She could not truly separate the reality from her fantasy that she could still save everything and yet have a clean house. To her, it was just a matter of reorganization. In reality, it was nothing less than a matter of clearing out a minimum of 75% of the volume of material in that house in order to pass inspection and be safe enough to live in.

While we worked, the weather fluctuated, but it mostly rained. The driveway, which had been covered by blue stone gravel nearly 40 years prior, had now transformed into a rich soil created by four decades of fallen and decomposed leaves and wood chips that had replaced the blue stone some time in the '90s. The huge 20-yard roll-off dumpsters that were strategically placed in the driveway began to sink into the mud as they filled up with matter from outside as well as inside the house. Marty had put down wooden planks, and even some discarded wooden doors that had been removed from the garage, having been saved from construction sites by my mother, years before. They were now being re-purposed to help keep us from sinking into the mud as we worked. But there was too much space to cover from the front door to the dumpster. There was always a spot where a foot sank into the mud. And as the rain fell upon the quiet little land of my birth and continued to drench us, my feet would get stuck in the mud with nearly every step I took. I made innumerable trips back and forth from the house to the dumpster with all manner of things that I discarded. And each time, my boot clad feet would sink deeper into the mud. And I began to feel as if this situation were never to end. I despaired, thinking that this was the worst moment of my entire life, not knowing if my parents would ever get back into the house, or rather if my mother's addition would prevent her from allowing us to get her back in.

While I was slogging through the mud, traipsing back and forth with things to be placed in the dumpster, I mused that things could not possibly get any worse than this. That my parents could be living in such filthy, unsanitary, inhuman conditions and that I was thus limited in my ability to help them. But I was not limited by my own abilities or by lack of funding; rather I was limited by my mother's own insistence upon things being saved, and in the most inefficient manner, so as to keep the progress to as slow a pace as possible. Often, I felt as if, when trying to help her, I were required to transfer a garbage pail full of water into a coffee mug, which was placed on the opposite side of a field, using nothing but an eye dropper to drain and relocate the garbage pail full of water—one dropper full at a time, one per trip. And the coffee mug had to be emptied each time before continuing, when it was full—and no provision for how or where to empty it had yet been determined. That is what it felt like; that there was always an obstacle placed in front of every task, and that the solution to that obstacle had not yet been reached or found. In this instance, I was grateful that there was a dumpster and not a coffee mug. But still, I knew that with each item I threw away, I was treading on thin ice, risking a major argument that could derail our progress. I ran the risk of my mother seeing it in the dumpster and fishing it out. Even while she knew that so much had to be thrown out in order to get back into the house, there was some kind of mental disconnect whereby she did not seem to comprehend that she could not just reorganize things and expect to have the placard removed. There was so much volume of mass to be discarded and nowhere to put it. I could not conceive of a solution. I was not sure that any of this could be accomplished. I felt as if there were no way out of this situation, like a bad dream that doesn't end, but just continues with no solution from one scene to the next.

But I just continued slogging garbage back and forth to the dumpster, my shoes sticking in the light brown mud in the same places each time. The discarded wooden planks lining different areas of the dirt driveway, now become mud from years of disrepair and lack of upkeep, provided only an illusion of respite from the mud. All I could do was keep putting one foot in front of the other. Later on, having read accounts of concentration camp survivors describing the forced labor at the various camps—like that of Primo Levi, whose book, *Survival in Auschwitz*, had a profound effect on me—I was reminded of my time slogging through the mud.[5] Obviously, I was a free man, with no war criminals holding guns to my head forcing me to work, and I do not mean to suggest that my experience was as traumatic or as potentially lethal as being in a concentration camp, but to me, if felt like my own private internment, an unjust incarceration.

This private Holocaust was of my own making; no one was forcing me at gunpoint to be there, as were Primo Levi or Elie Wiesel. It was only my love for my mother and father that was constraining and confining me, interning me there; as if I were held here, a prisoner to my family's sickness, forced to work

---

[5] Primo Levi, *Survival in Auschwitz* (New York: Simon & Schuster, 1995).

in untenable conditions, hardly able to stomach any food due to the stress and worry. For looming over our heads was still the threat of the seizure and demolition of our home if we did not comply. And that was enough. Worse yet was that we brought this upon ourselves. It was avoidable. I should have been a better son, a stronger person, and not let this happen to my family. But here I was, slogging through the mud, doing chores that should have been handled by someone else decades ago.

And similarly, I did not know if my parents would survive, possibly needing to be confined to a mental hospital due to their decline; or even if they did maintain their own residence, that perhaps they might die in a fire or succumb to a fall or contract a mold-borne illness. This was the start of my continuous worry about my parents and their safety. There was nothing for me but despair. I could see no end. And it was my mother's addiction that stood in the way of our salvation. We could deal with my father's lack of involvement. At the moment, he was not in our way. It was Mom's own unwillingness to allow things to pass through her hands without having to be saved for a project of some sort, that was the obstacle to my family's reinstallation in the house. I knew that even if I were to force my will upon my parents, proverbially tie them to a chair, and finish clearing out the house without their consent or their assistance, they would likely just begin to fill it up again anyway. I felt as if I could not win.

Still, I struggled onward, knowing that this was the only way anything could ever get done: just drive on. As the U.S. troops used to say during the War in Vietnam, as preserved in the Johnny Cash song by that name, "Drive on." Just drive on. "Don't mean nothing. Drive on."

Sell the House? Sticker-Shock

A few days into the task, Barbara and I had arrived early one morning at the house and Aimee and Charlie met us there to help with the day's work. The day was somewhat sunny, lightly overcast, a bit damp having rained in the last day, but not currently raining. The four of us stood at the mouth of the driveway, discussing what the day held, what tasks and what rooms needed to be handled. Charlie and Aimee brought up a difficult topic, making a suggestion that was honestly intended to make things easier on me. They had thought about this quite a bit and felt the need to get me to think about a potential solution. Aimee explained that maybe it was best for me to move my parents to California to be closer to me and to sell the house. The concern was that what if when the junk was cleared out, the mold and mildew was so unsuitable to human habitation that it would cost too much to repair the house. What if the mold was so deeply set into the walls or that the house was so structurally unsound that it would be useless to invest the money to repair it? Why not sell the house for the value of the property and at least get some kind of return on it so they could be closer to me? "After all," said Charlie in his somewhat monotone baritone voice, a slight accent from his upbringing in Israel, "it's too much house" for my parents.

Since the Dressler family were my friends, and Aimee in particular had been a very close friend for the better part of two decades and I trusted her judgment, I felt it necessary at least to listen and give any suggestion from them a fair assessment rather than just pooh-poohing it. However, my openness to the suggestion caused me so much pain that I nearly fell down in shock. It had never dawned on me to do something like this. Obviously, I wanted my parents closer to me. By that point, I had been living apart from them for 17 years, the very amount of time I had been in California; from the beginning of grad school, through my wedding, and until the present. We were very close, and the tendency of Long Island children to live in their parents' homes well past their majority had certainly not left me entirely. I wanted very much to have my parents near me, for them to help raise my future children, in order to keep an eye on my parents' well-being, and also just to enjoy the time I had left with them on this Earth. But I did not want to give up my ancestral home, the house that had been built by my grandfather—his final job—for his daughter and family, the house I grew up in. I did not want to leave that behind. And even more, I could not just leave the house as-is, with all the junk inside, along with the real treasures—family heirlooms, photos, my childhood toys and books, and so-forth. No one would buy the house as it was, even if it were their plan to demolish it and rebuild, having bought the property for its land value. It would still have to be cleared out. And in this market I questioned if we could even sell it at all. This was putting the horse before the cart. This decision was premature.

I had never even thought of this as a real possibility, and it hit me like a ton of bricks—just the notion that maybe this was the right thing to do and that if we were to invest tens of thousands of dollars in repair, we would be putting money into a pointless endeavor, wasting the money. I suddenly felt weak, very weak. I had to sit down for a moment, the gravity of the decision suddenly having hit me. This was the closest in my life I had ever come to fainting. Often, I would wonder how people (particularly women of old) would faint during stressful moments. It was alien to me, as I had never seen it in person, nor had it ever happened to me. But it was often portrayed in literature and film—women fainting in times of distress, throwing themselves fashionably and dramatically upon a fainting couch. Now, I felt as if it were close at hand. My entire world was collapsing around me. I was faced with a decision I did not want to make. I had not chosen to be here. I had not contributed to this problem, had I? Hardly. In fact, I had even tried many times to help my parents clean and discard. I had cleaned my own room before ceasing to live there permanently. Why had this happened to me? Why was I troubled so much on account of the sins of my parents?

I half listened to Aimee and Charlie, but I did not want to be there. I did not want to make that decision. Momentarily, I felt forced into the decision, as if it were a *fait accomplis*, the paperwork before me and pen in my hand, ready to sign. As if this were the only right decision, and I was an idiot not to see it. This, of course, was not coming from them, but from my own self-doubt. I knew that they were doing their best, attempting to give me what they considered good advice, out of love for me as their friend. But I could not handle it. It was too premature to even think about that decision. The house had to be cleaned out first anyway, didn't it?! Barbara, being more removed from the matter than I (since it was not her house, nor her fight), was able to think more clearly than I. She almost immediately responded resignedly to Aimee and Charlie that my mother would never agree to selling the house, so it was not even an option. Barbara did not give her opinion of whether or not it was a good idea, just that it was not an option. I was very grateful to her for saying this, for thinking this. She provided my way out. Barbara reminded Aimee and Charlie of the significance of the house to my mother, as I have written above, and she reiterated about my mother, matter-of-factly, "She'll never agree to it." I felt somewhat vindicated in my desire to see the house saved. I was overwhelmingly grateful that Barbara had said it, that the decision was taken from my hand. But I would never forget the feeling of shock that had come over me—it was slow to leave—feeling as if my decision to help clear the house was the wrong one, and that I was wasting my time. As if I were defeated.

When all was said and done, looking back, I am glad that we refrained from making this decision. It would have been gravely premature. I have always hoped to keep that house in my family for many generations to come, adding on extensions here and there, to accommodate my future children and grandchildren. But at that moment, it was too much for me to handle. I had never felt so close to utter shock and defeat.

In retrospect, the size of the house was not any part of the issue. In one sense, any amount of house would have been too much house for my mother. On the other hand, she was very adept at filling it. And so, rather than the size of the house, it was her sickness that was the issue. And my father's inability to help with repairs and upkeep was a side issue of this problem. A home in need of repairs, with a bit of extra grit and grime was not so much the problem. What was the problem was their inability to fend off the clutter, to be willing to throw things out and do so in an efficient manner. And that responsibility was on both of them.

The Flat Tire

On the only day that I took off from working at the house, my parents had a flat tire on their minivan. They noticed it while they were still in the parking lot outside of Barbara's place, where they were staying at the time. They called the Auto Club and a tow-truck driver from a local contractor came over to help.

Either they could not gain access to the spare tire on account of the mess, or it was no longer usable. Either way, the driver was going to tow them to the closest tire shop to get it serviced, but he was unable to get his lifts underneath the front of the car in order to raise it up, since there was so much junk inside the car from years of collecting and the nose of the car was now too low to the ground. After a bit of arguing with my parents, stating that they needed to empty out the car before he could help them, he left abruptly and unceremoniously. My parents called the Auto Club again and again, asking for a new driver. Again, the same guy came—described by my mother as being slow-witted and probably borderline mentally disabled, the poster child for the word "phlegmatic"—and refused to help them. During this time, my father was losing his composure and began to cry, realizing more and more that he was no longer in control of his situation since the onset of the Exile. Beforehand, his placating toleration of my mother's addiction was his way of coping, of staying sane, but it began to dawn on him that he no longer had any control at all, and his tears were an expression of utter despair. In this situation, my mother rightly took control, and she got on the phone with the driver's supervisor and the guy was convinced to stay. Somehow, he made it work and he towed them in. Several hours later, they had a new tire. However, this incident signaled another moment in which I would have to take back control to save my parents' lives. I was done pussy-footing around.

In the meantime, Barbara invited me over to have a pleasant meal with her and my parents—the only social occasion that we had during this whole two-week affair. I drove over to Barbara's, which was about twenty minutes away from our house. While Barbara cooked—and a tremendous hostess she was—I precipitously and proactively resolved to empty out my parents' car. I did it right there in the parking lot of Barbara's condo complex, in which the minivan was parked right next to the cement-walled, cordoned off area for her trash bins. I emptied out all the newspapers into the recycling bins of her community, saved what items were necessary and I discarded the rest in the garbage. Of course, my mother was exceedingly annoyed that I did this, claiming that she could do it herself, but that she didn't want to do it today due to her own exhaustion. I flatly said that I had a job to do and that she could go inside if she wanted. She attempted to work alongside of me for a while, but quickly gave up, saying that she could not keep up with my pace. Fine.

The things I found in there were preposterous. Not only did I find multiple duplicates of everything—umbrellas, flashlights and myriad other useful items which had gotten lost and then replaced multiple times over—but I also found all the lost mail (bills, checks, papers, etc.) that my father would retrieve from the mailbox and never bring into the house. I found bags of perishable food that had perished months before, creating stenches that had been covered over and hermetically sealed by layers of newspaper. I found, worst of all, rodent dung. It was likely small field mice that had gotten into the car, as no openings were large enough for rats (as there were in the house), but there was definite evidence for these small animals living in the car at one point or another. It disturbed me that my parents would allow themselves to live like this. I could not conceive that they in any way deserved to persist in this kind of existence. It maddened me. Despite my anger and exasperation, these were my parents and I loved them.

When all was done, the car looked amazing. Still gritty and full of dirt and dust, it was mostly free of debris and clutter—and most importantly, of rodents. All the remaining items being stored therein were neatly organized according to my tastes. On a cosmic and spiritual level, it seemed to me that the universe, in its inscrutable ways, gave them that flat tire—much to their dismay—to teach them the value of having that car cleaned out. While my mom had always insisted that there was no connection between what was going on inside the house and what was inside the car, always claiming that everything therein was either on its way to be taken to the recycling place or to the Salvation Army, the universe would not let my parents persist in this absurd belief. They needed to be made aware that the car would always be a handy excuse not to make progress inside the house. This vehicle, this conveyance, was just that—something that was needed in order to properly and responsibly take recyclables and donated items to their final destination. The universe was no longer willing to put up with their lying to themselves and to all their loved ones, especially me. The flat tire was the means of implementing that lesson.

While we were there, Barbara handed over to me a bunch of rat traps she had purchased to once and for all take care of the rat problem. They were mostly spring-loaded snap traps, but also some black plastic box traps with poison inside—like those one would see hidden in plain sight outside of restaurants if one knows what to look for. I would not allow any of the inhumane adhesive traps which catch hold of the animal and make no provision for its quick and compassionate death, just a weeklong fit of agony and starvation, leaving it to the discretion of the operator whether to provide any sort of euthanasia. I had an experience many years beforehand, somewhere in the late 1990s, in which I was unwittingly placed in a situation where I had to euthanize a group of mice which had become stuck to one of these traps. I took the most humane route and performed a mercy killing. The experience still haunts me to this day, and so I will neither use nor recommend adhesive traps. Barbara also bought some plug-in sonic devices designed to drive them out of the vicinity. All worked, at least inside the house. My only solace, while having to leave New York, was that my parents and the project were in Barbara's capable hands. She was committed to manage the rest of the cleanout in my absence, and if anyone could get it done, she would. But I knew that without me, and having to fight my mom for control, Barbara would tire quickly. My plan was still to return in October to help "mop up" the hopefully ending project and to give moral support to my parents from afar, reassuring them that I was going to return soon.

The next day, we went to a gas station that had a heavy-duty coin operated vacuum cleaner and we finished the job, leaving the interior of the minivan mostly free of dirt and dust. It was during this errand that I noticed most clearly how my dad had become artificially reliant upon his cane, and how his posture would temporarily bounce back if given certain instructions to stand up straight. When I momentarily took away his cane and directed him to stand upright and push his shoulders back, while helping me empty the remaining items out of the minivan so we could vacuum underneath them, he responded well momentarily, as if his back had miraculously healed and his rapidly scoliating spine had straightened. It seemed to me as if his issues were psycho-somatic, but he quickly returned to his hunched over state, as if his muscles had atrophied and become acclimated to their new, pathological position.

My Return to L.A. and The End of James

Working steadily on a daily basis, time ran short. I returned the rental van to the place where it came from and wrapped up any loose ends before leaving. Around August 29th, if memory serves me, I had to fly back to L.A. This was one of the hardest things for me to do, to leave my parents while they were still not back in their home. I felt like a cad, a neglectful son. Of course I was somewhat optimistic about some of the work that I had to do back in L.A. regarding some new professional opportunities for me, but it was still very hard to leave. When I was on the plane going back, I looked around for any senior citizen I could make conversation with, as if they could somehow be a momentary surrogate for my aged parents. I just wanted to have some sort of contact with elderly people—to try to show them respect and affection. But no matter how hard I tried or whom I spoke to, I knew that there was no substitute. My parents were not there and I could not affect them thusly. They were still in New York, struggling, and I was not there to help.

While I was still in NY, one of my other employers, a small startup university in L.A. that was Korean funded and was contracting with me to handle a lot of their incorporation and tax exemption paperwork, requested that I go to Korea for a publicity and fundraising event in late August. As soon as I had gotten back to California, I had to pack up and leave for Seoul, cancelling my first two class sessions at Loyola Marymount, the university where I most frequently taught, as an adjunct faculty member. Having to leave my parents' home in still unlivable condition, then cancel classes and rush to Korea was a real ordeal. It was far too much stress for me, but I did it anyway, as I knew that I needed the additional work to contribute to household expenses.

Back in L.A., while packing for my Korea trip, my mom called me on the phone to tell me of what had happened with James and why we urgently had to cut him loose as an employee. I couldn't conceive of why she would want him gone after all he had done for us. Evidently, my parents really liked him up to this point. The fact of the matter was that James had indeed been drinking on the job. But not lightly, as I had suspected and dismissed as a harmless personality quirk. My mom had seen all of the juice flavored malt beverage cans strewn about and had read their contents—which I had naively neglected to do. They were in fact alcoholic, and each day he was consuming numerous cans during work. But the proof was in the pudding. While he and Mike were contracted to work on the garage, there were several important items that my mother and I specifically asked him to locate and set aside when he came across them. Among them were some of my old toys and a child's replica fort my grandfather had built, as well as an artist's easel, and a dining room set of chairs and table. My mother had caught James and Mike, unfortunately too late, destroying the chairs, having already destroyed the easel. My mother was hurt. Some of these were family heirlooms, others were still-usable items. Their mistake was not due to a misunderstanding or simple carelessness, it was due to drunkenness. They simply could not be trusted. And interestingly, it appeared to me that James may have had some legal difficulties regarding transportation. As indicated earlier, he was always dropped off and picked up by a friend (whom he later identified as his girlfriend). His official story was that his truck was down for repairs. This may very well have been true, but a contractor without a vehicle is a contractor that can't make a living. Despite his skills in many trades, James seemed suspiciously desperate for work, and menial work at that. Notwithstanding the possibility that the downturn in the economy simply had hit his business hard, it was my opinion that his drinking had cost him his license, and possibly his vehicle. Things about James, as nice as he was, did not seem to add up.

So Mom concocted a story to release James from any further employment with us, without deliberately hurting his feelings or stirring up trouble. She stated that we simply did not have enough money to pay him for any further work, especially the interior of the house, and that we were just going to continue to use the help of family and close friends. This was not untrue, but if we had needed to employ James, I believe we could have borrowed a bit more funds from Barbara in a pinch. She desperately wanted to see this job done and my parents back home—and to get them out of her living room, as anyone would. But my mom felt that we couldn't afford to lose any more things, especially if it was due to drunken carelessness. The interesting thing was that she concocted a detailed explanation for James and wanted me to pretend that I was actually at the airport, ready to board my plane to Korea, when she arranged for me to speak with James on the phone to support her story. I got the sense that she even wanted me to speak loudly, as if trying to hear over the din of the jet engines powering up aboard the runways. Borne of her years of evading abuse, her tendency to concoct complicated, convoluted stories was sometimes helpful, but often ungainly and precarious for me to uphold. It was preposterously contrived and unnecessary, like a poorly written situation comedy where the plotlines are over the top, a melodrama full of clichéd turns of event. I refused to play that little game and just told James what needed to be said. I spoke to him briefly on the phone and he mentioned that he and Mike had had to kill two rats in the garage and had found the carcasses of several others. This, largely, was his explanation for the carelessness that characterized his conduct during the garage cleanout—that the conditions were so bad, that it was hard to salvage anything at all. Acknowledging this, I thanked him for his hard work so as not to rock the boat and cause him to be angry with us, and I said I looked forward to speaking with him again when I returned in October.

My mother paid him for the garage, which by this point was finished—though I never got the pleasure of seeing it fully emptied prior to its being filled up again with the things that were to come back from the offsite storage unit—and he left, none the wiser, really. In some ways, I was conflicted. I knew that the fewer people my mom had helping to complete this project, the longer it would take—partly due to the increased number of work hours each person would have to bear, but also due to her lack of supervision and tendency to obfuscate and sabotage—and that in some ways this most recent complication played perfectly into her unconscious plan to stall the cleanout and save more than should be saved. On some level, my mother thought that by simply organizing things, she could get Officer Barry to sign off on the house and get back in. She simply could not comprehend that it was decidedly a matter of sheer volume that had to be removed from the house. It could not be done any other way; Barry would not sign off on it. And this played right into her unconscious compulsion to keep hoarding. For me, though I really lamented the loss of the easel, since I used that growing up and it was made for us by Grandpa Arty, I knew that I had to view it as an acceptable loss, collateral damage. This job was dirty in the truest sense of the word, as well as figuratively. There would be casualties and things lost. That was the cross that I had to bear, having been a lax and remiss son who should have taken control of the situation much earlier. If I lost things that I loved, those were my punishments. If my mom lost things, it was the result of her sickness and the choices (be they conscious or unconscious, deliberate or not) that she made. She had made her bed and had to lie in it. James was a mere distraction. So the project continued with Barbara as my lieutenant and my eyes and ears, and with my mother plodding along at the quickest pace she could muster.

Barbara and Barbara

Barbara Simmons spoke with me by phone or by email fairly frequently after I had returned again to California from my Korea trip, which had lasted only a whirlwind two days, and was marginally fruitful. We spoke regularly about the progress, or the lack thereof. She was very honest in telling me that my mom was making very little progress and was in fact standing in the way of hers. I gave Barbara what encouragement I could. She and I agreed that on some level, the James affair played directly into my mom's unconscious wishes. Largely, it was just Barbara working in one room at a time, blazing through at a fiercely intense pace, and my mother plodding along, shifting from room to room, not really getting one thing done before going to something else. She would always claim that this was simply the way she worked, and that she was getting plenty done. But the proof was in the pudding. It *didn't* work. Simply put, not nearly enough was getting done. Barry wanted them to go more quickly, as did Barbara and everyone else.

It was around this time that my mom noticed that Barbara was getting exhausted. She seemed to be no longer thinking straight or making correct decisions about the dispositions of items. She was often throwing away useful and costly items simply because they were duplicates. Things that could have been given to Goodwill or some other charity had been thrown out, and my mother—ever the dumpster diver—noticed the items sitting on top of the dumpster prior to it being hauled away. There were new casserole dishes and oven pans, and so forth, which had cost a fair amount, and were now in the dumpster. My mom and I had a talk about it. I didn't like her solution. She wanted to ask Barbara to cease her work on the project. I didn't agree. But what could I do? So my mom, very truthfully, told Barbara that she was concerned about her and that she would like her to take a break and not come to help clean for a while. Barbara seemed to welcome this, even though she knew the consequences—that little would get done. But she was indeed tired out. So, my parents worked at the house during the day times and continued to stay at Barbara's place in the evenings, as there would be a hefty $15,000 fine if they were found to be residing (that is, sleeping) in the house while the placard was still in place.

The amount of cleaning that I projected would be done in the week or two after I left in August, had in fact been done. But most of that was done by Barbara. I had a fairly good grasp of what my mother and father were capable of and they did not surprise me or exceed those expectations. I knew that my mother did not have a grasp of the amount of volume that would have to be thrown out, nor did she understand that simply reorganizing things would not be able to correct the situation. It was simply a matter of getting things out of the house. She did not understand that, but insisted upon doing things her own way. While I was there, I had convinced her to some degree to trust me and my methods, since this was a dire circumstance, possibly losing the house. But when I left, Mom would no longer fully assent to my methods. She revolted against having Barbara as my "second", fully in charge of the cleanup in my absence. She vigorously and continuously asserted that she had lost enough control in her life, from her childhood when her mother persistently, deliberately, and maliciously threw out her belongings, to her adulthood in giving my father full control of everything in the house (a somewhat dubious perspective). It was a plodding pace that she had adopted, inspecting every piece of paper or notebook or magazine or newspaper in order to ensure that nothing of value would be thrown out. And of course, *everything* had value. It was a slippery slope.

But Barbara continued to check in with them daily while they were still staying at her place, and periodically reported back to me. She became justifiably pessimistic about the lack of progress at this point. She no longer had direct visual knowledge of the house, but she knew that the same dumpster—already full when she stopped working there—had not yet been hauled away, likely because my mother was pulling things back out of it. And I could not truly fault Barbara for her pessimism, since she put so much effort into helping us back on our feet and was now seeing the project stalled even more. And one particular day, during our phone conversation, she expressed real fear that the house would never get done. At the time, hearing this—and particularly in the way that she conveyed it—brought me down to the depths of despair. Being 3000 miles away, I could not take hearing that we were at risk of never getting my parents back into our home, and these kinds of emotional bombshells had a traumatic physical effect on me, putting a ball of ice in my stomach and guts that spread throughout my chest. So I had a talk with my mother about it, speaking candidly to her about how both Barbara and I were worried about the matter. She reassured me that things were moving along, even if it wasn't as quickly as I would like. I broke down and cried over the phone, exhausted and having reached my limit. My dad grew angry at Barbara for scaring me, but I somewhat gruffly reminded him that it wasn't she who had gotten us into this mess; it was my two parents and they alone. He was sufficiently chastised.

Throughout this time, Officer Barry had come regularly, every couple of days, to give my parents updates on what was still left to do. In his most recent visit, he was sufficiently pleased with the progress, which my mother conveyed to me in that same phone call, which heartened me. This, of course, may have been Barry's method of encouraging them, or it may have just been Mom's specious interpretation of his good nature. Regardless of whether or not it was true, I needed to hear some level of optimism in order to keep my sanity from 3,000 miles away. My family was an optimistic one, overall; that was our general tenor of life, our *modus operandi*. And at this time, I needed a dose of optimism, particularly from my mother, even though less than a month before, I had seen that her take on the situation was simply unrealistic and her assessment untrustworthy. Nevertheless, it helped me to hear it. But I think on some level, this particular experience galvanized my mother to work harder and stop messing around. Seeing what she had done to her only son, her beloved child, had a negative, but compelling effect on to her. From that point onwards, her attitude changed and I felt she had grown beyond some of her addiction, as witnessed by her subsequent willingness to finally bring in an outside agency to help.

Greener Cleaners

During this time, I began to research various agencies in the New York area that would either assist elders or provide cleanout services. I was desperate to try to get something for my parents, knowing that they were now working on their own. They had occasional help from Marty and Phil, but now Charlie's back problems had caught up with him and prevented him from doing any further work. I suspected that the plodding pace of the situation, with no conceivable end in sight may also have had a demoralizing effect on him. Pamela McManus, from APS, had handed the case over to her successor, Cathy Chung, who was very nice but equally ineffectual in helping to find some kind of assistance for my parents in this affair, be it volunteers from a local church, or a government run service to help elders like my parents. Letters came in the mail, more formalities than anything else, stating that the county was there to help and could offer support services, but none ever materialized—empty promises to make some government office look good or make them feel better about themselves. Officer Barry tried to arrange something through the town, but once again, documentation of my parents' finances was necessary in order for them to qualify; they were unable to locate said documentation with the condition the house was in. But Barry came one day and expressed his own concern that things were not proceeding quickly enough, stating that he only had a certain amount of time before his own supervisors were going to force his hand and require him to either fine my parents or bring in the town workers to take over the job for them. The latter case would have been particularly disastrous, resulting in a crew of workers coming in and emptying out everything that they saw fit just as had been done in the historic Collyer Brothers case—picking up anything that looked like trash and indiscriminately discarding it without concern for its value as a family heirloom or condition of being important notes or papers. And ultimately, my parents would have been charged for the cost of the services; more money that we could not afford to pay.

So, Barry lit a fire under them and when I came up with a viable company that could help finish the cleanup, my mom was finally open to the idea. It took a little bit of reassuring her, to the effect that they would not just come in like gangbusters and throw everything out before her eyes. But there was still a matter of funds being an object. If she paid them their rate to come and do their job, she had better not waste their time standing in their way and allowing them to leave without the job being done. Done means done, and Officer Barry was the final arbiter of that condition. If he wasn't satisfied, my parents would have to pay more to get the company to return. Money wasn't a plentiful resource in our family at that moment.

So, I introduced my mom to the idea of Greener Cleaners, whom I had spoken to by phone. The owner, Frank, was a nice Italian-American guy, and truly sympathetic to my case. He offered an excellent rate that was based on the truckload of debris carted away, and not by the hour, and he was also willing to be very careful about not indiscriminately throwing out my mother's prized belongings. So, when I had sufficiently convinced my mother of the efficacy of having this company come out and do an estimate, I made the appointment for them. Frank came out to my parents' house the next day. When the walk through was over, my mom called me to give me the news. The whole job would cost about $1400 and he estimated that it would require two of his big dump trucks, each of which were about the size of the 20 yard dumpsters that had until recently sat in our front yard. Mom approached Barbara about lending her the funds to cover the cost. Barbara, delighted to see the prospect of progress again, immediately was more than willing to lend her the funds. She thus came through for us again, even while not directly involved with the labor.

So, within a few days, Frank came with his trucks, my mother having done as much as possible to separate out the savables from the junk, and the family heirlooms from the dross. They came with several workers, each carrying large plastic bins the size of large garbage pails that they filled and then dragged out to the dump trucks. They worked quickly and my mom had to keep an eye on them in two locations, both the living room and the master bedroom. They filled bin after bin. Mom did what she could to get important paperwork out of the way and save what shouldn't be thrown out. It was very hard work and she struggled to keep up with them. Ultimately, they emptied the entire living room of all the unnecessary debris that was there, leaving only the furniture and shelved books. They also emptied about half the bedroom—including the mattress itself, which had been compromised by rodents—but were unable to fit the remaining debris into their trucks. They were packed. It still amazes me to think that two elderly adults, and not very large ones at that, could amass so many dumpsters full of junk in their home.

Officer Barry was there, perchance, and he kept an eye on the workers. Frank later told my mom that Barry was a bit rude to him, sort of sticking up for my parents' well-being and expressing great suspicion of Frank. Barry had said to Frank that my parents had become "sort of friends" to him and that he didn't want Frank taking advantage of them in any way. Barry scrutinized Frank's pricing and his methods, much to Frank's dismay and discomfiture. He said he wanted Frank to come back as soon as possible to finish more cleaning and to give my parents an even better price. My mom and Frank had a bit of a chuckle about this later on. This was quite an indication of Barry's kindness toward my parents, going above and beyond the call of duty.

After the job was done, two dumpster sized trucks filled in several hours—far ahead of their anticipated schedule—they left, suggesting that they could come back again soon to handle the remaining volume of trash that was left in the house, sizeable as it was. Barry suggested strongly to my mom that she have them back soon. In my post-event phone conversations with her, I also encouraged her to have Frank back, but she explained her reasons for not doing so.

Unfortunately, it appears that a small metal box containing older issue coins of collector value (maybe worth a couple of hundred dollars—at the most) was emptied and its contents taken. The box was left, the coins were not. Evidently, one of the workers saw an opportunity to make some change. My mom chose not to bring this to Frank's attention, for fear of hurting his feelings; it was probably out of his control. Nevertheless, it served as a handy excuse for her not to have them back. And moreover, Mom wasn't sure that she would be able to financially afford a second visit from them. This disturbed me, as they were so close to being done. There was still the rest of the bedroom, the Den and the Sewing room to do. Barry would not let the house pass inspection without these rooms being done. My only hope was that my mom could obtain more assistance through the town or volunteers that had been repeatedly promised by the County Adult Protective Services. But none of these ever materialized, much to my dismay and exasperation, so my mom had to continue to work on her own, with occasional help from Marty or random family friends who stopped by to help with a chore or two.

Daily Phone Calls

During these many months, I began to speak to my parents by phone daily. It seemed like they needed the emotional support, and that was all that I could give them while I was not physically present. I also needed to know for my own emotional state that they were alright. It seemed to help. Prior to the Exile, I usually spoke to them about once per week, as any good son should. When the Exile began, the frequency of phone calls increased accordingly, and some time in October or November, it became a daily ritual and continued even beyond the Exile.

I had promised my parents, as well as informing Officer Barry, that I would be flying back to NY sometime in October in order to help continue the cleanout. I thought this would help on many levels, not only letting Barry know that family was continuing to help, but also to give my parents some moral support, even if I could not do much in only the few days that my school gave me for mid-semester break. So, I made reservations, once again asking Dave Feuerstein for some help with free air miles from his amassed points. I was to fly to NY for five days, travel time inclusive, from October 14th to the 18th.

October Trip

When I returned to New York again in October, the cleaning had indeed slowed down. Barbara was still not coming to assist, my mom having asked her to take a break. My mother was essentially doing it all by herself, insisting that she was getting loads done. When I arrived, things simply had not progressed to the level that they should have, given the amount of time that had passed since I had left in August. We had of course had Greener Cleaners there to help on that one occasion. Both Frank, the owner, and Officer Barry felt that Greener Cleaners should have been brought back for a second visit. Things were still in such a shambles. A lot had been removed by them, and I was pleased to see that, but there was still so much left to go.

Shortly before I arrived, the discounted rate for the storage unit was about to expire, leaving my parents with the prospect of a huge monthly bill for storing a huge amount of material from the house. Since the garage bays had been cleared out by James, as his last job for us, they were now able to receive the items that needed to go back in from storage. On one of the last available nights (I kept telling my mom not to wait too long and leave it to the last minute) before the discount disappeared, Charlie Dressler helped my parents load up all the boxes into a van and bring them back to the house. As it began to rain, several boxes of books split open and spilled all over the ground, getting wet. As my parents cleared them away and got them to dry safety, my dad sustained a minor hernia which would not be noticed until several months later during a visit to the V.A. hospital. In the meantime, it just blended in with his usual difficulty walking.

Nevertheless, the storage unit was cleared, the deposit returned, and the garages were now beginning to get filled again. As mentioned earlier, my mom insisted upon using black plastic garbage bags for saved items, rather than boxes, since she felt she was unable to lift the boxes, but could drag the bags. As it was, the bags were now filling the garage and were unable to be properly stacked, leaving us with haphazard organization in the newly cleaned and re-filled garage bays. Marty took note of this and was a bit dismayed about it, indicating to him my mother's lack of grasp on reality; and yet she would insist that this was the best way to do things, refusing to see anyone else's logic. She knew best. It was this very disconnect in her thinking processes that was at the heart of the hoarding disorder. Realistic perspective was put aside in favor of an idealized perspective that simply did not exist.

So, for about two days during my October trip, I rearranged the garage. Having first begun to work alongside my parents inside the house, I realized that this was futile. They were not making enough progress and I was too tired to argue with them. I figured I'd leave that to Barry to convince them that they simply were not getting done quickly enough. But I realized that if I stayed away from them and remained in the garage, reorganizing everything as best I could, that would be the most efficient usage of my time for the few short days I was there. I totally rearranged the left bay of the two-car garage, stacking boxes perfectly and leaving excellent pathways to the electrical panel, as Barry had required of us. Phil was there to help for part of the two days. A sweet, simple man, he tended to stray a lot, going outside to smoke cigarettes and take cell phone calls from…I knew not whom. But he could be depended upon to lift heavy things when I needed him to, so I would periodically call him back inside and ask him for help with specific tasks. He didn't talk much, but always had a pleasant demeanor and the hint of a smile on his face. I occasionally grew exasperated by his frequent disappearance, but his presence was never a burden on me, as he stayed out of my way most of the time and was helpful when needed. He just required specific direction in order to be of assistance.

While I was working in the garage by myself, I would frequently hear rodents rustling about in the furnace room, currently out of reach from where I was working, obscured by walls of bags and boxes. Evidently, they were still around to some degree, having not been driven out by the traps Barbara and I had set months before. Enraged at the entire situation, I would frequently take a moment from my work to yell at the rodents to be gone, as if they represented or embodied my parents' sickness, and coming to represent my helplessness in this situation that my parents had created. As I worked, I would periodically take long wooden sticks of flexible wall molding that were stored nearby from some old construction project in the house, eight or so feet long—long enough to reach the furnace room from where I was working on the other side of the garage and over stacks of boxes—and I banged and slapped them against the door jamb to make enough noise to scare the rodents away for a while. The sticks wavered and flapped against the wood noisily, unruly and uncontrollable. I wanted the rodents gone, to leave my parents alone, just as I wanted the mess to merely go away. An exercise in ritualistic futility.

I worked and worked. My presence was a boon for my parents' morale, but I knew that my effectiveness had severe limitations. I could only hope that by maximizing the space in the garage, it would allow more things to exit the house in an efficient manner and, if salvageable, to go neatly into the garage. It rained a lot for the few days I was there. It was chilly, like the Octobers that I grew up with, and the relatively warm garage where I worked became a haven to me, protected from the outdoor chill as well as the insanity that my parents wallowed in—having created it—within the house. If it were not for this tragedy that continued looming over my head every moment that my parents were barred from living in our home, perhaps I would have thoroughly enjoyed the weather—delightfully dreary and gray, Autumn leaves having already fallen, crisp air that was breathed by several generations of my ancestors, settling in this new land, so far from the old country. I had always loved the cold, Autumn weather of Long Island, but I could hardly enjoy it at this time; so I savor it in my memory, in retrospect, as if it were a lost moment that was merely captured in a photograph that I can look back upon at will. This image, painted in dark earthtones captured in time-lapse, is seared into my mind. That while I was there, the Long Island Autumn continued to deliver alternating days of chilly October rain interspersed with humid, cold, gray days when the sun never shone from behind its impenetrable blanket of cloud cover, accentuating bare, angular branches of denuded trees, stark like scarecrows against the gray, ashen Autumnal sky.

Rona White

On Friday, October 16th, while I was chauffeuring my parents around to handle a few chores—the bank, the post office and so forth—a welcome respite from the house, there was a very disturbing incident.

After leaving the post office, in order to avoid crossing busy lanes of traffic to make a left, I turned right and then into the parking lot of a fast food restaurant diagonally across the street, so that I could turn around and then head South; I often used this method to ensure safety. While I was waiting for oncoming Southbound traffic to subside so I could make the right turn to go back towards home, a woman attempted to cross in front of our vehicle, out of my field of vision, and was nearly hit by me. It happened at approximately 12:40 PM and the weather was still rainy and cold. I was in the driver's seat of my parents' Dodge Minivan, with my father in the front passenger's seat and my mother behind him in the middle row of seats. I had already crossed the threshold of the sidewalk so as to better see traffic, beyond some natural obstacles. When I entered the threshold, I did not see any pedestrians in my vicinity from either direction. As I was attempting to make a right turn, I continually watched my left flank to see the oncoming Southbound traffic, which was very heavy and required my continual attention. I had already checked to my right and saw no one nearby, but there was a fairly dense hedgerow to my right which must have obscured my visibility from seeing the woman's approach until she was already right in front of me. My mother later commented that she was looking at the pedestrian as she crossed in front of us and the woman did not pay any attention to where she was walking, casting a downward gaze and having little care for her surroundings. So when a break in traffic finally opened, I began to make my turn and suddenly found myself in contact with a thin, 50-ish light-skinned African American woman in a dark blue overcoat. She evidently attempted to cross in front of me at the last minute—crossing right to left. When my car began to move, I turned my gaze straight forward and, luckily, in an instant I saw her. I stopped short. Simultaneously, she turned towards me, coming out of her somnambulant daydream, and she deliberately slapped my hood with her hands and began to shout at me, claiming that I had been looking right at her and that I had seen her and that I had intended to hit her. Obviously this was not true, and a preposterous accusation. I was looking in the other direction when she began to cross in front of me, and I had already viewed the right side of my vehicle a few moments prior and had seen no pedestrians in my view. And I most certainly did not attempt to hit her on purpose. What would be the purpose in that? What could I possibly have to gain by doing that?

Startled and concerned, I instinctively began to apologize profusely through the car window as she continued to shout at me, eyes ablaze with anger from other incidents in her life that obviously made her feel disempowered. Evidently, she did not know that we were both suffering from life's vicissitudes and that I was not the enemy. Still shouting, she demanded that I give her my license. Realizing the right thing to do, I backed the car up to a nearby parking space inside the parking lot. I exited the vehicle and continued to apologize and attempted to calm her down. I asked if there was any personal injury to her and she responded that there was none, but she stated that if I had continued to move forward, I would have taken her leg off. She gradually calmed down as I helped her realize that I had not in fact been looking at her, but was looking at oncoming traffic. She realized that my not seeing her was not intentional and she finally gained her composure down, accepting my apologies.

We went over to the car and she began to speak with my parents and me. I was trying to get some paper to copy down my information for her, as a formality of course, since no actual contact had been made by my vehicle, other than her punitively slapping the hood. While my mother got out a piece of paper to copy down my California driver's license and cell phone number for her, I instinctively or intuitively decided to confide in her and I told her, somewhat out of earshot of my mom and dad, that my parents were homeless and I was driving them around, trying to help them while I was in town. This was, perhaps the first time that I had used the word "homeless" to describe my parents in their predicament. One might argue that they were not, since they owned a home and had a place to stay on a friend's couch. But in reality, there are many different kinds of, and reasons for homelessness. They were essentially no different than other people who had left their homes and families due to mental illness or addiction, subsequently living on the streets or in flop houses. I had told her this as my mother got a pen and paper for me, and the woman could see clearly all the junk that was still in my parents' car—even after I had cleaned it out during my previous trip in August, the car now being filled with items for donation. The junk solidified the appearance of their transient state of residency and she softened a bit more. She said that she, too, had been homeless at one point. She told me her name: Rona White. She spoke with my parents for a few moments, showing them great concern and respect. She asked me to please make sure I take care of my parents, perhaps having struck a chord in her.

Toward the end of our conversation, I gave her a $20 bill as a sign of good faith for her troubles and suggested that she buy herself dinner on me. She accepted, and we concluded our conversation, which had now become cordial and friendly. She and I gave each other several hugs over the latter half of the conversation, having made peace. I once again checked to make sure that she was unhurt and she reassured me that the exchange of information was merely a formality. She then went about her business, mentioning that she had to catch a train.

I got back into the car, still very shaken. In some ways, I was angry at myself—primarily because I had been less than sufficiently careful about continually checking all directions. If it had not been for my guardian angels, perhaps I would have been responsible for injuring this woman. In addition to the guilt that I would have felt for harming her, I would also have had more legal troubles than I would care to handle, especially at this time while my parents were still in unsafe conditions. It would have made my life more difficult than I could imagine. But I was also angry at myself for letting her yell at me like that. It reminded me of all the times in my childhood that I had been unfairly yelled at by people, authority figures and other children alike—even my mother—having not done anything wrong but being in the wrong place at the wrong time. My training was to apologize as soon as someone began yelling, whether it was my fault or not; it was instinctual. If someone was angry, it must be my fault. And this situation reminded me of that. Rona was reacting to her own hardships and I was in her way. Unfortunately, I had my own hardships as well. Thankfully, in this case, my instinctually contrite attitude was able to help disarm and ameliorate the situation. Nevertheless, it hurt my pride and stuck in my craw that it always seemed to be my responsibility.

Later that afternoon, I called the insurance company to report the incident, as a precaution. I first spoke to Maria, who told me that the report she took would indeed be considered an "incident" rather than an accident. She informed me that since I was driving someone else's car, I would have to report it to their insurance company. I did so, calling my parents' insurance company and giving them the facts as well. Tamesha, the woman from the second company, said that if 30 days passed and Rona didn't contact them, it will be closed out and deemed "incident only." Of course, Rona only had my information and not the insurance company's number. But she would have called my cell phone if there were any subsequent need. I sincerely hoped that she never would contact me to follow up and obtain my insurance company's information, since I had enough on my plate and there was no actual injury as far as I could tell. I waited with baited breath over the next few months, but nothing materialized and no further contact followed. I continued to pray for Rona's health and well-being, believing that we were karmically linked.

But here was the heart of the matter. My parents were homeless in their very home. I repeat: homeless—in their very own home. That is what this incident reminded me. They did not have the legal right to reside there, but they owned the place and were required to fulfill certain obligations before being allowed to move back in and reside there. It was a real eye-opener for me. Perhaps on some cosmic level, Rona needed to see a young man taking care of his homeless, elderly parents for her own edification. Perhaps she needed a boost of optimism. I cannot know what the universe had planned in this situation. But I have always believed things happen for a reason and that God is very much in charge of our education as humans. And for myself, I was reminded of how fragile life is, that I could have seriously injured or killed this woman if I had not been more vigilant. That in an instant, even my own parents could be taken out of this world. That in an instant, a dog escaped, got killed, and brought the authorities to see their squalorous plight and ultimately save their lives from an accidental death in their own home.

Marty's Talk

The day before I left to return to Los Angeles again, Marty and I agreed to have a heart to heart talk with my parents, at the house. As the dull October sunlight shown through the windows of the unlit living room, he and I sat with them and did not mince words when we asserted that we still did not think that things were going quickly enough. We challenged my parents to do better, suggesting that perhaps they didn't actually want to get back into the house, citing their slow pace as either a stalling tactic or a level of obliviousness to the facts. They were receptive and did not argue with us. But while we demanded that they obtain more help and more assistance in getting the house done quicker, my mom still insisted that she wanted things done her own way. On some level, Marty and I were frustrated, but we also were able to make my mom understand that the way she had handled the garage and its totally disorganized re-filling was yet another symptom of her persistent suffering from hoarding. Marty and I forced my parents to agree to do a better job in organizing the garage and to continue to search for inexpensive options to obtain help in finishing the cleanout. Barry's promise of finding town funding or volunteers, as well as the County Adult Protective Service's promise of finding volunteers or funded help were still our best options. Unfortunately, these never panned out.

My parents and I continued to clean more that day, with my now helping them inside the house. And inside the house, my mother was slowly sifting through papers to see what could be saved and what thrown out, producing an occasional garbage bag of things to be put "somewhere else" and the even scarcer bag to be thrown out. My father at this time continued diligently vacuuming the same small patch of bare linoleum tile floor in the master bathroom, thinking it cleaned and put behind us, thinking that he was making tremendous progress, yet surrounded by piles of garbage that still needed to be sorted and disposed of—either deluded by his obliviousness, or his altered perception of cleanliness after having lived for so many years with my mother's hoarding. It was as if he, too, were blinded by the junk, and blinded *to* the junk, in the same manner that my mother was. He too had become inured to its presence. And when my mother or I dirtied up the area that he had just vacuumed in the process of removing more junk, he would get upset that we had dirtied the area. He had the same reaction at a later date when Officer Barry came during one of his many visits during the process, checking up on the progress, and gave his assessment of the bathroom. Barry stated that still more needed to be done to consider that room finished, noting that the shower curtain rods needed to be cleared of the clothing that was hanging from them, jam-packed and preventing the showers' use, and that there were still several piles of newspaper and books in the way of full accessibility to the bathroom. It upset my dad that although he felt he had done such a good job in vacuuming the bare patch in the center of the room, Barry still would not sign off on the bathroom. It was as if my father could not see that vacuuming a little dust and shreds of newspaper was NOT what this affair was all about. He was like a little child who simply could not understand the nature of the task at hand and was frustrated to tears about his helplessness to either ameliorate or comprehend the problem. Even Mom had spent unnecessary time and energy selecting and fluffing up decorative throw pillows to place attractively on the reclining chair that stood uncharacteristically in the front hallway to please Barry's eye the next time he inspected. And yet the twin showers in the mid-century modern master bathroom (oddly placed side by side, one with a tub and the other without, being a walk-in shower) were each filled by dozens of pieces of clothing hanging from the shower curtain rods, preventing them from being used without temporarily moving them to another location and then moving them back. The shower, on the left, was the most frequently used—and not so frequently at that—while the shower/tub combo on the right had not been used in decades, jam-packed with the same old clothing that my mom had placed there to be sorted through but was never addressed. Sitting on the toilet, I always found myself staring at the same dresses that cousin Patti had gifted, second hand, to my mom, with Mom's promise to either donate or restore them. One, a Dan Beauly, had sweat stains in the armpits and was unwearable by Patti, but it stayed there hanging from the shower curtain rod for nearly a decade, a symbol of Mom's habit of taking on a task that she would never accomplish.

But neither of my parents really could comprehend their complex relationship with hoarded junk. That was what was so frustrating. That they just could not understand. And I was the only one who was fully capable of understanding that some things in the house indeed needed to be saved (as few others did, except for my mom), being family heirlooms or items of sentimentality, while everything else needed to be discarded (as most others knew, except for my mom). I was surrounded on all sides by people who only saw their own conception, their own limited perspective, of the problem—those who simplistically wanted to throw away everything, and those who wanted incomprehensibly to save everything. But I was hindered by people with more say than I had, who could not understand the complex nature of the situation.

It struck me as surreal that my parents' house was so warm and comforting to be inside during the cold and rainy—almost wintry—weather, reminiscent of the many years I spent living there, considering that as comfortable as one might feel, it was illegal to reside there, to remain there overnight. The physical warmth—mixed with the slight improvements in cleanliness that we had made since August—was deceptively comfortable as I worked inside the house, in the still, musty air, heated by baseboards concealing copper piping filled with scalding hot water that zipped by throughout the house at lightning speed, propelled by an electric pump connected to the oil burning furnace, located in the oil burner room of the garage. It created a sense of normalcy that contradicted the fact that this was still not a home, but a work zone while no one was legally permitted to live there under the conditions of the placard. It would have been no worse if there had been a big crack down the center of the house due to an earthquake that hit it and rendered it a disaster area. Either way, we were surrounded by junk, some pieces less sanitary than others, and my parents had created this together. And I had stood by, mostly helpless, watching it happen.

And so my mother continued to go through loads of old clothing and newspapers from around the house and have only a small bag of garbage to show for it, as Dad continued to vacuum the same few open spots like a little child. Maddening as it was to me—the lack of perception on both their parts—I continued to do what I could while I was there, convincing myself to ignore the seeming futility of the whole affair. I had to drive away the very real fear that this project would never get done with the two of them as the only real regular participants in the labor.

Vito's Ladies

The last day that I was there in October, Vito—my grandpa's well-loved former protégé, who continued to be the family plumber—had arranged to bring over two ladies who were retired and did some cleaning work on the side and were willing to give an estimate for the remainder of the job. Vito arrived at the same time they did and came in to make the introductions. The two sixtyish—possibly Italian American—ladies were nice enough, but somewhat well-dressed for cleaning assistants in my opinion; it struck me as odd. They looked around, saw the place as it was and left after about fifteen to twenty minutes. The place actually looked much better than it had in August. It was no longer an outright death-trap, but was now just a very cluttered house. There was nothing absolutely pathological about it at this point, comparatively speaking. Frankly, I did not see anything that would dissuade these ladies from taking the job to help out with cleaning. They said that they would call my mom and get back to her with an estimate if they were able to take the job. But when all was said and done, a few days later, they politely declined to take the job. The just said that they were too busy at this point in time. The reality, I am sure, is that they could not handle that kind of cleanout. We were out of their league, one might say. They were used to light cleaning at rich ladies' houses. We were more of a janitorial job that required a "man's back" and not a "lady's touch". So, once again, we were on our own.

My mother continued to try to get volunteers through the County APS, which had promised workers from local churches, and could not come up with anyone—even with the promise of payment and not just the expectation of free labor. One would think that with the current economy and so many people out of work, that someone would need some work and would be willing to help out some elderly people who needed some cleaning and renovation. Either there was a conspiracy in which every APS and public safety officer tacitly told all of their potential contacts, "Steer clear of these folks, they're out of their minds" (I jest, of course), or the universe did not want my parents to saddle their problems on anyone else and were going to be forced to handle this themselves.

I left in the evening of a rainy Sunday, October 18th. I left from Islip MacArthur Airport, and I cried when I left, knowing that my parents were still not in their home. I continued to fear, every day, that something might happen to them—in line with Kim's warning that they should have someone to watch over them and take care of them—perhaps a car accident on the way back to wherever they were staying, or something equally tragic. It would be a long time before I could shake that feeling, well after the Exile was lifted.

Back to L.A.

So, with that short trip over, I went back to Los Angeles to resume teaching and working at my various other part-time jobs, including several consultancies and the filming of a DVD lecture series—I worked about 60-80 hours a week, doing the equivalent of about four half-time jobs at that point. I continued to call my parents on the phone each day, usually while they were at the house working. They often stayed there until late at night and then left to go back to Barbara's.

My dad, after a while, got very tired of going back to Barbara's late at night and many times tried to convince my mom that they should just stay over at their house. Either forgetting about the potential $15,000 fine for occupying the house while still placarded, or just being careless about it, his lackadaisical attitude concerned both of us. Mom insisted that she didn't want to get fined if the police happened to roll by and see a light on at night and found two elderly folks sacked out behind a door with a placard on it. Dad just insisted, blithely and somewhat obtusely, "But it's our house!" This happened day in and day out. Even Barbara suspected that they were sleeping in their car in the driveway at times that they did not come back to her place until very late. While this would have allowed them to remain close to their home and to work late, still remaining in compliance with the mandate not to reside in the home while placarded, it was dangerous for two older adults to be in an unheated car at night during the cold weather. I pressed the issue with my mom about whether she and dad were staying in the car. She denied it, conceding that sometimes they would stay very late, cleaning, and she did admit that on one or two occasions, they would find themselves napping in the car, but that they would always make it back to Barbara's. More obfuscation of facts, prevarication.

While they were at Barbara's, they began to grate on her nerves. And who wouldn't be annoyed by these very eccentric and somewhat self-centered old folks? Once again, I jest. But these two people, some of the most generous and compassionate people I know, can certainly wear on a person. Recognizing this, they decided to give Barbara a break and take some of the other relatives and family friends up on their offers to let my parents stay with them for a bit. So, off to cousin Vic and Cookie's they went. Cookie was the adopted sister (though genetically a distant cousin) of Vic and Marty Green (a different Marty than my first cousin, Marty Merget, who was the son of Mom's brother, Arty). Vic and Marty were Mergets on their mom's side, being my mom's first cousins. One will notice that there are lots of Martys and Barbaras in my family. Marty and his wife Marian were both now deceased; Vic was Marty's twin. Cookie had become the caretaker of Marty and Marian's developmentally disabled adult daughter, Amy, who had survived them when the two had passed away, one just after the other. Cookie moved into the house with Amy to be her caretaker, and Vic would often stay over, also having just lost his own wife to cancer, and later moved in as well. So, Vic and Cookie had offered to put my parents up for a while, knowing their situation and having been greatly helped by my mother when there were legal troubles involving the evil woman who had initially been appointed executrix of Marty and Marian's estate, and therefore Amy's legal guardian. This nefarious woman, Lisa, had begun to plunder Amy's inheritance and therefore her maintenance, lining her own pockets with impunity. She and her henchman, Kevin—an erstwhile family friend, prior to revealing his true colors—began to harass Cookie, spy on her, deny her the funds she required for Amy's maintenance, and be all around bad people. When the family went to court over the matter, my mother had given hundreds of hours' worth of time and attention to help them through legal preparations and paperwork. Vic and Cookie knew what kind of generous person my mom was, and they saw fit to help her out in return.

So my parents spent about a month and a half on their couch, subsequent to moving out of Barbara's place, now serenaded by several dozen parakeets, canaries, chickadees, and so forth, and slobbered on by a huge Saint Bernard named Brandy, as well as a smaller toy poodle. It was delightfully noisy. But they didn't spend much time there anyway. They were at Green Gardens most of the time, still cleaning up at a plodding pace.

At this time, Officer Barry knew that he had higher-ups in the department watching and he wanted my parents to finish up this project soon. He began to give them slightly harsher deadlines. Nevertheless, they were still alone in their labors. At times he was pleased with the progress he saw since his last visit; at other times, it was insufficient. When insufficient progress had been done, my mother would experience a sense of loss or disappointment. There were a number of times that I would phone after an inspection had taken place, and I could readily hear the dejection in both my parents' voices. I wished that I could have been there. In fact, I knew exactly what needed to be done. But as long as my mother was "in-charge" of this project, things would not get done in a timely, efficient, and expeditious manner. In many ways, her highly specific questions to Barry about the details of his cleanliness criteria—few of which would be satisfied anyway—served as a stalling tactic, masking her unconscious resistance to change, like doing jumping jacks to simulate work when only real progress is needed. So I decided that I needed to get my mom into a program that would help her through this stage of stagnation, a detox of sorts. When I had broached the issue with her in the past, of seeking some kind of specific help regarding her compulsive hoarding addiction, she stated that she was fine going to Kim to help her, even though he did not specialize in hoarding disorders. Or that if she needed some specific work, she could work with Marty—who although he was a competent therapist, was not versed in hoarding disorders and the newest techniques of behavior modification either. He was also too close to the situation to be impartial. Old habits die hard.

Professional Cleaners

When I was back in California, I continued researching various agencies and services, both governmental and private, that advertised assistance for estate cleanout, hoarding, even forensic cleanup (for the uninitiated, that means post crime-scene cleanup!). They were all very kind when I spoke to them, but they were all far too expensive. I thought to myself, how could a hoarder—often not working or financially insolvent due to mental illness—afford these kinds of services? Are these people crazy?! Perhaps they only catered to the rich and famous hoarders who were eccentric millionaires. I know that actress Delta Burke, whom I adore and admire, went public with her compulsive hoarding addiction a few years before our Exile. I was so pleased to see that someone as wonderful and beautiful as she had been so humble and honest as to proclaim her proclivities to the world and show us her faults and foibles. I thought that perhaps she might become the Betty Ford or Tipper Gore to the hoarding set! And perhaps these businesses were charging rates in anticipation of a mass revelation of celebrity hoarders requiring their services.

Nevertheless, I began to research various mental health clinics that specialized in compulsive disorders such as hoarding. A few psychiatrists that I spoke to by phone were very focused on prescribing drugs. I knew my mother would not like that, and neither did I. A few other individual practitioners, psychologists, social workers, and a few psychiatrists, focused on hoarding and were more open to talk therapy and only resorting to drugs when necessary. However, the one that I was able to reach that was the most affordable as well as geographically closest to my parents, was highly pessimistic. He said, specifically, that in most cases when the family member comes to him, rather than the hoarder him or herself, there is usually no success. I found that to be too pessimistic for me to deal with. When I spoke with my mother about it later on, and quoted that to her, she also did not feel comfortable going to someone like that.

I did find one clinic, however, that was highly thought of, took Medicare, and was not too far away. They focused on behavior modification methods, talk therapy, nutrition and occasionally pharmaceuticals. They also, as part of their intensive programs, would send out someone on a home visit to help with the progress. I thought that I couldn't find a better fit. I spoke with my mother about it. Her first reaction was "No, I'm not going to bring people into my house and pay them to tell me that I have to throw everything out!" Of course, that was her fear, not the reality. It would be nothing like that. The key to these types of therapies, as I had come to see, is the process of helping the patient make their own decisions and not taking control from them; the latter would be a surefire path to failure. But she had her preconceived notions. As time wore on, she began to soften to the idea, but still wanted to put it off until the future. Her ironic statement was, "I don't have time to go to these kinds of intensive programs; I'm trying to get the house cleaned up so we can move back in." The utter irony of it, which she clearly did not comprehend, was that with her current addiction and state of mind, she was less likely to finish the job than if she took a few weeks to do the intensive program, having counselors come out to the house to guide her through the process and even participate in the labor. In that case, she might actually finish quicker. But she didn't see it. So I told her that I would give her some time to think about it but that I would begin to bug her about it if she did not make better progress. It was about this time that I began to tell her very candidly that I thought she was "stubborn and willful". I asserted that her adult son had gained some wisdom in his life and that she should listen to him and stop dismissing his good advice. This initially struck a nerve with her and hurt her feelings just a little bit. But as time wore on, she realized the sense of what I was saying, and we came to chuckle about it. Eventually, this became a token, a perennial jest between us, that she and I would laugh about her being "stubborn and willful."

Toys and Dolls

Early on in my mother's therapy with David Grand, she began to make a connection between her hoarding and my grandmother's compulsive throwing away of my mom's belongings, an indication of loss of autonomy. Grandma Jeanne had a tendency to throw things away—anything. She was known for throwing away things "accidentally". Grandpa Artie had saved up money, during tough times even, and bought her a nice set of silverware—real silver silverware. Piece by piece, the set dwindled, inexplicably. Occasionally, my mother would find items in the garbage, having been accidentally thrown there in a fit of plate clearing—some of these silverware pieces were among them. A few were saved. Before too long, the set was no longer complete, in fact it was decimated. These nice things given to her by her loving husband, she felt she did not deserve. Unfortunately, it affected everyone else. And the sickness did not stop there. All her life as a mother, she would go through cleaning fits, insisting that my mother choose certain items to give away, items she cherished, sometimes giving her the choice, a Sophie's choice—like a political prisoner who has to choose between saving one of her two children—while at other times she would simply wait until my mother was not at home and would clear out what she did not want her to have. When young Barbara would return home after school—or from work, later in her early adulthood—she would find things out in the garbage, at the curb, sometimes soiled and irretrievable, other times vaguely salvageable. Sometimes, she would only find vestiges of the items after the garbage men had already picked up the trash. And on occasion, Mom would simply notice her favorite things missing and would ask Grandma Jeanne what happened to them. The answer was terse and simple: "I was cleaning. And they had to go."

I will not deny the possibility that my mother was always a bit of a "pack rat", saving a variety of things. She had always been a saver, even in my early childhood. But I remember her being relatively organized. By contrast, my grandmother's illness, however, caused her to see any bit of volume of clutter as deplorable; this caused her to purge things that were not hers, leaving those around her to be vulnerable to her fits of cleaning. Self determination and autonomy were lost in the process. It is no wonder that my mother began to hold onto things later in life. She lost so many wonderful and cherished things earlier on. Some of these had, or would have, monetary value if sold. Grandma Jeanne did not, or would not, see that. She only saw the need to purge for whatever reason.

A few brief illustrations may be worthwhile. In her childhood, Mom lost an old-fashioned player piano that had been given to her by a family friend. It was beautiful and it worked well; the friend just no longer had a use for it. It could play tunes autonomously, by design, but also could be played manually by the pianist, and had inspired in her a desire to learn how to play. She begged for piano lessons, but Grandma resolutely said, "No, they would cost too much." And since the piano took up too much space, Grandma forced my mother to give it to relatives, whose boys proceeded to destroy it, literally. The sight and sound of its gradual destruction by rambunctious cousins stuck with her for the rest of her life. As another example, a big, beautiful handmade doll house that Great Grandpa Andy (Grandpa Arty's father and my mother's favorite grandfather) had fashioned especially for her as a place to store all her most prized dolls, was requisitioned to be given away to the neighbors across the way, since they had some little girls whom Grandma Jeanne thought could use the doll house. Ultimately, it wound up as a doghouse and was relocated outdoors, in the back yard, susceptible to the wind and rain and all the elements so that eventually, it fell apart. Mom cried at the ignoble and highly avoidable demise of that precious gift.

All of her "Collectors' Comics" were given away, a franchise of classic comic books that are now priceless. All my mother's dolls were gradually culled and picked off, like a wolf picks through a pack of caribou. Some were ordered to be given away. Others just disappeared. Beautiful porcelain dolls, many with tremendous sentimental value, some that today would be worth thousands of dollars as collector's items, were all singled out. A three-in-one Trudy doll from the 1940s, various other dolls found today on eBay, connected to very sizeable prices—all such dolls thrown away. Even in my mom's adulthood, Grandma Jeanne would find the last remainders of these when she would visit my house to babysit for me. She would begin to "clean", even though forbidden to do so, and with a sheepish smile she would confess when pressed about where certain items had gone, that she had thrown them out. "They were old…they were dirty…they were just clutter…," or even, "I don't know what happened to that." And all because Grandma Jeanne had some inexplicable compulsion to "clean", and perhaps some hidden desire to see the trappings of childhood disappear. One can only guess why the sight of dolls and happy childhood things disturbed her so much. We can only speculate what she had suffered as a child, that she was now denying or hiding from, to make her behave so irrationally. It's no wonder that my mom was so intent upon saving things. And no wonder that she had such fierce emotions about her belongings being touched or their disposition decided without her input or knowledge.

Mom always had a feeling of animism, even in childhood, that made her feel as if the toys themselves had souls, could feel and think and love. Many of us have a little bit of this sentiment. It is a vestige of childhood dreams and imagination. Anyone who has seen the popular series of movies, *Toy Story*, can understand and participate in this. Humorously, I have heard people say that *Toy Story 3*, which deals with the idea of children outgrowing their toys, is the movie that can make grown men cry. It's true, as I can attest firsthand. But Mom would tell the story of Grandma Jeanne throwing out her last doll, sometime in my own childhood, when Grandma came to visit, cleaned, and left. It was as if it were one last show of dominance over her daughter, to seek out and destroy her last vestige of childhood joy and innocence. To find the very doll—a plastic faced, plush bodied toddler styled doll that my mom had actually named Barbara after herself, since it somewhat resembled her—and trash it. That was the ultimate offense that she could sustain, as if it were deliberately directed at her, an attack on her very person. And it hurt—deeply. Mom described herself imagining the doll lying in a garbage heap somewhere, crying for her, wailing, asking why she had been abandoned. Indeed, this animistic sentiment, imagining a soul and a consciousness in any artifact of our childhood, is very natural. But I believe that it was even more ingrained in my mother—whose childhood had been so defiled and prematurely lost, sold, given away—than most other people. This doll, and all others like it, represented her—her own childhood self. Given to the wolves, the monsters that were pulled together by her grandfather, Lawlie, and then ravished by them, torn apart. That was the child she was crying for. That was the child that was lying in a garbage heap, crying, wailing, pleading for salvation.

And some of this seems to have found its way into my own childhood and my own consciousness and sensibilities as well. As far back as I can remember, I imagined my toys with consciousness of their own, as if they were entities, and I often mused that they came alive at night and moved around without my knowing. And to this day, I even invest them with some sense of spiritual aliveness, and I feel somewhat guilty for having been rough with them at times during childhood play. For this, I even feel the need to seek their forgiveness. Whether this is evidence of my own delusion, or simply a normal emotion, only the wisdom of the ages can tell. Yet for nations that have for thousands of years invested hypostatic personality in flags, statues, ships, monuments, and even in the nations themselves, I do not think that this is so odd or abnormal.

But I do have recollections of the inexplicable compassion and sorrow that I have felt for toys I have witnessed being abandoned or destroyed throughout my life. I remember in my childhood seeing a little doll of Sesame Street's Big Bird, sitting against a tree in a public park in Philadelphia, wondering where its owner was, sorrowful at the likely outcome. I remember even as a young man, working as a Summer custodian in my father's school district while on Summer break from college, having an inexplicable feeling of sorrow and compassion for toys I saw in a classroom that I was cleaning. A few hand puppets or dolls of a little king and queen I remember, thinking that I prayed they would be loved and taken care of by children and never thrown away. Of course I have no idea whether this prayer was answered. To think of the likely outcome still saddens me inexplicably. And this sentiment has carried into my later adulthood as well. I remember a few years ago begging a friend of mine, who was clearing out his old childhood toy collection, to spare his toys from being subjected to the target practice that he had planned for them at a local outdoor desert shooting area. I reminded him that not only could they still serve a needy child, but that they also had served him well in his childhood and were more than just inanimate objects; they were the repository and the seat of the loving energies that he had invested in them as an innocent child. They were, therefore, sacred, representing the very innocence that we cherish in children and have a responsibility to safeguard. I'm sure my words were lost on him. It may be that I am deluded to talk about vibrational energies and such "nonsense", but do not forget that only a century ago, talk of radio waves and nuclear energy would have been met with rigorous ridicule about such nonsensical claptrap. Yet, today, we daily listen to the radio to hear news reports about debates in our Congress over the safety of nuclear energy—claptrap, indeed!

But the bottom line is that, even beside the natural and inherent animistic belief that may be engendered in me, either as a result of vestigial childhood imagination, or from a higher consciousness about the forces that unite our universe and are only just being discovered by experimental sciences like Quantum Physics—even besides all these—I have somehow internalized the struggles that I am very aware both my parents went through as children, and I feel somehow oddly responsible to save them. Every doll, every lost toy, every stuffed animal, somehow is representative of the little Richard and the little Barbara that are nestled deep in the past and the current consciousness of the people who would one day grow up and create me. Somewhere in my unconscious, I knew what they had suffered. Somehow, subliminally, genetically, I could feel and understand it. And the natural feelings of male nurturing, the defending father consciousness that is deep within the unconscious of every normal male, and is so very ingrained within me, personally, is exactly what seeks to save my parents, across time, from their tormentors. And yet in reality, I cannot accomplish this.

This is why, when they first were removed from their home and experienced the Exile, it struck within me a tremendous feeling of paternal defense, as the Father archetype is responsible to defend the tribe and the children from the proverbial saber toothed tiger entering the cave. I knew that it was up to me to drop everything and try to save our home, to save my parents. But I could not be there more than a little while, as I have described in this book. And while I was separated from them by the distance of a continent, I prayed a lot. I even found myself engaging in very superstitious behavior, much like the ancient peoples who thought that by making a sacrifice or a votive offering to a deity, that they might secure the safe return of their relatives traveling on the treacherous roads and seas.

One of the things I remember from the period of the Exile, while I was still in California, working my job as a professor while my parents toiled (or gave pretense of toiling) in their squalorous home, was the following. Many years before, as a teen perhaps, I had read a small cartoon story in the children's magazine, *Highlights for Children*. The story, told mostly in pictures, depicted a little lamb (anthropomorphized and dressed in human children's clothes, replete with jacket and cap) that had become separated from its mother in a busy city and had gotten lost. From what I remember, vaguely, it asked a policeman for help and was ultimately reunited with its mother, happily. But this notion stuck in my mind for decades. That idea of this poor little lamb, so very anthropomorphic, so helpless—with all of the obvious metaphorical connections and Biblical motifs of "a lamb led to slaughter", Jesus as the "lamb of God", dying vicariously for our sins—stirred such compassion in me. I never knew why. The idea of losing one's mother, or either of one's parents, was abhorrent to me. And so when my parents were endangered—by their own doing, one may argue—it all became very clear to me. They, as children, were representative of the lamb archetype. They were that lamb. They were the helpless little innocents, lost and unloved. It was my responsibility to save them, I felt. And when I would pray, or meditate, and sometimes I would do so while hiking in the mountains near my L.A. home, during this time of the Exile—unable to help, being so far away—I would endlessly repeat to myself the mantra, "Save the Lamb." It became an obsession to deal with the helplessness I felt. Every step that I took, every moment of every hike, every mile I would push myself, devoting one more bit of energy to my meditative novena, my prayer for my parents' wellness, for the helpless little "children" that they were, both now as adults and during their physical childhood, every bit was devoted to the powerful spell that I was weaving to save them from impending doom, from doom that across time had already devoured them—in the 1930s, in the 1940s, and even, in their hearts, until today. For them, I would be willing to suffer, to exchange places with them, to hurt for them, to travel for them, as any good son would, as any Father figure would. My mantra became a compulsion. Helpless, three thousand miles away, I took to doing whatever I could imagine to save these lambs in my life, chanting over and over again in my practical helplessness, "Save the lamb". I was saving the little lamb figure in the cartoon in that magazine; I was saving the lamb that was embodied in my parents. I was saving every lamb that was suffering in the heart of every abused and abandoned child. That was my intent.

The Final Months

In November and December, things were getting colder in New York. Barbara was concerned that with the drop in temperature it was going to signal the inability of my parents to complete the project. They no longer had a dumpster at the house. They were manually depositing black bags at the edge of the driveway when full. Barry put increased pressure on them. He demanded that they get a new bed, since the old one had been taken by Greener Cleaners; he wanted them to be able to sleep on their own bed, like two human beings. He did not know, of course, the problems that might still stand in the way of that, but at least the sentiment was correct. You can lead a horse to water, as they say, but you cannot make him drink.

So, my parents bought a new mattress for the master bedroom. They bought a new dishwasher, which Vito, the plumber, installed for them. They even purchased a new refrigerator, which ironically was an inch too tall for the cabinetry that had been built around the original fridge. So, another family friend came one day and jig-sawed out a little bit of extra clearance for the top.

Melissa and I began to plan a trip to visit my parents for the Winter holidays. This was the time limit, as far as I was concerned. If my parents were not back in their house by Christmas, I was going to have to take over the matter again, and then spend my holiday hiring another cleanout crew—perhaps going back to Greener Cleaners, whether my mom liked it or not—to finish the job. I knew that my mother's addiction was the main thing preventing them from being back in that house. With the rapid pace of progress (a fever pitch to be accurate) that Barbara and I had sustained during the first ten days of the cleanout, the house should have been entirely done by October. No question about it. That was, in fact, the original intention behind my trip in October. It was going to be a sort of "mopping up" operation, in which I could help with rug cleaning and buying new furniture to replace what had to be discarded due to rodent infestation. But it didn't work out that way. And when December came and Melissa and I made our travel arrangements and bought tickets, I made my intentions known to my mother in no uncertain terms. I said, "I don't intend to come to New York and not stay at my own house. If that house is not done, I will come and take over and finish the job by hiring a cleanout crew. You will not like the results if I cannot stay at my own house." My meaning was clear and Mom understood.

Of course, Melissa and I knew ahead of time that even if my parents were allowed back into the house by that time, we would not be able to stay there ourselves, on account of Melissa's allergies to dust and mildew. I knew that the smell of the mildew would not be totally gone by the time we arrived, but I was sure that by putting that kind of threat upon my parents, they would work that much harder to finish. Having them back in the house was my only desire. Melissa and I had no problem staying at my grandmother's old apartment, part of Aunt Bobbie's house, about a twenty minute drive away. So we just planned for that scenario.

In the meantime, my parents did work harder. Barry gave them strict guidance and would check in on them weekly or more. At times, Mom would put up obstacles, asking about exactly how Barry wanted things done, as if he were there as an interior designer. And he made it known, "I'm not here to redecorate. It doesn't matter how the drapes are. I just want to make sure that there is sufficient egress and pathways in case, God forbid, we need to come in here with a gurney." My mother's inquiry, however, was a sort of stalling tactic, in my opinion. On a few occasions, she was disappointed that they had not already passed inspection. In fact, Barry made it very clear to them what still needed to be done: the kitchen counters needed to be clear, the Den needed to be clean, as did the bathroom and the Sewing Room. And his definition of clean did not include any details about style or decoration, but focused exclusively on the pathways through the rooms and proper egress from the entry of the room to any windows or exterior doors. In the end, he was very lenient on them. He realized that they were working alone in this. When all was said and done, the Den and the Sewing Room were left largely untouched, still full of things. He must have realized that they generally did not use these rooms, so it was not as much of a safety risk. And getting them back into the house by Christmas, with all the major rooms accessible with proper egress, was more important than having every single room clean. To some degree, I was disappointed that there wasn't more of a threat over their heads to force them to get all those rooms fully cleared out and livable when they had the chance. And this was our chance to make the best of a terrible situation and get the house truly cleaned. But the advantage of this, however, was that they were back in their home, safe and sound by the time Melissa and I arrived just after

Christmas (our work schedules and flight prices would not allow us to arrive any earlier). But the disadvantage was that at some point in the future, I would have to come back and continue the job to finish cleaning those rooms. And in addition, the mold, mildew and other pathogens would still remain in those rooms.

The best news we received was that on December 23rd, 2009, Officer Barry gave my parents the go-ahead to remove the large yellow cardboard placard from their front door and to resume their legal occupation of their home. Even though those two rooms—the Den and the Sewing Room—were still untouched, the rest of the house was sufficiently clean to his satisfaction, with all signs of rodent infestation now gone as well, for the time being. He felt comfortable letting them move back in. The Exile was now, officially, over and quite significantly, 37 years to the day after they had first moved into the house in 1972—tremendous symbolism as my grandfather had ensured that the house was ready for occupancy by Christmas that year.

Inspector Barry asked them if they wanted to tear up the placard. They said that they would keep it as a souvenir, to remind them of what they had been through and what never, ever to let happen again. I had mixed feelings about this, of course, since the excessive saving of things is exactly what got them to the place they were in, in the first place. But one more item saved as a souvenir would not hurt, I supposed. Especially one so significant. So I kept my mouth shut. My only hope was that they wouldn't lose it under more piles of junk.

When my mom called me on my cell phone to tell me the good news, I was helping my mother-in-law, Lynne, at her art gallery, since her workers had gone home for the holidays. I stood in the carpeted back area, receiving the welcome news from my mother, who had a melodic, celebratory tone in her voice as she delivered the news, almost singing, of their final visit from Officer Barry. I gave a tremendous sigh of relief, and kept the call brief, as the gallery was still an active business for the holidays. In the few seconds that followed, I welled up with tears, standing on my own in the back room, contemplating the gravitas of the moment, and humbly thanking God for his benevolent and divine providence. When I had gained my composure, I shared the news with Lynne, who was overjoyed as well, having been kept apprised of the goings-on over the last few months. Then I called Melissa shortly after to pass along the news.

A slight rain had come over Studio City, California, where Lynne's shop had stood for over fifteen years, and it finished quickly, leaving a double and even triple rainbow over Ventura Boulevard. Lynne called me outside to view it, and I looked up over the row of one and two story businesses to see three rainbows stretched over the sky as far as I could see. As soon as I saw one, I looked higher and saw the next, concentric circles arched across the sky, one above the other. I took it as a trebly good omen—that our troubles were finally over. Maybe it had nothing to do with my efforts, my prayers, my meditative walks and hikes, but in the end, my parents and the house were saved. Yet I was under no misapprehension about my parents' continued and perpetual safety. They had demonstrated their increasing vulnerability. Even after the Exile, I continued to recite the mantra, quietly to myself, "Save the lamb; save the lamb."

Richard and Barbara Greenberg, Chino, California, October, 2008

Greenberg Family, MacArthur Airport, Islip, New York, January, 2010

Arik and Dad at Loyola Marymount University, 2005

CHAPTER SIX:
AFTERMATH OF THE EXILE

The day after my parents were allowed back into their home, they contracted a small carpet cleaning company to come and steam clean the old white shag carpet in the living room. Evidently, this was where they planned to have Melissa and me stay, as my bedroom was still only partially cleared, and still a zone full of dirt and rodentine pathogens. But the living room carpets were not dry enough to replace the furniture in that room by the time we arrived in New York, which was not unexpected. So, Melissa and I just continued as planned, and stayed at my grandmother's old apartment at Aunt Bobbie's house, at Mergetland. This arrangement afforded Melissa and me some privacy, comfort, and more cleanliness than my parents' house could offer at that point in time.

The day after we arrived, Melissa and I visited the house. Much of the egregious mold smell had gone, but there was still a level of mustiness that would have bothered Melissa's allergies had we attempted to stay there. I was very satisfied with the level of progress that had taken place. While we were there, I helped move the remaining furniture back into the living room—including the newer couches that my parents had bought to replace the old ones that had been discarded—revealing the full level of openness that was now visible at the house. But it also revealed the level of disrepair that the entire house suffered from. Sliding glass doors were heavy in their tracks, slowed by decades of grit and caked grease, and their glass fogged with mold that had settled between the double layered panes. Handles had broken and locks were no longer fully reliable, forcing my parents to place wooden bars behind them in their tracks to ensure proper security when they left the house. In the main areas of the house, there was still a level of clutter that was visible here and there, but it was no more than it had been in perhaps the 1990s, when I was in grad school and would return for summer breaks, or perhaps even a few years prior to my marriage when things were cluttered, but still livable. Observing the kitchen, which was still not fully cleared of clutter, but was certainly usable, I remembered the fight my mother and I had had just a couple of years prior about retiling the kitchen floor. I considered that while things were not yet where they needed to be, I was grateful to see progress to the point where my parents' environment was relatively safe. Seeing Melissa standing in the kitchen with my mother, talking (even though she was still somewhat disturbed by the lingering scent of mildew), Dad and I relaxing in the living room, I didn't care about the kitchen tiles peeling up, or the cardboard that was spread out upon the bare particle board subfloor to cover it and protect stocking feet from splinters, or the remaining clutter that made things look old and shabby, and still caused us to sidle around things in order to traverse from room to room. I was, for that moment, happy.

So, we spent as much time as possible visiting with my parents at Grandma's old apartment, so that Melissa could benefit from the comfort and cleanliness which that place could offer. It was a small, but comfortable apartment attached to the Mergets' house, which had been converted from their longitudinal, two-car length garage back in the early 1970s. For myself, I would have been just as satisfied spending time in my old home, but that would have to wait. And, of course, we experienced more than one argument between my parents—a function of their still suffering marriage, in addition to the slow deterioration of my father's short-term memory, mixed with his depressive state, dependent as well upon my mother's persistent addictive and somewhat realism-challenged personality. It was a deadly mixture. He would get cranky, she would perseverate; they would argue; we would observe. It was painful for Melissa and me to have to sit and watch, especially since we had a bit more objectivity about the situation and felt obliged to help disarm things a bit. We did our best to do so on one or two occasions, helping to save an otherwise pleasant day from the depths of misery that my parents' own *danse macabre* had grown proficient in producing.

And while we were there, Melissa took some yoga and belly dance classes at local studios nearby, to keep from going batty from the monotony of "Greenborg" inertia, the depressive cloud that could often waste an entire day and distract a person from one's chores so that you wouldn't even be able to leave the house and get started on your day until nearly sunset. She had the right idea: just get out and do something; don't wait for everyone else.

It was during this visit that I witnessed my dad do something careless while behind the wheel of the car. My parents, Melissa, and I were in Northport, one of our favorite places: a little seaside fishing village that held the school where my dad had taught for many years, along with the health food store we had shopped at since the early 1970s. It was part of the Town of Huntington, which also held Dix Hills. We had just finished shopping there and had a little meal of delicious and healthy organic foods, much to Melissa's delight as well as Mom's. It was dark when we exited and returned to the car, which was parked in one of the diagonal street parking spots, right in front of the Trinity Episcopal Church, which was just one door down from the health food store. We had loaded up the groceries and buckled ourselves in, ready to go home for the evening. Dad pulled halfway back out of the parking spot in front of the church, then turned the wheel left and headed forward without sufficient room for the rear of the vehicle to clear the rear quarter panel of the car to our right. I heard a somewhat mild, but unpleasant crunching sound, as if molded convex steel panel had buckled and indented under pressure, and then crinkled. Dad seemed completely oblivious of this faux pas, and I shouted for him to stop. I became enraged, jumped out of the minivan, looked at the other car for any visible damage, and saw none in the pale yellow light of the street lamps. I ran back around to the driver's side and demanded that my dad exit. I immediately took over driving, unceremoniously scolded Dad for not paying attention, and left him sulking in the back seat like a chastened child. In retrospect, I felt terrible about how I had addressed him and punished him like a teenager who just experienced his first fender-bender. It took away his autonomy, how I handled it, but I was trying to protect my family and was still in a state of denial about Dad's declining mental state. By blaming him, I was able to maintain my own delusion that everything was fine and that my dad was just as capable as he had always been; he was just being lazy and needed correction. This would not be the last time I made a mistake in how we dealt with Dad's health.

One evening while in New York, I was at the house with my parents, while Melissa was elsewhere, likely back at Mergetland. The three of us were sitting in the newly reopened living room, taking some time to relax and review all that had happened in the last year, when Vito called on our house phone. My grandfather's former apprentice and our family's longtime plumber had periodically called to check in on my parents in recent times, knowing our predicament. Vito was in some ways extended family to us and did not stand on ceremony. During one previous visit to New York during the winter holidays, while Melissa and I were staying at my Grandma's old apartment at Mergetland, Vito had stopped by unannounced, just as he used to with my grandmother, even after Grandpa had died, checking in on the widow of his mentor. His knock at the door had startled us, as we were not expecting guests, but it turned out that he just wanted to check in and say hello, and to meet Melissa for the first time. She was charmed by Vito's down-home earthiness and his unpolished old-time New York accent as he asked us, "What do youse two do?" inquiring about our usual New Years' plans. With this, Melissa had just experienced an age-old New York phenomenon, her first "pop-in".

Vito knew that my parents were back in the house and the Exile ended, having installed their new dishwasher right about the time that the placard had been removed, but he still continued to check in with them at times. That evening, I answered the phone, being closest to the handset and seeing Vito's name on the caller ID. Initially, I had him on speaker phone, wanting to share his call with my parents; that was our usual protocol with family calls like this one, a sort of group conversation. Vito's tone was pleasant, and we exchanged basic greetings, but I could hear a bit of consternation in his voice, as if there was more to say. I had not yet conveyed that he was on speaker phone or that my parents were right nearby, and he launched into a line of inquiry that I immediately knew would not be appropriate for my parents to hear.

"Lee, can I ask you a question?" he probed politely but with a decided eagerness in his baritone, gravelly voice, calling me by my birthname. I had come to use Arik in my mid-teens, but most of the older family members and family friends still persisted in referring to me as Lee, as they had always done.

"Sure, Vito."

"Do you ever get mad at your parents?" he continued, thickly accented. By this point, I knew it was time to quickly turn the speaker phone off before continuing the conversation. Thankfully, Mom and Dad seemed oblivious as they sat there, one on the couch, and the other in a nearby office chair that lived in the living room. Both of them were tired from the day and a little bit groggy, just enough to not take note of where Vito was going with this. "I mean really mad?" he finished, by the time I had been able to switch off the speaker.

"Of course I do, Vito," I answered, trying to be as forthcoming in my conversation with him but not allowing my parents to know what was going on for fear of hurting their feelings. I could tell that Vito wanted to unburden himself about what he had seen in the house over the years, the amassing of junk and the deterioration of the house that he helped to build with Grandpa back in 1972.

"Do you ever wish your dad would grow a set of balls?" he continued, and I was grateful that the phone call was no longer audible to my parents. "I mean, all that junk in the house that your mom collects, and he just stands by and lets it happen." I continued the conversation as best I could without giving my parents any clue about how personal this was, but I answered Vito's questions in the affirmative, agreeing that I wish things were otherwise, and was somehow able to convey that I was getting them the help they needed to get better. He made apologies for speaking so boldly, but said that it really bothered him to see the condition of the house that my grandfather had built. I felt the same way. As we finished the phone call, I couldn't help but feel a bit insulted for my father's sake, especially the way Vito spoke of my dad's subordination to my mom's will in such an unhealthy situation. But he was right, and I did feel that way—for many years, I wanted my dad to stand up to Mom's insanity, her addiction, her insistence upon having things her way when it was dangerous and damaging to everyone. I relished that he was a gentle soul who adored his wife so much that he would do anything for her, but I wanted him to be the traditional male—for just a moment—and set our family right, to protect us from the hoarding, to protect us from Mom's illness. But Dad had his own problems and was unable to act in that way and it disappointed me greatly.

Vito and I finished the phone call in a few minutes. He was satisfied in knowing that we were on the same page and that I was not deluded about the abnormality of our living situation. My parents hadn't had a chance to speak directly to Vito; but with a few statements relayed back and forth between me as the intermediary, Vito said he'd call them back in a few days. Mom and Dad seemed satisfied, and none the wiser about our secret conversation that took place in plain sight.

Despite the dark moments, most of this visit was truly refreshing for me. It was during this visit that we took my dad to visit his brother, Howie—from whom he had become estranged—so they could reunite. In the process, we met several younger cousins whose acquaintance I had never made since their birth; Melissa and I were delighted to have helped orchestrate this. In fact, it was really Melissa's efforts that brought this about. She insisted that we had these young cousins that she had never met due to family unrest, and that she wanted to make their acquaintance. That we were always spending time cleaning up my parents' problems, and she wanted to have some joyful, relaxing family time with cousins for a change. So she had made inroads with Uncle Howie and cousin Steven, the eldest, and made plans to bring my parents down to New Jersey to see each other and patch things up. When we arrived in the minivan in front of their Cherry Hill home, my having driven, I witnessed my dad and Uncle Howie hug for the first time in several years. At first, when they approached each other on the sidewalk outside the house, there was a bit of palpable tension—my dad saying something like, "Howard, we have some things we need to talk about", followed by Howie's response, "Yes, we do." But it was immediately replaced by hugs and feelings of instant reconciliation, as if they had both forgotten what had caused the rift between them. In reality, I cannot say who was at fault. Two brothers, my Dad five years older, had often fought, held grudges. Perhaps one was too quick to speak, making off-the-cuff remarks that hurt the other's feelings; perhaps the other was too quick to interpret malice in the remarks of the other, being simply silly or folksy in his banter. Even during my wedding, four and a half years prior—the last time they saw one another—relations were chilly between them, due to their perceived rift. I have heard it said that Jews have the memory of elephants when it comes to slights. But all was forgotten by the time we entered the house and were surrounded by the bustling household full of younger cousins and their parents and grandparents. Among these were my first cousin, Steven and his wife Deana; and Ellen, Steven's sister, who was my age; and her husband, Bob.

As we sat around the living room, swarmed by little cousins that were Steven's children—ages 5, 10, and 13 at the time, all doing their own thing, chattering and playing video games, comfortable with their parents and grandparents, and their Aunt Ellen—my dad leaned over to me at one point, seated in his chair in the living room, and asked, *sotto voce,* "And whose children are these, again?" I gently reminded him that they were Steven's children—Steven, his nephew. Dad's lack of awareness bothered me a bit, knowing in my heart that this was not normal for him. I convinced myself that it was merely because he had never met them and because this was an emotional day.

Uncle Howie and Aunt Liz had gotten my dad a chocolate cake in honor of his birthday, which had been just a few days prior, on January 9th. It was brought out after a late lunch, as a surprise. Initially, it seemed as if Dad maybe had forgotten that he had just had a birthday, and so his response was a bit cool, pleasantly approving with a squint-eyed smile not too dissimilar from a contented, sleepy housecat, but not overly exuberant. I had seen this facial expression on him many times before; it was a sort of go-to resting countenance that conveyed a sort of blissful disconnect, an oblivious tranquility. Noting this look, I suspected that maybe Dad didn't understand at first that it was his cake, perhaps assuming that it was for someone else in the household who had a recent birthday. But he gradually warmed up to it, chocolate being his favorite flavor, and it sank in that it was obtained in his honor. We all took part in the chocolate—except Mom whose health food diet had not included store-bought cake for decades—and my cousins and Melissa began to quote the old Bill Cosby routine about being a very popular father when he fed his children chocolate cake—this of course was years before revelations about Cosby's sex crimes became public. Dad repeatedly accepted seconds and thirds while at the table, as readily as Aunt Liz offered, and even occasionally dipped his fork into the dregs that lay around the cake dish, now mostly abandoned and discarded by satiated family members, as if it were his personal plate. I was charmed by his freedom and boldness, and perhaps I happily ignored his obliviousness of social convention—nothing that he ever would have done in earlier years.

When we left New Jersey, I was grateful at having been a party to reuniting my dad with his brother, and helping give Melissa the gift of newfound cousins. And when Melissa and I left New York a few days later, I had a general feeling of accomplishment and satisfaction that the house was sufficiently clean to be able to house my parents and keep them safe. I knew that there would be more cleaning necessary in the future, and I did not relish this fact. But I was able to put it aside and focus on the positives of the present. And overall, it was a very good visit.

Summer Visits

In June, 2010, I came by myself for a week or two to help my parents do some more cleaning, which I had promised to do, and also to get some quality time with my parents after all they had been through in the last couple of years—and the last ten months particularly. We didn't get much cleaning done while I was there, unfortunately. The intent was to handle the Den at this point. But I found it daunting every time I looked in there. It was still full of junk, as if it were the last holdout of the house's former state. So I conveniently put it off till my next visit, making plans to come again in August. Meanwhile, we had some wonderful visits with extended family, including a visit to see Uncle Howie and Aunt Liz in New Jersey, deepening the rekindled relationship between him and my dad. During my return visit in August, we took the opportunity to make a trip to Maine to see Jack, my father's best friend from childhood.

Jack and Dad had met during childhood, growing up in Port Jefferson, NY, just as the war was ending. Dad had just moved there from Brooklyn, to what was at the time, the "boondocks", out in the undeveloped wilderness of Long Island. When they first met, Dad, a lonely child, was sitting on the sidewalk, burning ants with a magnifying class. Jack approached and introduced himself and instantaneously knew that they both had the same warped view of the world and would become fast friends. They understood each other. Jack was one of his first friends there and was rapidly accepted into the Greenberg family as an honorary member. As an Irish Catholic, he marveled to learn about all the exotic foods and customs of what it meant to be a Jew. They stayed friends for many years, both entering the Armed Forces around the same time and later pursuing careers in education. They fell out, however, shortly after my parents' wedding, when Jack's alcoholism caused him to misinterpret my dad's intent in placing Jack's little son at a separate table from him and his wife of the time—the couple was on shaky ground, heading toward divorce, and Jack seemed to think that Dad was trying to drive Jack and his son apart; of course this couldn't have been further from the truth, but such is the effect of alcoholism, and Jack and my dad lost contact.

Although their rift was complete by the time I was born, I grew up hearing his name with great fondness, my dad introducing me to the concept of cinnamon toast, which was Jack's favorite, along with all manner of stories about him. In the Summer of 1994, as I was languishing at home alone in NY, nursing a broken heart from my breakup with Melanie, my first serious girlfriend post-college, and as my parents were away in New Mexico looking for property during a poorly timed trip, I received a phone call on the house phone from a John Calloway, asking for a Richard Greenberg who grew up in Port Jefferson. I was overjoyed to be the one to answer. "Jack Calloway?" I exclaimed excitedly, as if he had spoken his name wrongly. I instantly said that he had the right house and that I knew exactly who he was. I introduced myself as Richard's son, Lee Arik, who had been born after Jack and Dad last spoke, and that my parents were away on vacation and that I knew my dad would be excited beyond words to hear that Jack had called. We spoke for a little bit and got to know each other. He shared that his alcoholism had been a major contributor to his falling out with my dad, and he informed me that he was now clean and sober for many years and a regular participant in AA. He was also happily remarried. I promised to give the message about his call to my parents as soon as I possibly could.

When I next spoke to my parents by phone, that evening at their motel in New Mexico, I told the story and my dad was indeed overjoyed. He and Jack spoke later that night on the phone, sparking the rekindling of a friendship that should never have been put on hold, but only got closer now that they were older and wiser. A year later, Jack and his wife Karen came to Long Island to visit during the Summer, driving the ten or so hour drive from Maine where they now lived in a sleepy and idyllic little rural town. Being that it was during the Summer, I was grateful to be there to witness these two old friends reconnect. Fittingly, we all met up in Port Jefferson, where their friendship had begun fifty years prior. The year or two after that, the three of us drove up to visit Jack and Karen in Maine, further cementing the rekindled friendship between Dad and Jack, but also establishing Jack in my life as an honorary uncle of sorts. We would speak occasionally on the phone about life and philosophy, and I was grateful to be able to visit in person as well. Over the years, our families grew closer and I continued to think of Jack as a second uncle, a very important figure in my life, an older friend whose wisdom was always shared humbly and freely, who helped shed light on my dad's life and mindset, and as someone whose presence in my dad's life eventually helped ground him during some of the tough times that he experienced with my mom's hoarding.

When Jack began to see my father's mental decline, he and I would speak about it, and he would share with me his concern and consternation. The Exile had been hard on Dad, as I mentioned, and Jack picked up on that. He noticed that something changed in Dad, and that he no longer seemed to have a response to what was going on around him, as if he had closed off and stopped recognizing that his life was in shambles. Their phone calls became less lively and interactive, with my dad speaking in generalities and platitudes, leading to an early dismissal, often saying that he'd tell Jack what has been going on "next time we speak", and next time would never come. Jack being on the opposite end of the political spectrum from my dad—Jack being conservative and my dad progressive—they had always had lively conversations about politics during the last decade of their friendship, since the rekindling. But as of late, seeing that my dad was less connected to life than before, Jack would often try to playfully provoke him with deliberately incendiary conversation topics about politics, just to try to get Dad involved, but to no avail. This deeply saddened Jack, as if the Richard he knew and loved were disappearing.

But this trip, in the middle of summer but during a lull in the hot weather, Jack had a chance to see my dad's changes firsthand. I drove us up to Maine and we stayed over at Jack and Karen's house—my parents in the master bedroom of the main house, and myself on a cot in the living room—while Jack and Karen stayed in a little cabin on their property that was the first structure they had built and lived in when they purchased their forty acre plot of land a few decades prior. We spent a good amount of time driving around in two vehicles, one following the other, looking at the scenery, newly built houses, a lake, and other sites, since Dad's difficulty walking was a bit of a hindrance to taking longer jaunts that required any distance of walking. One afternoon, as Jack and Dad and I were waiting for Mom and Karen to finish shopping at an antique shop, we sat in Jack's truck and talked. Dad eventually fell asleep in the passenger seat, nodding off quietly as Jack and I continued to converse. At some point, Jack looked over at Dad, and turned back to me, the two of us silently acknowledging this change in Dad's behavior. I confessed that this was happening more often with Dad, that he would just nod off at times. Jack understood, and offered sympathetic words of support. Not much more was said. Nothing else was needed.

During this visit, we happened upon a lake in the area of Maine that Jack and Karen resided. It had rained earlier that day, but by now it had stopped, so we took a drive and stopped to see the vista, still bearing a slightly dreary, misty ambiance that reminded me of the mythical Avalon. In the area around the shore of the lake, there were some ducks. My dad spotted one duck, which was lame; it had a limp, and had a bit of trouble keeping up with its companions. Something about this really touched Dad. Maybe he identified with it, what with his own limp. Maybe he saw himself in that duck. He was visibly concerned about the animal, and said so—that he felt sorry for it. Even in the midst of his difficulties with memory, I could see that Dad had compassion and really identified with the downtrodden. And something about seeing Dad's response truly moved me, but by this time I had only just begun to decipher why, as I shall elucidate below.

****

At one point while I was in NY this trip, I looked in the garage and saw a couple of recently acquired, small pieces of furniture that my mom must have picked up from somewhere, with her newly spacious minivan that I had helped to clear out. I was annoyed at her and I went to chide her, somewhat gently but with paternalistic displeasure. She had both a ready excuse as well as a sheepish look to go with the proverbial egg on her face. She was sufficiently chastised. I made it known that I did not intend to put up with another Exile experience. She assured me that she would not make a habit of this, but had picked up the item under such and such circumstances and did not want to pass it up. For the moment, I decided to put the issue aside, hoping that I would not have to deal with another crisis, and simultaneously not looking forward to the fact that I would indeed have to spearhead additional cleanouts of the garage and the house in order to stay ahead of my mother's addiction.

I had hoped that with a new bed, my parents would resume sleeping in the master bedroom in their own bed. But during this trip it became apparent to me that my parents had, for all intents and purposes, resumed their earlier sleeping arrangements of sleeping on couches opposite one another in the living room. The bedroom was vacant, still symbolic of their relationship. And my room had begun to be filled up with clutter again—things that needed to be moved out to the garage, books, boxes, and so forth. And perhaps this was somewhat symbolic of their sense of loss at my absence, the thought of filling the "empty nest" with more branches and twigs, to continue the metaphor. Nevertheless, I was a bit annoyed at this, since I had desired, intended, to sleep in my own bedroom. But perhaps this was a bit of a Godsend, since my parents had not had a chance to fully sanitize my room from the presence of rodents since the Exile. I would not want to lay my head unwittingly near old rat dung. So I was to sleep on one of the couches in the living room. I could tell that my parents had not fully thought this out: two couches, three people. So I demanded that one or both of them go and sleep in their bed. Initially, they suggested that I take their bed, a seemingly noble gesture, but I vehemently declined, insisting that it was theirs to sleep in first. I am glad I did that. So both my parents tried the bedroom. I took the longer of the two couches, the one by the tall, sliding glass doors—one of which I had clambered through during the Exile, the first day I entered. But now I was comfortable enough, all things considered. I was just glad to be back in my parents' house, knowing that while it was still not ideal, it was safe and livable.

The first night, Dad said he did not get a very good night's sleep. So the second night, he went back to sleeping on one of the sofas, across from the one upon which I slept. It was kind of nice to sleep that way, being close to at least one of my parents, whom I did not see often enough. The next night, it was my mom who fell asleep on the couch across from me, with the cat (Kitty-cat Rotten, the aging mackerel tabby who came to live with us in 1992) on her lap, and so my dad then went back to the bedroom. They switched off like this the entire time I was there, so I took advantage of every moment I had to be near my parents, even in sleep. It nourished some sense of childhood safety and comfort in me, even though now it was I who was more of the adult than they.

It was during this visit that my mother confided in me the fact of my parents' lack of physical intimacy, corroborating what Kim had said to me the year prior. I never did inquire about the gory details, nor did I really feel it appropriate for me to know. But suffice to say that it engendered in me a tremendous amount of sympathy for both of them. As we sat in the minivan in the parking lot of a Trader Joe's near Mergetland, waiting for Dad to come back out after picking up some groceries, Mom merely reiterated that my dad had gradually crowded her out of the bedroom, always strategically placing junk on her side of the bed late at night, prior to her retiring, as if to say, "Don't come in here." And eventually, when challenged by her about this behavior and his intent, he admitted that he no longer felt comfortable staying in the same bed. Curiously, I had, since that time, seen them stay in the same bed when on vacation, so the parameters and dynamics of the arrangement were lost on me. But at the time, all I could do was put my arm around my mother and comfort her, saying, "I'm so sorry…I'm so sorry."

Pertaining to the causes of this marital difficulty, it was during this trip that my mother and I had the opportunity to do some work with my dad in excavating his own childhood abuse. He had received some advice from various therapists to do some meditative exercises designed to comfort his inner child from whatever abuse he had suffered in his youth that was still not readily available to his conscious mind, being suppressed as a defense mechanism. But it was at this time that these were first uncovered, more fully than ever before. Dad seemed significantly more willing than previously to get them out, and was naturally somewhat embarrassed about the subject matter once it was revealed to us. It is to this matter that I now turn.

Stuffed Animals

It was no secret that my dad was very angry with his father, who had died nearly thirty years before, when I was still a young teen in 1983. His father had been a self-centered, contentious man, who considered his two sons his competitors, rarely had a kind word for them, and largely abandoned them when he sent them to live with his sister after his wife's untimely death in 1955—Dad being twenty, and Howie at the tender age of fifteen. But I never knew why my dad's outright antipathy for his father was so great. Grandpa Charlie, as he was known to me, was called thusly to distinguish him from Grandpa Arty, who was merely called "Grandpa". I felt that Arty had earned that monomymous designation; Grandpa Charlie had not. Charlie had changed his name from Isidore—or Israel (no one really knew until we saw his death certificate)—at some point in his youth to Charles to fit into the still Anti-Semitic environment of the America he grew up in—to be more "American" and less Jewish. Throughout my childhood, his presence as a grandfather was a bit of a mixed bag. He would bring hip and stylish new girlfriends to meet us when invited to the house, and he would talk about going "dahn-cing" with them—by all accounts, much less dancing than inexpertly pushing them around a dance floor, attempting to seem elegant—which made him seem somewhat dashing, trendy, and youthful in my eyes. Even though he was hard to get to know and rarely offered any warm and welcome glimpses into his personality, occasionally he would surprise me. At cousin Steven's bar mitzvah, when I was still around 9 or 10, Grandpa Charlie danced with me in a way that one would expect grandparents to do with their grandchildren. For a moment, I felt close to him. My parents later tried to disabuse me of thinking too much of this, suggesting that he was only showing off for the other adults. I cannot say whether that was true or not, but my opinion of him was colored by both my desire to have a closer relationship with him, and also by the disappointment of feeling his emotional distance.

He would call my parents out of the blue and start arguments. Sometimes he would try to invite himself over with little advance notice, and be annoyed when they would request a little more time to prepare, on one occasion coming over and then leaving unceremoniously when dinner was not ready quickly enough. I witnessed numerous arguments over the phone in which he would lay guilt trips on my parents for not inviting him over more often. As my parents described the relationship, it was always a game of one-upmanship, trying to appear somehow more refined than they were or to establish that he was in the position of dominance and to keep his adversary—son, daughter-in-law, or whatever—off guard. It annoyed my parents to no end that he had promised me a tool kit as a gift, one with electrical supplies representing his trade as an electrician, but it never materialized. When he would call us on the phone and inevitably ask to speak to me, his pointed question to me was, "How come you never call me?" This automatically set up a dynamic between us in which I, the child, was somehow irresponsible and unloving, and always at a disadvantage, the unwitting and unschooled participant in a game that I could never win. I had received a birthday card from him somewhere in my pre-adolescence, about 8 or 9 years old perhaps, that featured a beautiful drawing of a train coming through a tunnel, but the ready-made inscription read, "On your birthday, Grandfather...." I couldn't figure out why it didn't say, "...Grandson." My parents later explained that this was in keeping with Grandpa Charlie's carelessness in regards to how he treated people and that it was likely an oversight in choosing the card. The last straw for my dad in his relationship with his father was that Grandpa Charlie had been telling people that his sons were doctors, referring to the two sons of his live-in girlfriend, Florence, as his own. This hurt my dad very deeply. Evidently, having two sons that were a highly regarded school teacher and a successful electronics salesman was nothing for Charlie to be proud of.

When I was 13, he contracted cancer and was in the hospital with not much longer to live. My sense of guilt got the best of me and I made a concerted effort to call him on the phone near his hospital bed, stating to him that I was finally calling him, as he had always asked me to. He responded coolly and changed the subject, proceeding, in his state of hospital dementia, to inquire of me if I "had seen a yellow tray around here somewhere." Dad, hearing my side of the conversation reassured me that Grandpa Charlie was no longer himself and not to concern myself with answering logically about the tray. But the idea that he had lost his grasp of reason disturbed me. When Grandpa Charlie died, just a week or so later, I accompanied my dad to the hospital morgue to identify the body, something I had never even known was customary or required. In the cold, dim room, the body was displayed, still, supine, and I noted how Charlie's flesh had diminished from his sickness, having always been a bit portly with a bit of what I imagined as "roast beef" below his chin, the fat of years of eating such; that feature had lessened. And now, his eyebrows were more chiseled than I had ever remembered, and the word that came to mind was that he looked "handsome". Dad declared, beginning to well up with tears, "That's him," as if to say, there is no doubt that is the body of my father. We left and ordered a simple pine box for his burial, as was Jewish custom.

After Grandpa Charlie died, I did not cry, and I felt guilty about that, as if I had betrayed him or had finally proven that I was an unworthy grandson. For years, it bothered me, but eventually I forgave myself, realizing that the lack of closeness was not my fault. But I also took pity on him, thinking of the fact that at the age of 2 or 3, his own father had left his mother with nine children, causing little Isidore to have to sell chewing gum as a mere toddler on the streets of Philadelphia, hardly the kind of experience that engenders good childhood development and healthy relationships in later life.

At the time of Grandma Ethel's death, my father was twenty years old, and in his second year of service in the Air Force; my Uncle Howie, his younger brother, was only fifteen. Their father was unable to care for them in any material way other than paying the most meager of bills. It was at this point that my father's younger brother went to live with their Aunt Sadie Gluckstein, Charlie's Sister, and came to see what kind of woman she really was. My uncle would later relate about her that she "never missed an opportunity to berate" him. Evidently, her taking him into her house as a teen did not include giving moral support and encouragement.

My father already knew what kind of woman she was, having spent large amounts of time at her house being supervised by her as a small child. But it would not be until many years later that he truly remembered the damage she did in his life. He always remembered her as a snide, bitter woman who took every opportunity to belittle him as well, and he marveled that her children could grow up so sweet and so unlike their mother.

"Richard! Where's all your hair?!" she commented to him sardonically at some point in his twenties, having not seen him in a while, and noticing his receding hairline.

"I keep it at home in a cigar box," he retorted snappily, which was lost on her as she had already turned her attention somewhere else and had not heard him. This was standard fare for her. But in 2010, he finally was able to remember what kinds of experiences he suffered as a child.

I remember during the times that my mother had remembrances of her own abuse, relaying the experiences to my father and me, my dad would usually ask me—in front of my mother—the stilted and leading question of, "What do you think about what your mother suffered?" What should I think? When someone tells you about such horrible torment, what are you supposed to say or think? I guess my dad was at a loss for words, but his question always seemed like some sycophantic attempt to flatter my mom, or to fill an uncomfortable pause, or to remain on her good side. It would annoy me, not because I did not agree that she deserved our sympathy, but because it seemed forced or inauthentic. It seemed that there was something else behind it. I finally began to find out what that something was. Evidently, he had suffered his own traumatic abuses which he had repressed as well.

In 2010, during a temporary break in his therapy with Kim several months after the Exile was over, one spiritually oriented therapist my parents were consulting suggested that my father should connect with his inner child and do some kind of visualization that would help to comfort him from the suffering he had experienced. My dad was resistant to it for quite some time, choosing to keep his sullen and somber and depressive moods fueled and untreated by any attempt to disarm or ameliorate them. When I was home visiting them in June—about six months after they were allowed to go back into the home—I convinced my dad to let me guide him through a meditation like what the therapist had suggested. My mom and I had my dad lay down on their bed and take part in a guided visualization. In short, I asked my dad to speak directly to his young self (around the age of 7, which is the age the healer suggested to focus on) and to offer him encouragement and love. It was not a new method, but something that I had seen used before in many self-help and therapeutic techniques.

Gradually, my father began to realize that his 7 year old self had things he wanted to talk about that had every connection to his current reality and problems. Young Richard began to talk about the things that were done to him. We pushed him to share, to divulge. My father relayed his memories to us, through the viewpoint of his 7 year old self, as if narrating to us what he would have said. It became evident that Aunt Sadie was not normal. She gathered to her groups of people who had perversions in which they wanted not only to sexually abuse little children but also to witness them being abused. My father, at this point a small innocent child of seven, was like fresh meat to these people. He was helpless to their adult machinations, much more wily and devious than the naive child.

Richard recounted to us, bravely, what had happened in one particular circumstance. A group of people were brought in to Richard's bedroom in Brooklyn while Sadie was babysitting for him. He was presented stuffed animals to play with. Among them was a gray elephant that had earlier been given to him by his Grandpa Louis, his mother's father. He loved that toy. The strangers brought a brown horse as well, as a sort of 'gift' or a ruse. The situation seemed strange to him. He was uncomfortable. He knew there was malicious intent involved here, exuding from these people. Suddenly, he was grabbed by Sadie by the back of the neck and was forced down onto the bed. In an instant, the stuffed animals were forced into his orifices—his mouth, his anus—both the elephant that he loved as well as the newly arrived horse. The shock he felt, the betrayal, was inexpressible. Then, suddenly a man came forward to sodomize him, but now with his phallus and not merely inanimate objects. As Mom and I encouraged and even urged my dad to continue to bravely narrate this incident for his own catharsis and mental health, he stuck for a moment on the descriptions of what was done to him. And as I pressed him a bit to describe the matter further, with an outburst he shouted the word, "Sodomy!" as if it was the key to the whole affair. "Do you know what that means?" he challenged, loudly, irate, as if to give a name to what he suffered.

He continued to narrate how little Richard's innocence was taken as he was subjected to this horror. Then, just as suddenly, the animals were taken away and discarded, having been soiled and now become evidence of the strangers' crimes. Richard was taken away to be cleaned up before his mother returned home. But one part of this that he would finally disclose to us was that his own father, Charles, was present—not as an active participant, but he had helped to organize this. There was even the hint that money had exchanged hands over this event. My dad would later ruminate, analyzing the situation in retrospect, that because this was during WWII, times were tough. Money was in short supply. A deviant person with a little bit of money could command other people to become accomplices in their sins, while little children were forced to be the unwilling victims. It was similar in format to what my mother had experienced at almost the very same point in history. But the most poignant part to me was that these stuffed animals, one of which was his favorite toy given to him by a beloved grandfather, were used as the tools, the implements of his torture, and then taken away from him, adding insult to injury. For some reason, I fixated on those toy animals—as if they had suffered too, given what they meant to that little boy—just as much as the little boy himself. I weep for that little boy and for what he lost—his innocence, his ability to place trust in those who were assigned to love and protect him. And I weep for that wounded little boy that still resided deep inside my father as an elderly man.

My father cried quite a bit as we wrapped up this session, comforting him. Within several weeks, he would forget this whole experience of the meditation, much to my shock and my mother's. We did not realize that his short-term memory could be that poor. Had it been just a tall tale, made up by a man who wished to throw the spotlight off of his marital difficulties and the daily arguments, one would think that he would remember the generalities of this session and merely lose track of the details. But he remembered none of it at all. When it was mentioned to him, he was surprised, as if we were trying to convince him of something that simply wasn't true. Trusting us, he was forced to believe that something had come out of that session, but he could not remember exactly what.

I came back for my second Summer visit in August, this time to really try to do some work on the Den. In the course of our time together, my mother and I led my dad through another meditative exercise in a similar vein, yielding more extensive results than the last one, revealing more of the memories that I had indicated above. A comparable experience was raised in which a group of people were brought in by Aunt Sadie and began to hit and sodomize him, treating him like a piece of meat. And even another experience surfaced in which his aunt barged in on him while he was taking a bath. He tried to cover up his private parts, but she stood there leering at him. Though vague and foggy, the clouds of memory began to clear to and suggest that she forced him to perform sexual acts with her—further assailing his innocence. Ironically, it was years later at a family gathering that Sadie turned to my dad, as if to share some piece of important news, and proclaimed to him only for his ears, "You're a creep!" Nothing more, no explanation or supporting evidence; and then she left the conversation. Whatever demons lurked within her demanded that she accuse my dad of being the very thing that she was—a creep. Evidently, she was a very sick individual. The thought strikes me of how many other children she may have abused or facilitate being abused. The small comfort I take in knowing this is that—if these allegations are in fact true—she will now be remembered by my readers as the pederast and pervert that she was, her misdeeds exposed to history and unforgotten.

It was around this time that Dad had been brutalized by other, older boys in the Brooklyn neighborhood, perhaps sensing his submissiveness—caused by abuse—through their own bullying senses. It was also around this time that he was coached by the older kids to begin to abuse animals. He remembered being told by local boys that sometimes there were too many cats in the neighborhood and that some of them had to be killed so that the others wouldn't starve. He remembered being coached how to hold kittens under water until the squirming animals stopped moving, submitting to a larger more powerful foe, just as he did with the perverted adults who held him down. After moving out to Port Jefferson on Long Island—then considered "the country"—it was frogs and ants that were his more usual victims, not waiting for the coaxing of older, more sadistic children. These were things that he later said he was not at all proud of. My mother and I, both very strongly compassionate toward animals, were saddened by knowing that my father had been "one of those kids" who abused animals. I am still disturbed by his participation in perpetrating more misery. I empathize and hurt on behalf of those innocent animals, and I still wish that he had been less apt to direct his anger at helpless beings. But I do understand it in the context of a small boy who had been tortured by adults and had no recourse for justice or retaliation, and I sometimes felt that my mother would unnecessarily and uncompassionately berate him for the choices he made, heaping further abuse on him in retrospect. He later would jokingly muse that he is now the slave to our family cat.

Other experiences surfaced. Each time, my father had difficulty remembering the previous ones, but he gradually remembered more of them each time. He began to come to grips with having been sodomized by groups of people, orchestrated by his aunt and even, to some degree, by his own father. That his innocence was stolen from him. That it indeed affected his relationship with his wife. That when years later, he experienced marital difficulties with his wife, and ceased sleeping in the same bed as her, these early childhood experiences were partially to blame.

The threat was seared into his mind that if he were to tell anyone about any of this, they would kill him. And even if he did tell, who would believe him? After all, they were the adults and he was just a child with an overactive imagination. He was forced to forget. "Forget," the ghosts of his abusers whispered to him in their thinly veiled threats. "Just forget...," they said, just like so many other children have forgotten the things done to them in early childhood when they could not speak up or speak out, only to suffer for it for the rest of their lives and only perhaps later in life, to even deign to remember small parts of it.

We were as loving and supportive as we could be when orchestrating these guided meditations. But just like before, my dad had once again proceeded to forget a large portion of those restored memories, as if they were too difficult and painful to handle and address head on. As with the earlier instance, within about a week to two weeks, he had forgotten all about these experiences. When reminded of them and their subject matter, his memory was jogged, but still foggy on the subject. If he had been making these up, my assumption would be that he would quickly assert something along the lines of, "Yes, I remember it now; it's all coming back to me." But it was not so. In fact, within a month, he could not even remember the session with my mom and me, guiding him through the meditation that allowed him to retrieve these suppressed memories. It seems that the amnesiac curse invoked by the abusers, so many decades before, had been an unbreakable spell, or at least one that only abated for a moment before returning, as strong as before. But the benefit from knowing about them was not lost on my mother or me. It gave us greater insight into my father's personality, his issues, and his potential problems in the future.

The underlying medical cause of this amnesia, most likely, was a function of his deteriorating short-term memory. It was on this trip as well, that he had an experience late at night in which he awakened from a deep sleep and found himself disoriented. He was unsure of where he was, even though he was in his own home, sitting upright on a couch, having just awakened from sleep. He was frightened and I was glad to be there to comfort him. It was things like this that began to worry my mom and me more and more. He had been checked for Alzheimer's and cleared of any suspicion of its onset. As we were later informed by doctors at the VA, the likelihood was that these were early warning symptoms of minor vascular dementia, possibly linked to vitamin deficiencies and low blood sugar due to his poor diet, which was a function of my parents' inability to efficiently navigate their hoarded home for so many years. His depression as well had contributed to this overall mental deterioration and loss of short-term memory and was also likely related to the amount of mental energy it had taken to suppress these memories from his early childhood.

Much like how I feel about my mother's abuse, I lament that I was not there to defend my father. Forgiving and overlooking the moments in which his obliviousness to the world around him was at its worst, I felt compassionate understanding for the little boy who grew up too quickly and was forced to forget what was done to him; causing me to vow to fight the injustices done to children in our world, and to any innocent person, for that matter. For that little boy—my father, Richard—and for that little girl—Barbara, my mother.

"Nama, Mama…ZIZZA!!!"

It is interesting to note that both my parents had emergences of abuse memories during that August visit of mine. It was as if they both felt comfortable enough, having me there, to deal with the memories. It was, however, a bit stressful on me to go from comforting one parent during a pain-filled remembrance of severe sexual abuse to talking the other parent through a dissociative episode connected to severe sexual abuse. And all of this without a formal degree in Psychology; my formal training, afterall, is in Religion.

My father woke me one night during that August, 2010, visit. He said that my mother was crying and that he attempted to speak to her, but she wouldn't talk to him, as if she were angry with him for something. Believing that I could help, he had decided to awaken me and asked me to check on her. Coming near to the master bedroom door, I heard the distinct sound of my mother repeating some mantra-like phrase repeatedly behind the closed door. I knocked. She would not answer, but I heard the repetitive mantra. I opened the door and saw her sitting up in bed, with several colored flashlights that she used for color spectroscopy therapy lighted and positioned near her on the bed—another one of her peculiar forays into alternative medicine and spiritual healing. She kept saying something like, "Nama, Mama", in somewhat plaintive questioning tones, again and again and again. It seemed like a prayer she was engaged in, but I could not get her to address me directly. I entered and sat on the bed in front of her, realizing suddenly that she had begun another dissociative episode, like the first one I witnessed her experience in 1993. I had seen these several times since then. They were somewhat scary to witness, but they were nonetheless very cathartic for her and always very revealing. David Grand, the family therapist, had reassured me that these were a very good thing to have happen, since they would always reveal some deep, hidden, and till now forgotten abuse from her childhood. They could be traumatic for Mom to go through, but they were always for the best. I had comforted her through several in the past when they had occurred and although I was often concerned that she would not return to normalcy from such a state, this was not a concern David shared.

She kept repeating, "Nama, Mama" and sometimes even "Nana, Mama," occasionally changing her intonation to be more or less plaintive or sometimes even insistent. She did show some signs of recognizing me, and seemed to feel safe with me, but she was attempting to communicate with me in a pre-verbal mental state. This was surely from her early childhood, perhaps no older than 1 ½ to 2 years of age. She was somehow able to express to me that her mother had been involved in this abuse memory. Ever present in my mother's abuse memories was my Grandma Jeanne, who, as previously mentioned, had evidently suffered from split personalities and would often brutally torture my mother—on more than one occasion, to the point of death. I could discern that Jeanne's father, Grandpa Lawlie, a cousin to Mafiosi and no less deranged than his daughter Jeanne, was part of this newly resurfaced memory, too. As I have also mentioned earlier, he had evidently abused my grandmother—possibly sexually—and had left her mentally and emotionally compromised, now also a willing accomplice to his persistent crimes against children. Jeanne was now his assistant, perhaps during the moments of her change of personalities, and she would help him to abuse her own daughter, Barbara. This torture began when my mother was very, very young. Knowing that the youngest victims are not often believed when they 'tattle', she was an easy target, nothing more than an animal to them, a plaything that could be toyed with and tortured with no regard for her humanity.

There she was, sitting in front of me, an old woman, pitifully expressing the mind of a young child. Using her hands, feebly, in a stabbing motion, to depict something, she kept saying, "zizza, zizza!" For quite some time, I could not conceive of what she meant by this. It finally became evident to me that she was attempting to invoke scissors. She was describing, in a pre-verbal, juvenile mindset what the monsters had done to her—rather in the current moment of dissociation, what they were presently doing to her, as if in real time, being described to me in a play by play commentary. She would not come out of her dissociative state for quite some time, which of course concerned me. She continued to give me descriptions of what had been done to her, using the language of a one-year-old, as if it had just happened and she were still bleeding, trying to tell me so that I could prevent it from happening again. Each time she would express a new statement, I would try to understand her and would repeat back to her my interpretation, to obtain her acknowledgement. She would either nod yes in her baby-language, or would shake her head and keep trying to explain. This horrendous assault upon a helpless child had taken place nearly three quarters of a century ago, but in her unconscious, it was fresh, the wounds still flowing with blood.

She continued to make a sawing, stabbing motion with her hands, describing how the scissors, held open so that only a single edge was exposed and employed, were used to cut her in various places, including her arms, her thighs, and even her genitalia. Lastly, they were held over her eyes, more as a threat than with any actual intent to blind her—a threat that if she told anyone, she would suffer even more than ever. She continued to cry, imploringly, "Nama, Mama!" as if to say, "No more, Mama," gradually leading up to a crescendo of crisis as she described the scissors being held over her eyes, shrieking, "ZIZZA! ZIZZA!" repeatedly, at full pitch.

She was able to express to me that she had attempted to go to her daddy and tell him, but that he was unable to understand her due to her lack of verbal skills. All she could do was cry and produce ill-formed words that he could not comprehend. He would comfort her, but her mother, Jeanne, had covered up what truly had happened. Jeanne would perennially disguise the cuts and bruises deliberately sustained as if they were the result of little Barbara's clumsiness; she would often decry how clumsy her daughter was. But the only clumsiness was in her choice of family. As I watched and comforted, I kept thinking how pitiful this was. I had so much compassion for this little child—in the body of an old woman—but could do nothing other than comfort her and curse the memories of the monsters who had done this to her. After a while, she finally did return to the present moment. It took perhaps a full fifteen minutes for her capacity with language to return. Part of me feared momentarily that she might be intellectually crippled from the experience, unable to speak without slurring her words, like the victim of a stroke. But having seen her in similar dissociative episodes like this before, experience taught me that she would be okay, perhaps even better and more self-aware and emotionally healthier after detoxifying these memories.

This was, indeed, not the first time I had seen her go through these. I had helped her through numerous others, being there to hold her hand during the remembrance and to help her process the information afterwards. Several therapists had talked to me about it after the fact and had debriefed and counseled me on the best actions to take and what the value of these remembrances was. Sometimes I was not there to help, and my mother had to go through these either in therapy sessions or with my father as her comforter. She would later convey to me the information gained and experiences recovered. I was grateful for this as it helped to paint a clearer picture of her life and personality. One of the most difficult episodes for me to deal with, as the son, was the aforementioned episode in which some of Grampa Lawlie's friends, gathered for a regular session of child abuse, and had nearly killed my mother, when evidently, someone had taken a hammer to her skull during their orgiastic ritual of abuse. They had gone too far and nearly killed the chattel that they needed for their ceremonies. Spirited away to a hospital far from home, where the family would not be recognized, the cranial lacerations and potential fractures were not fatal, and were treated. But my mother relayed that she had a moment of spiritual awareness, perhaps akin to an out of body experience, in which she was asked by an angel to decide whether she wanted to persist in this life or whether she wanted to abandon ship and to die. She chose life, because she knew it would devastate her beloved father if she were to die. Despite her severe sufferings, which continued for quite some time after this, I am glad that she persisted, or I would not have been born and had the opportunity to discover and learn from this marvelous person so many years later.

Had she been able to tell her father about this particular experience with the scissors—had he understood—one would hope that he would have believed her. He adored her, and on some level he suspected something, but felt helpless to do anything, as it was his own precious wife who was given charge of this even more precious daughter during daytimes. How can one question the sanity of your own wife? Especially if there is no damning evidence to suggest her insanity—no smoking gun. It was all carefully hidden. Explained away. And after all, Grandpa Lawlie was a barber by trade; there was never a shortage of scissors around. But my Grandpa Arty knew there was something amiss. So, throughout my mother's childhood, he would constantly remind her to be careful, going so far as to show her newspaper clippings about people who were careless and had gotten killed or kidnapped or suffered some such fate that resulted from their carelessness in the face of danger; all so that he could warn his daughter of the dangers of life and possibly prepare her for when he was unable to protect her from it. Such was his response to his helplessness.

But he did not know who the very culprits were: his own wife and his own father in law, accompanied by whatever deranged friends they could call upon in the middle of the day and usher out before being noticed. They would often ensure the silence of my mother by threatening to kill her beloved father, Arthur. Whether this was a task they could have accomplished is another matter. He was a big, strapping man who could have killed his scrawny father-in-law with his bare hands, let alone a baseball bat or whatever other implement came to be in his hands had he found out what crimes against nature the little man had committed against his own kin. But Arty never did find out. The monsters had convinced my mother that they could indeed kill him if she were ever to rat them out. Perhaps they might have tricked him in some Byzantine way, using their Sicilian wiles that our tribe became so well known for, feigning loyalty to him on account of blood ties and then perhaps killing him in the night, when he could not use his massive strength against them. Who knows? But suffice to say that Arty did not know. He never found out. But his daughter survived, mainly on account of her knowledge that one person—her father—did love her. He loved her more than anything. And she wanted to protect him from discovering the harm that was done to her. She in some ways had to become an adult before her time, to become the protectress, the parent, while the monsters were torturing her and threatening to murder her father. And she suffered torture at the hands of the monsters for several years more, perhaps up until the age of seven. She willingly suffered so that her beloved father would not have to.

It was at times like these, these dissociative episodes, that I felt the most rage toward the perpetrators that had committed these crimes against my mother. It was times like these that instilled the most compassion in me for this poor little child, grown up, brilliant yet somewhat broken. They caused me to have more compassion for her when there were moments when I could not bear her addiction to junk. These moments made her more human and more understandable to me, less insane and more a victim of circumstances, still trying to self-medicate with her drug of choice—junk—seventy years later. I would feel like I wanted to go back in time and protect her from her abusers.

But I could not. I could only try, somewhat feebly, to protect her from herself. I had as much love for her as she had for her own father, Arthur, whom she tried to protect when he could not protect her. And I felt just as helpless to protect her as he did. It was my cross to bear, as it was his, but I had been born too late to make a difference.

There have been moments in which I have questioned whether any of this abuse happened at all—to either my father or my mother. Were my father's recovered memories of abuse—so quickly forgotten after retrieval—merely the concoctions of his mind, a function of his deteriorating mental state? Did Mom make up everything about Lawlie and Grandma Jeanne—not deliberately, but as a part of her mental illness—an easy scapegoat? Could I be sure that she was correct in retrieving these repressed memories? Had I been conned, swindled, into believing an elaborate lie, as innocent as its fabrication may have been? Had I become a slanderer by believing her allegations? How could I ever know the answer to these questions?

Regardless of whether the most minute details of their memories are true, the likelihood is that something very traumatic happened. This kind of abuse against children is well-documented and not entirely uncommon. That is for sure. On occasion, I have heard people discount the idea that there are groups of people who ritually abuse children, who thrive on the torment of helpless little children. I believe that to deny this would be to discount the existence of evil in the universe. There are people who are so sick that they abuse the helpless. Maybe they are not of a religious nature, but the abuse is systematic and ritualistic, their groups often cult-like. It has been documented during countless massacres and genocides in human history, not least of which were the Killing Fields of the Khmer Rouge, the Armenian Genocide, and the Holocaust. And it happens on a daily basis between adults and children, even in peacetime and in civilized nations. Occasionally the children die. And occasionally, the abusers are caught and punished. But more often than not, they get away with their crimes and the children grow up to be broken, stunted humans who carry the scars of this abuse with them throughout their whole lives, sometimes with more functionality than others. Sometimes, these monsters band together and support each others' sick and twisted pursuits so that they may more effectively feed their addictions without getting caught. My mother was a living example, testimony to the existence of these cults, if you will.

At times, I still cringe at the memory of hearing her crying, "Nama, Mama....Nama, Mama....Nama, Mama...." and her shrill shrieking, "ZIZZA! ZIZZA!"

A Babydoll Cries

Subsequent to this story, I must divulge a personal detail. Sometimes, in the back of my head—especially around the time of the Exile and afterward, and while writing this—I imagine that I hear a baby doll crying "Mama...Mama!" It's something I know I've heard before, perhaps in TV shows, or cartoons, or in toy stores. The mechanical sound of a recorded voice, inside a child's doll, crying "Mama...Mama!" Sometimes it hits me, and it makes me feel moved with pity. As if somewhere, some doll is without a child to love it and take care of it. And I have been faced with this many times, seeing a doll or a toy that is discarded or lost and no child anywhere to love it. It pains me to see it thrown away. At times, I've been tempted to pick it up and bring it to some kind of charity whereby it can be given to a child that needs it. At times in the past, working janitorial jobs, I have been faced with the task of discarding such toys, and wondering why I have such a distaste for such a task, a simple chore of discarding a piece of plastic. I knew it meant more to me than just the task at hand.

But ultimately, it became evident to me that it was not such a simple thing. It was not merely about the toy, despite my very deep-set animistic tendencies. It was the cry of my mother's inner child, the cry of my father's inner child. I was pining for the lost youth of both of these people—and millions of others like them the world over. So alone, so afraid, forced to do things, unnatural things, that some depraved adults wanted them—nay, forced them—to do. Each of them survived periods when adults were allowed to get away with forcing children to do things that should never even be imagined. In those times, prior to the rise of individual therapy and counseling for the sane—as a casual thing that did not reflect one's need to be involuntarily confined—in those times, it was easy for a grown up to say that a child was lying, or was making up stories. That he or she was simply not to be believed. "Who would believe a child over me, an adult?" they would say.

And I hear, still, the voice of that doll, crying, "Mama...Mama" the way that little Barbara and little Richard must have cried. And sometimes I imagine that I hear the voice of a small girl, happily proclaiming, "Daddy!" in a way that my mother must have done when she would finally see her daddy, after long periods of time when he was away working, during the War effort, during WWII, during the Depression. When he returned, unknowingly putting an end to the torments and machinations of his father in law and the man's gang of pederast friends—if only temporarily. It is a joyful sound, that little girl's voice, beginning on a high note, the first syllable accented, as if to express surprise at his return. But it is not simple unadulterated joy. It is mixed with incredible sadness, the respite of which would only be temporary, till he went away again to go to work. I still hear her voice and wish that I could prolong that feeling of safety in her voice. I wish I could console her and fight off the bad people who harmed her. But no one could. Not even her father, who was unwittingly ignorant to the whole ordeal. And she faithfully kept it from him as best she could, threatened with his demise should she ever speak of it to anyone. Had he found out about it, he would have flown into a rage and killed his father in law, and as many of the man's friends as he could locate. With his bare hands, or with a baseball bat. And he would have wound up in jail. Not an option, she thought when considering the outcomes. And perhaps they might have been able to actually get him, caught unawares, in the middle of the night, sleeping off the exhaustion from a back to back shift aboard the warships on their multi-day shakedown cruises out of Brooklyn or New Jersey. Perhaps Lawlie might have taken a razor blade (barber by trade that he was) to Arty, during sleep. Who knew? She did not want to take that chance. So she forced herself to forget, that she may never even be tempted to give utterance to what they had done.

Or Richard, seeing things done to him by strangers, perhaps to bring in money for the family during the Depression, sold for a moment to deranged people to be toyed with in a manner that no toy should ever undergo. It was a form of child slavery, what they did to him. They left him emotionally broken and confused, nowhere to go, no one to tell. They berated him and made him take a vow to never speak of this. A code of silence came upon him, lest they get him and do even worse. So he, too, forgot, till nearly 70 years had passed and he was forced to remember by a wife and son who were concerned about his memory lapses and his increased moments of confusion. And the curse of amnesia would be so strong that he would forget again and again, even when reminded. But meanwhile, as a child, he found himself filled with rage, unexplained rage, causing him to do things to small animals that he would later be ashamed of, taking his anger out not on those who harmed him, and not on himself, but on those smaller and less powerful than he, egged on by older, meaner boys in the neighborhood who saw his vulnerability. This would not last long, but it spoke volumes about his sense of self-worth. I can still hear him crying as well, calling for his mama, who was away, perhaps shopping, or somewhere else. And she would not last long in this world either, literally dying to get away from whatever evil lurked in that family. Whether she knew about it consciously or not, she knew about it with her heart and she soon died of breast cancer, leaving him and his brother half-orphaned at the ages of 20 and 15 respectively, and their father, a widower. And for the rest of his life, his wounded child inside would cry bitterly for the loss of his beloved mother.

Finally, the Den

After all this soul searching and cathartic activity, my mother and I did finally spend one August afternoon in the Den, cleaning things out. She did most of the sorting—since it had been her safe haven during the worst of the Pre-Exilic period when my parents sequestered themselves to different areas of the house—and she wanted to be careful about what papers might have been hidden in there that should not be lost or carelessly handled. Ultimately, she was able to get the longer of the two couches that were in that room cleared off. Cousin Marty stopped over for a brief visit and we gratefully used his back to help me get that couch out of the room—by the very window that Sonny-

Boy had jumped out of on one of two occasions, and the very window that my mom had illogically suggested my dad should have used as egress rather than destroying the front door knob. And so we got it out through that window and out to the street. Thankfully, only a few months before, sometime after the Exile was lifted, in a very serendipitous event, a local concrete company was doing some work up the street and had a fair amount of crushed concrete aggregate left over from their job and needed to get rid of it. They saw our driveway and approached my mom, who happened to be out there talking with Cousin Vic that day. They offered her the whole load that remained, just enough to cover about the first half of the driveway—from the street to a few yards away from the existing concrete apron. And they were willing to pack it down with their roller-compactor, all for a few hundred dollars. Knowing the general costs of this sort of thing from his experience in construction, Vic approved, encouraging Mom to take the deal. She did, paid cash, and about an hour later, there was a new section of usable driveway where there had previously been only mud. Thankfully for this, Marty and I were able to walk the couch to the street without having to deal with muddy ruts and potholes for at least part of the driveway.

We knew that the room had been compromised by the presence of rodents, but we did not know how badly until now, since the entire floor was still covered with newspapers. When we got the sofa outside, we noted that the rats had chewed a hole in the cloth covered wood of the front skirt panel of the sofa and evidently had begun to make a rats' nest underneath, directly below where my mother had slept for several months.

Mom took a few pieces of the brass casters off the bottom of the sofa, claiming that the metal should be recycled. In reality, she was holding on to some shred of the couch and her sentimental lament for ruined dreams and expectations. This couch cradled her during the worst times of her adulthood, when she could not make her marriage work and while her hoarding addiction was entirely out of control; but simultaneously, this was the couch that had been bought, second hand, to redecorate what had become the "Arthur A. Merget, Sr. Reading Room", the Den that in the '80s had been redone in honor of her father, her protector. He had sat on it when he was still alive and he enjoyed that room. It was something that he had touched and cherished, a vestige of what he had done to help make the house livable during our brighter times.

So, we left the couch there by the street, having scheduled a bulk item pickup with the sanitation company. It would be gone by the next day, and the space inside the Den where the couch had been would allow for further cleaning in the future, when Mom got around to it. Meanwhile, some of the dust and pathogens in that room had gotten up into my nasal passages during cleaning, and within hours I began to develop a summer cold. While we visited my Dad's brother and wife—Aunt Liz and Uncle Howie—in New Jersey the next day as the last social visit of my New York trip, I had gestated a full-blown upper respiratory infection, replete with sneezing, sniffling, and nearly constant nose blowing. I was now, once again, a casualty of Mom's hoarding addiction.

I flew back to Los Angeles the next day, quickly on the mend, but still suffering. But the one thing that stood out in my mind was that even though we had removed one couch and placed it by the street, there was still the love seat to match it, as yet in place in that room, covered by more papers and junk, likely having been permeated by rodents as well. The rodents were no longer there, however; we had handled that during the Exile with the traps and plug-in sonic anti-rodent devices. But the damage and the pathogens were still strategically hidden in various places that may yet be uncovered. But more than that, even, there was the original sofa that had been hauled out of the house by Greener Cleaners during the Exile, having formerly been stationed in the living room. It was the chocolate and vanilla striped tweed couch that I loved to sit on as a child and still exists in many childhood photos of mine and continues to exist in my mind as a piece of that era that feels as though I can nearly reach out and touch, if I were to try hard enough. It was there for us through many decades, from the beginning of our lives there, right up until the Exile. It had a mate, a love seat which had already been discarded as part of the cleanout. But somehow, this one would not fit into the last dumpster onsite during the cleanout and it was strategically placed in front of the garage, where my friend Gerard's desk had once been, rotting away in the elements, covered by a tarp. The couch had been left there since the Exile and had not yet been discarded, fully eight months later. It was no longer good to use, as it too had been permeated by the presence of rodents. The living room now had newer, though also second hand, sectional sofas in it, located where my parents were currently sleeping. But this old sofa, well worn and well loved, stood upended, between my old Chevy Nova and the garage, half covered with a tarp, so as to shield it from getting too waterlogged from the rain and snow, that it might be easily carried to the front of the driveway to be picked up. Many times, I had reminded my mother to get either Phil or Marty to help carry it to the edge of the driveway to have it carted away, but she always had a handy excuse, such that Phil hadn't come in a while, or not on the day prior to the garbage pickup and they didn't want to be fined for having it out there too long, or that Marty was often in a hurry when he came over, or that the wind wasn't blowing the right direction or something similarly preposterous to allow the couch to be left there in the driveway for even longer. And it had been there since the end of the Exile—for eight months since that time, to the time of this book's first few drafts. I finally got my mom to admit, speaking honestly, that she was having trouble with letting go of the couch. "It feels like failure....It feels like failure to me," she confessed. I sympathized and I expressed what words of comfort and solidarity that I could. I understood. It felt like failure to me, too. The whole affair—the Exile.

And a Year After That

When I began to write this book, it slowly emerged in the form of various disconnected episodes of a memoir. I began that project on some level even while my parents were still out of their home during the Exile. I put whatever time and effort I could into the project, often more as an attempt to express my anguish and pain during times of disillusionment with my parents' behavior and lack of progress in the cleanout of the house. Later, after the Exile was over, and they were back in the house, I continued to write, when the moment struck me, knowing that at some point I would have to put my nose to the grindstone and get it done. When I was unable to afford to visit my parents from the last time I saw them in August of 2010 onwards—due to the financial vicissitudes of being an adjunct professor—causing my parents and me considerable pain on account of our closeness, I became inspired to do everything I could to change my finances, perhaps by publishing a successful book that could help other people who similarly dealt with loved ones that suffered from compulsive hoarding disorder. Thus, during this enforced time of separation, I began to really focus on completing this book. And so, beginning in May, 2011, when I had finished teaching classes for the Spring semester, I stepped up the pace and gave myself the mandate of finishing the book. I also unrealistically swore that I would not only finish it, but start my next book, too. While this did not happen, I still galvanized myself to make this book a priority. And by the middle of August, 2011, I had proudly finished my first draft, intending to put the project down for a month or so and work on a revision in the middle of the Fall, hoping to find a publisher by the end of the calendar year. But Providence had a different time schedule for me, and a host of other revisions in store, as the reader will see.

Writing this book, I made sure to receive my dad's fully cognizant permission and blessings, as well as my mom's, to tell this story. My main remaining concern, of course, is what my dad's relatives might say when they hear reports of his early childhood abuse, something they have never before expressed knowledge of. While all of the abusers are deceased, some of their descendants are still alive and may be quite embarrassed to recognize their forebears in this story. Knowing that they are kind people, I sincerely hope that it never causes them any pain; for this very reason, I made every effort to conceal the true names of those individuals. I suppose only time will tell.

As for my mom, she had already begun to tell the story of her abuse publicly. David Grand had enrolled her in an art exhibition on Long Island a few years prior to the Exile, showcasing the art of abuse survivors. It was at this particular exhibition that my mom had very boldly provided an overview of her abuse during her presentation to those viewing her beautiful ink drawings of animals, noting not only that she "had been abused," but also that she "*is* a survivor," an important distinction and a sign of her gradual healing.

It is noteworthy to tell the reader that when I first mentioned to my mother that I was considering writing a book about my experiences during the Exile, it was still prior to my parents' return to the house. It may have been during my visit in October of 2009, perhaps, that I had said to her, "Mom, when we are done with all of this and you guys are back in the house, I think that I'm going to write my memoirs about what happened." Her answer was succinct and quite surprising to me. "I'll bet you don't," she said rather quickly. For a mother who was always extremely supportive and encouraging of every endeavor I had ever undertaken, from the most elementary to the most outrageous, this was certainly not her usual, supportive self, but indicated to me some deeper fear or misgiving on her part. I left it alone at the time. Months later, when I had begun the task in earnest and had told her about my strong start, I broached the issue with Mom about her having initially balked at the idea and having even been somewhat dismissive. She apologized to me and explained that she had originally been quite a bit reticent about the idea and reluctant to give her support to something that showcased what she was still very embarrassed about. She noted that it was not so much the abuse that embarrassed her, but her ultimately unhealthy reaction to the abuse and to my father's issues, resulting in her self-medicating through a hoarding addiction. It was her fallibility and her human foibles that were what she was most embarrassed about. She had allowed her sense of shame about the house to stand in the way of being fully in support of something so terribly important. And it was important not only for our family—something cathartic and very healing—but also for the world. Since that time, she became entirely supportive of this project.

Sometime in 2011, about a year and a half after the Exile had been lifted, Mom wrote a narrative of some of her abuse. I had invited her to write something firsthand that I could include in my book. She knew that I would be including her abuse memories as part of my narrative. Both she and I felt that much of this was the source of her hoarding, hence its relevance. She wanted to contribute something to the tale of our experiences as a family, so that it would not only be my voice speaking. I was grateful for this, and continue to be grateful, many years later. It seems that much more important now to have her firsthand testimony of what she suffered. She handwrote four pages, and I have transcribed it here exactly as she shared it.

Written prior to 08/23/2011

My Dearest Son, I'm writing this to you as the one & only person who could give an accounting of why your life in our family has held such strangeness & at times such mystery. Living through to my 7th decade, I've come to think perhaps the greatest mysteries are those we create for ourselves. Since you are 1 of 1, my only child, I felt a parental responsibility to do what I wished had been done for me: that is, someone explaining why our extended family does what it does = keeps secrets (some from ourselves) because we felt the need to have a defense from frightening truths.

I was born into a normal, working-class American family or so I thought. It was normal if you consider just how many thousands of American families hide uncomfortable facts from their children, their relatives, their friends, their neighbors & mostly themselves. Some families have skills uncommon: their members are gifted artisans, craftspeople, singers, dancers, writers, builders, teachers, scientists, doctors, brilliant thinkers. Others have abilities that suggest needing to deal with undesirable facts & habits.

I am speaking of alcoholism, drug addition, family abuse. We fit into this last category, and based on how many men, women & children in our society awaken each day to these uncomfortable realities, I feel justified in saying there is a strange normalcy to spending lives in, as Thoreau said, quiet desperation. Many people in the US, in the world, would put the accent on the desperation, but if you are a child, your demand is on the quiet part. Children can do that best, for that's where they come from. They most recently had no speech, no ability to let another person realize that help, an intervention was needed in a life & death, right-now, right-here, going on under everyone's nose, behind [p.2] everyone's back, & maybe it was not yet something that little child could verbalize, to ask for outside rescue.

People in every part of life in the U.S. of A are "bouncing about" seemingly experiencing a normal, common sort of wake-up, eat breakfast, go about their business & deal with jobs & the home they come to at the end of an 8-10 hour shift. But some of them go through the wake-up, there's no breakfast & their business is to endure a physical beating that won't show much of a wound & an emotional attack that leaves no marks on anything but their personal behavior & untrusting view of life.

I am sad to relate that I was one of those children, but I didn't "know it" until my 54th year. You ask how is it possible to not know you were "treated badly" for years?

It is more than possible, it is absolute necessity, or you won't be able to go on as if nothing is wrong. So you learn how to keep terrible, frightening secrets all the while you're trying to go to school with your homework completed & correct, chatting with classmates about the funny thing your dog did yesterday, & all the while your mind is closing doors to torture rooms, & your chatter is covering thoughts of being wrapped in huge newspaper pages & tied up with dead kittens in your lap. Dead kittens strangled in front of you because you cried out in pain & made noise that could have been heard by the upstairs neighbors in the 2 family house Grandma & Grandpa rented. Kittens were always in plentiful supply so they could be used as a threat. "If you keep screaming, if you don't do what we say, we'll kill this kitten & [p.3] it will be your fault." Nobody in the neighborhood ever counts how many kittens from the last batch are left, & you know THEY will kill that kitten & you "know" it will be your fault because you said, "No, I don't want to drink from that whiskey bottle. It burns my throat & makes me feel like throwing up," & if you still hold your mouth closed or try to spit out the whiskey THEY force on you, another kitten will be drowned in the bucket of water, or have its neck broken, & I can't watch it anymore, I can't play with it anymore. It just lies there on my lap & it's my fault & I'm sitting here wrapped in this newspaper & the kitten is here keeping me company, but not in the way I'd ever wanted. How long will THEY keep me here with this poor dead kitten? Why didn't I stop THEM? Why didn't I do what THEY said? I can't let them kill any more kittens. I have to be good. I have to do what THEY say. Next time, I'll be good. I won't cry when THEY cut my knees. I'll hold very still when THEY put my head in the bucket & I'll try to hold my breath longer next time so I won't swallow that soapy water. I'll be good. I'll be good. Please somebody help me be good...And I'll never say again that I'll tell my Father because THEY said THEY'D kill him if I told & I know THEY would, because I've seen THEM kill 3 kittens already & there are 5 of THEM. THEY could kill my Father. I have to protect my father. I have to save him. I have to save the kittens. I can't tell anybody ever. "Don't ever tell anyone. Just forget what happens here." THEY are right, I'll try to forget, cause I can't tell anyone if I don't remember."

So, the process of defensive forgetting begins & over many weeks, many months, [p.4] many years, nothing is left to tell because forgetting makes it be that nothing ever happened.

My mother & Aunt Fran & Grandma are out on a Saturday of shopping in Department stores for curtains, bedspreads, sweaters, shoes. But Grandpa Lawlie stays home to take care of me because I don't have Kindergarten on a Saturday, & he phones his friends to come visit as soon as Mommy & Auntie & Gram leave.

And then people come to visit. Some of them I don't know. One lady is a Nurse; she comes from her job at the Hospital & she's still wearing her white nurse's uniform. Sometimes she brings hyperdermic needles she sticks into my neck & makes me feel dizzy & go to sleep.

That man with red hair & very white skin & freckle spots all over his body, the one THEY call "Red" almost always visits. He never raises his voice, he whispers & always brings me candy, but he does strange things. He has the other 2 or 3 people put me on the dining room table & hold me down & then he puts things into my ears & mouth & down below. Sometimes it hurts, but I can't cry or scream because I have to protect the kittens, & protect Daddy. I love Daddy; I want him to be proud of me. I have to save his life because when the War is over, he'll be able to be home with us all the time; he won't have to work in the ship yard & stay in New Jersey overnight & he'll protect me & THEY will never visit again, or hurt me ever.

****

When I finished the first draft of the book by mid-August—calling it *The Exile*—I was still full of zeal and enthusiasm, so I only took a few days off prior to beginning a full revision of it, throwing aside my earlier intentions to give myself a break. This effort yielded a second draft, completed by August 20, 2011, the second anniversary of the date that I arrived in New York to help begin the cleanout, the day after the Exile had begun. This was an extremely significant and auspicious occurrence for me. It seemed to me as if that chapter of our lives was over, granted some closure by the angelic and providential forces that propelled us through this period and sustained us through the Exile. But as it turns out, the story was as yet unfinished. More had to happen before I could put down my pen. Much, much more.

At that time, I did fear how the house's condition may have changed for the worse since I had last seen it in August, 2010, knowing my parents' tendencies. And truly, my fears may have been valid. A year is a long time, and people don't change their ways that easily. Subsequent to the Exile, it had occurred to me that the only way to ensure that my parents would not resort back to their former dynamics, producing another crisis of monumental proportions, would be for me to make periodic arrangements to clean house for them. I would have to do it very firmly, yet with tremendous understanding. Thinking this, I realized that I might still have to get my mother into some kind of intensive program for compulsive hoarders, something that she had always been loath to do, fearing the loss of her autonomy to any outside authority figure.

The other issue was that, as they aged, I would want to move my parents to wherever I was currently living. I feared that with their addictive dispositions, they might not be able to handle themselves in that environment. Kim had suggested this to me, when he visited our home during the Exile. He foresaw that I might want to move closer to my parents, or have them move closer to me, in order to keep an eye on them. Surely, I did indeed have a desire to be there to take care of them. In fact, having a very old-fashioned sensibility, I had come to consider it a privilege to take care of my parents, as they did for me when I was a child. I continued to feel great pain from being unable to spend time with them as they aged. Notwithstanding some kind of ailment that requires twenty-four-hour medical care, I had never intended to let them live in a nursing home or anywhere other than right next to me, and it had been a long time hope of mine to reunite my family for the first time in decades. I had always desired to have my parents right alongside of me, able to enjoy their future grandchildren, and also where I can keep an eye on them so that I do not have to worry about the actions of two sets of children or teenagers. But above and beyond that, I had missed out on so many years of joy with them, living so far away. I have lived in California since 1993, when I began graduate school, and have continued to live here, through the beginning of my career as a professor, through the beginning of my marriage, and till the present. By the time of the Exile, I had missed almost twenty years with my parents, rarely seeing them more than once a year. I began to think that if Melissa and I were to be able to afford a slightly larger house, perhaps one with a separate entry and apartment for my parents, I could move them out here to live with me for the majority of the year, still keeping our Long Island home that was so hard won, and spending Summers or holidays there with them. When the subsequent events which I will relay hereafter came to pass, I continued to maintain faith that a higher power had just begun to reveal his divine plans to us; that perhaps we were being propelled toward that desired goal.

Just over a week after I finished editing the second draft of this book, a tropical storm that was originally called Hurricane Irene spread over the Eastern Seaboard and swept throughout the Northeast, touching areas of Long Island and leaving whole neighborhoods without power. At 9:30 AM Eastern time, on Sunday, August 28th, 2011 (ironically, my parents' 43rd wedding anniversary), a 65-foot-tall Oak tree that had for decades provided shade for our house, uprooted itself in the pouring rain and driving wind, and fell flat on the back half of my parents' house, doing over a quarter of a million dollars' worth of damage. Despite the tragic nature of this event, the tree fall was the spark that touched off a symbolic fire which cleansed our lives of further dross. It led eventually to the full cleanout of my home, to be fully renovated and restored to its former glory, the way that Grandpa Arty had left it. But it was also the harbinger of even more drastic changes that would come. Most of all, it inaugurated a new phase in my religious and spiritual journey. It triggered a dramatic shift in my understanding of God, and the role within our lives of Providence and Divine Will. Thus began a maturation of my spirituality, from the trusting, childlike faith of my youth to a more complicated and often troubled relationship with the Divine, which like Kushner and Wiesel before me, wrestled with God's omnibenevolence, and the problem of why God permits bad things to happen to good people. In this journey, I would be called upon to put away the things of childhood, like the Apostle Paul, and to finally become an adult (1 Corinthians 13:11).

"But who can endure the day of his coming? Who can stand when he appears? For he will be like a refiner's fire or a launderer's soap." (Malachi 3:2)

****

Dad at Green Gardens, January 2010

Dad, January 2010

Mom & Kittycat Rotten, Jan., 2010

Mom at Green Gardens, January 2010

Dad and Arik at Green Gardens, January 2010

Mom, Dad, and Arik in Cherry Hill, NJ, January 2010

AFTERWORD

The Exile continues with the next installment in the trilogy:

I AM THE EXILE

For further information on purchasing the next installment, please navigate to the author's personal website, www.DrArikGreenberg.com,

Or to the publisher's website,
www.EnlightenedReligionPress.com

THE EXILE

BIBLIOGRAPHY

Ginsberg, Allen. *Kaddish* in *Selected Poems, 1947-1995*. New York: HarperPerennial, 1997.

Grand, David. *Brainspotting: The Revolutionary New Therapy for Rapid and Effective Change*. Boulder, Colorado: Sounds True, 2013.

Levi, Primo. *Survival in Auschwitz*. New York: Simon & Schuster, 1995.

Miller, Alice. *For Your Own Good: Hidden Cruelty in Child-Rearing and the Roots of Violence*. Translated by Hildegard and Hunter Hannum. New York: Farrar Straus Giroux, 2002.

Tolin, David F., Randy O. Frost, and Gail Steketee. *Buried in Treasures*. New York: Oxford University Press, 2007.

<u>Musical works</u>

Cash, Johnny. "Drive On." *American Recordings*. American Recordings. Released in 1994.

ABOUT THE AUTHOR

L. Arik Greenberg (B.A., Wesleyan U.; M.A.T.S., Claremont School of Theology; M.A., Ph.D., Claremont Graduate University) is the inaugural Clinical Assistant Professor in Interreligious Dialogue. His first book was entitled, *"My Share of God's Reward" Exploring the Roles and Formulations of the Afterlife in Early Christian Martyrdom* (Peter Lang, 2009). Dr. Greenberg employs his primary training as a scholar of New Testament and Christian Origins as a jumping off point for his academic and social activist work in interfaith, with a particular focus on the diversity of belief within early Christianity as a model for modern ecumenical and interreligious dialogue. An ardent advocate of religious tolerance and interfaith dialogue, he is founder of the Institute for Religious Tolerance, Peace and Justice. Dr. Greenberg has served the Theological Studies faculty of LMU since 2003.

He began writing *The Exile* in 2009. It has been a labor of love.

Made in the USA
Middletown, DE
23 April 2023